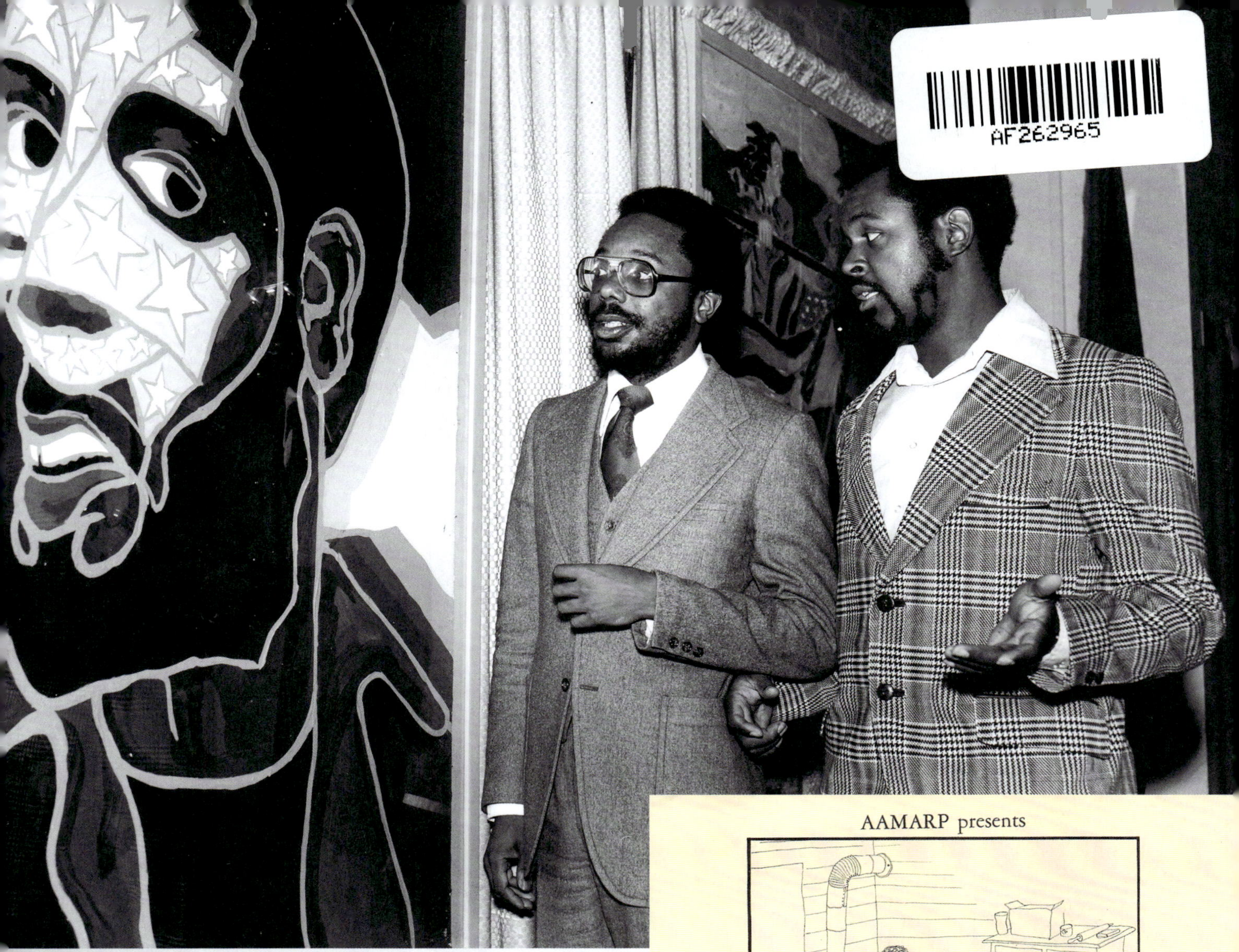

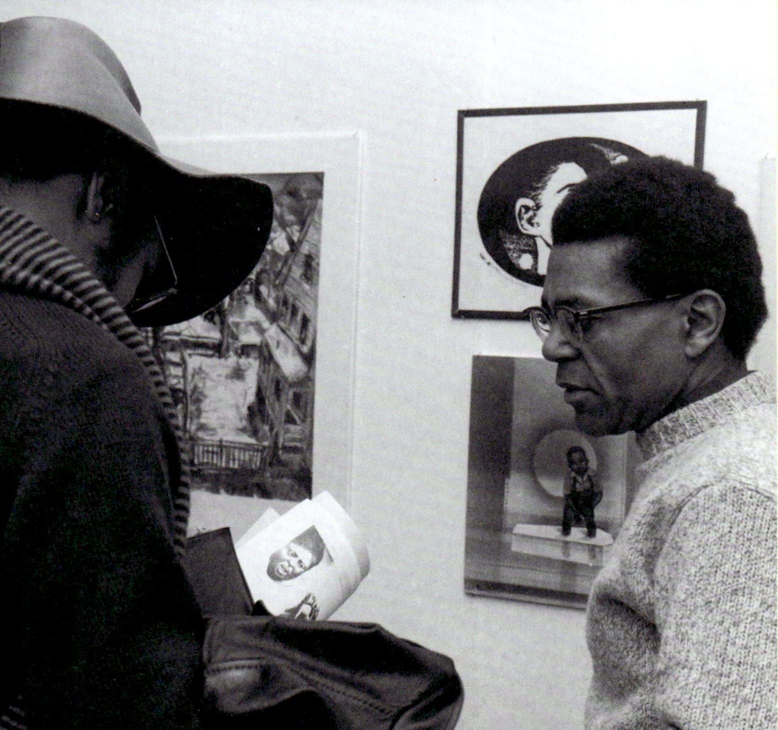

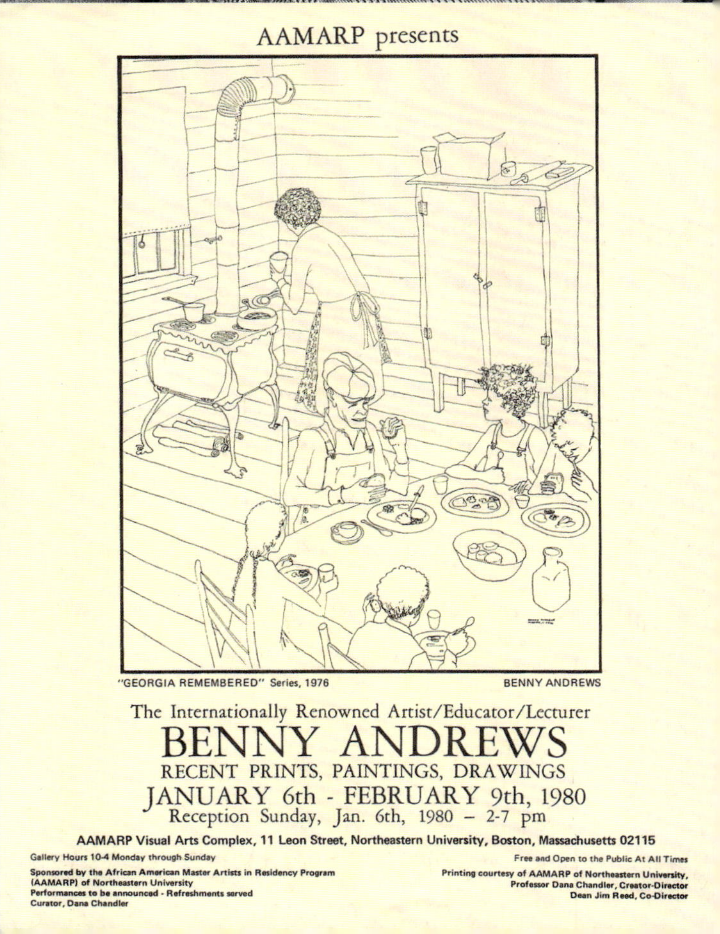

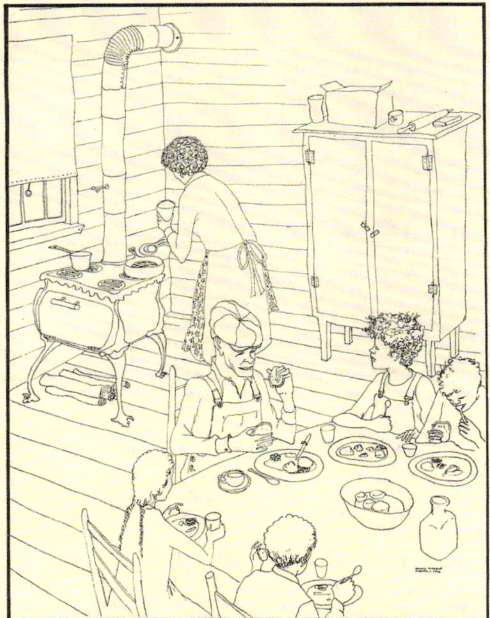

AAMARP presents

"GEORGIA REMEMBERED" Series, 1976   BENNY ANDREWS

The Internationally Renowned Artist/Educator/Lecturer

BENNY ANDREWS
RECENT PRINTS, PAINTINGS, DRAWINGS
JANUARY 6th - FEBRUARY 9th, 1980
Reception Sunday, Jan. 6th, 1980 – 2-7 pm

AAMARP Visual Arts Complex, 11 Leon Street, Northeastern University, Boston, Massachusetts 02115

Gallery Hours 10-4 Monday through Sunday

Free and Open to the Public At All Times

Sponsored by the African American Master Artists in Residency Program
(AAMARP) of Northeastern University
Performances to be announced - Refreshments served
Curator, Dana Chandler

Printing courtesy of AAMARP of Northeastern University,
Professor Dana Chandler, Creator-Director
Dean Jim Reed, Co-Director

SAY IT LOUD

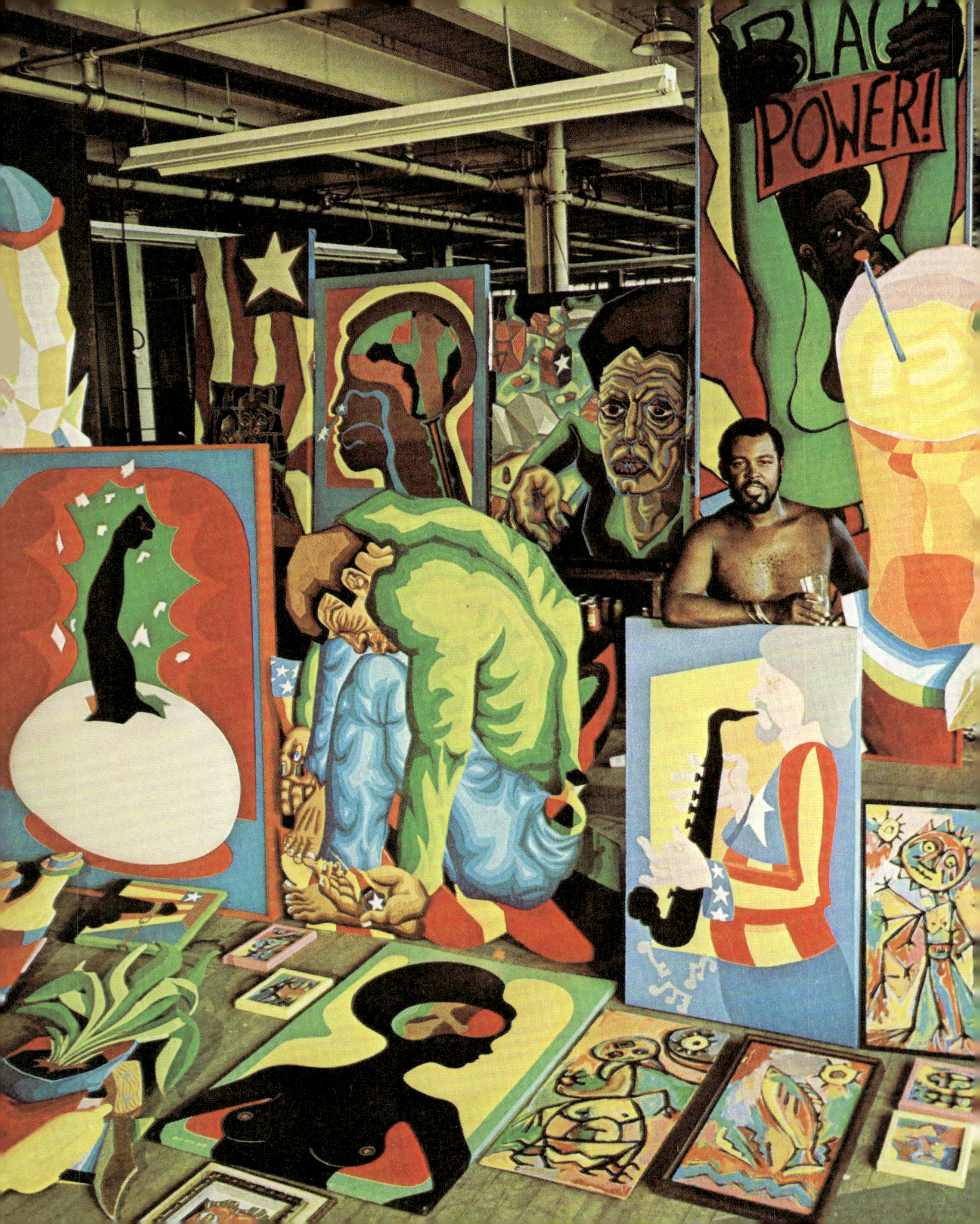

BLACK
POWER!

SAY IT LOUD

AAMARP 1977 TO NOW

Edited by
JEFFREY DE BLOIS

The Institute of Contemporary Art/Boston

DelMonico Books • D.A.P. New York

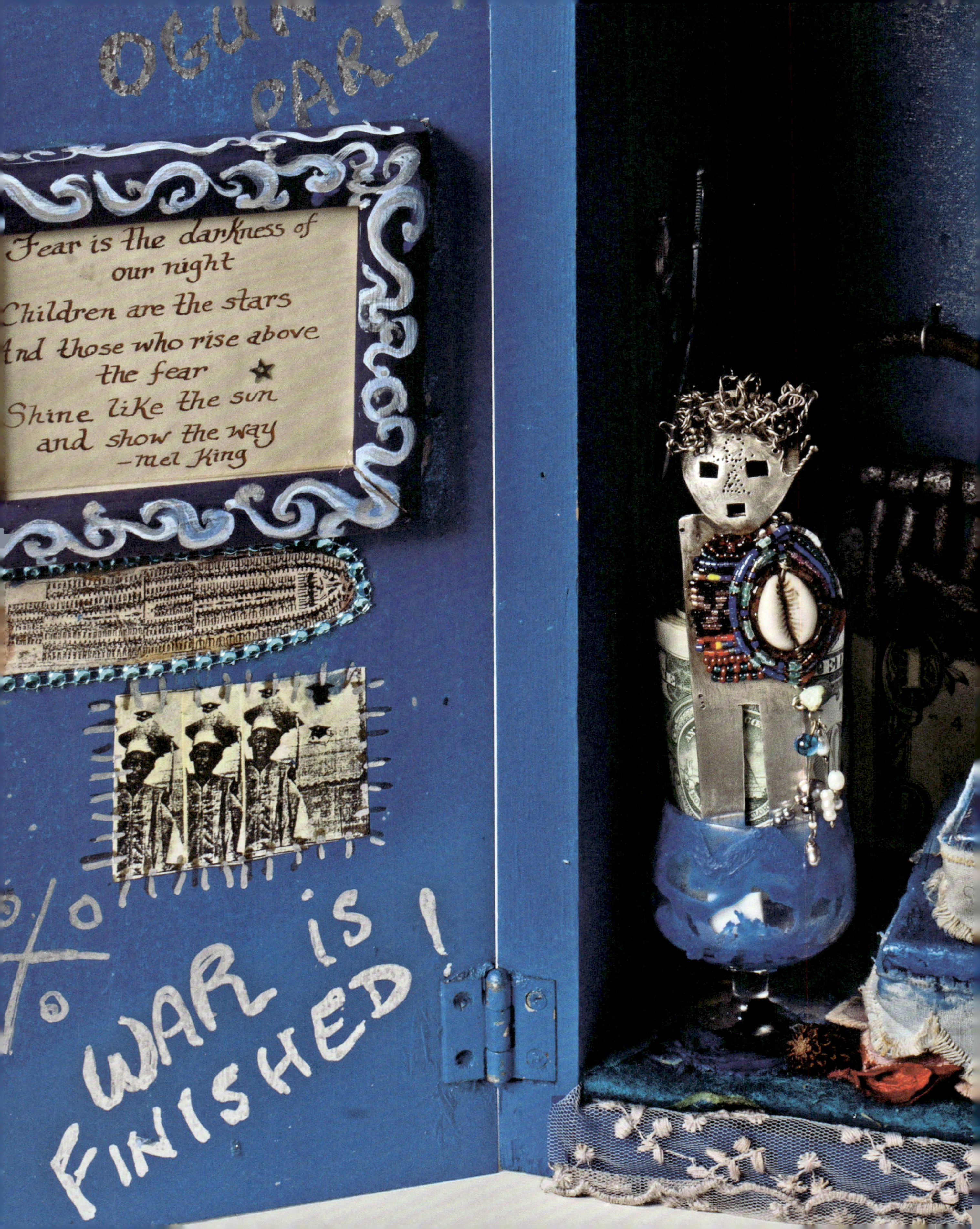

OGUN PARI

Fear is the darkness of
our night
Children are the stars
And those who rise above
the fear ★
Shine like the sun
and show the way
—mel King

WAR IS
FINISHED!

Contents

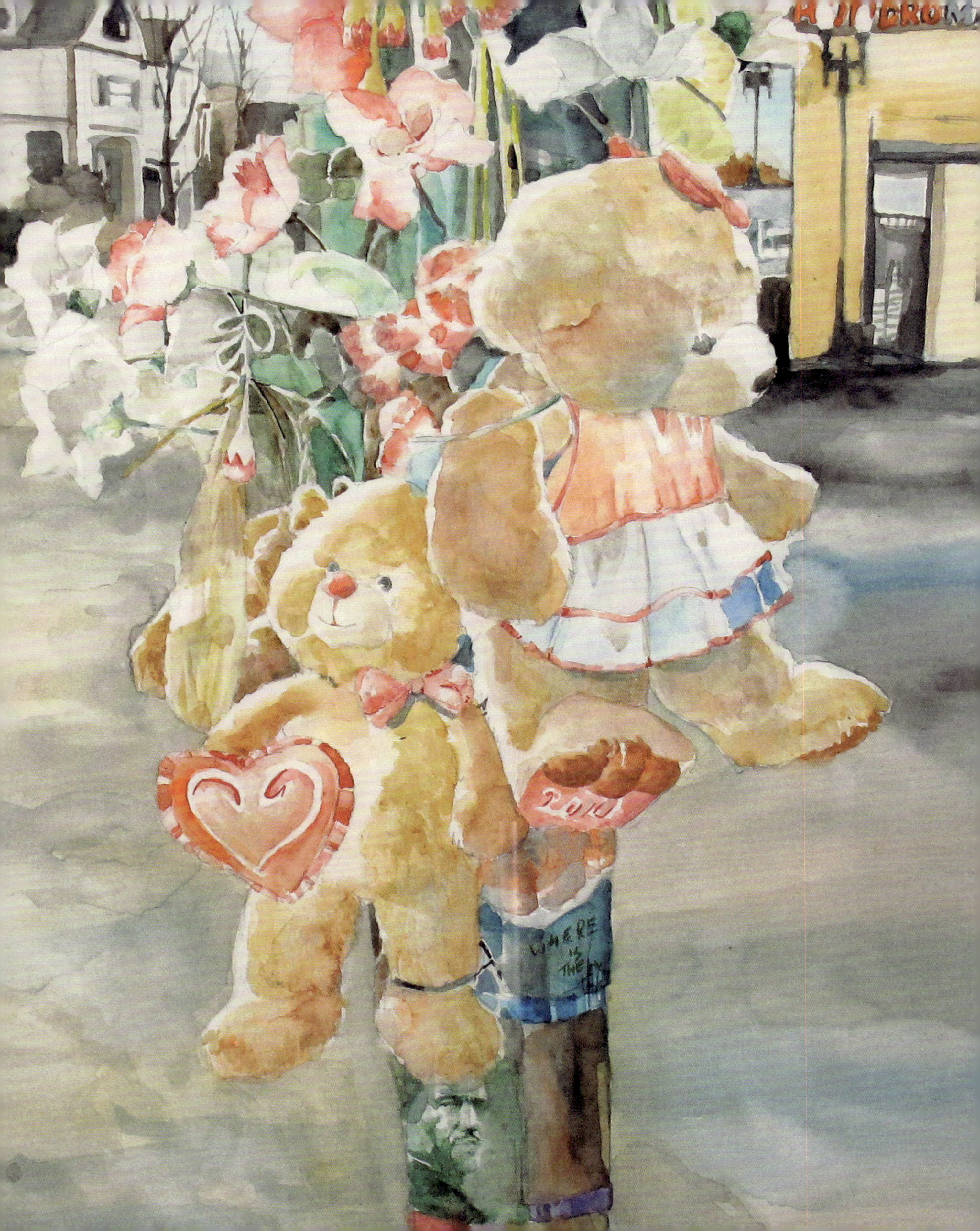
WHERE IS THE

Director's Foreword

The African American Master Artists-in-Residence Program (AAMARP) at Northeastern University is first and foremost a space of community. Founded in 1977 by pioneering artist, educator, and activist Dana C. Chandler Jr., AAMARP was one of the first and only in-residence programs primarily for Black artists in the United States. Since then, it has been dedicated to "aesthetic and philosophical freedom," according to Chandler. Crucially, the program provides studio and exhibition spaces for Boston artists, fostering creative exchange and collaboration in a city where artist studios are increasingly at a premium. For nearly fifty years, AAMARP has centered expansive ideas of community—that artists are integral members of their communities—and that community can be made both with those close to home and much further afield. This includes students of all ages, artists of all disciplines, and people of all walks of life. The program offers a model of openness and inclusivity to be celebrated. For his rigorous vision and leadership, we dedicate this project and publication to Mr. Chandler and his legacy.

A peripatetic history has brought the collective and the many artists in its orbit from Leon Street on Northeastern's campus, to Huntington Avenue, to Atherton Street in Jamaica Plain, but AAMARP's ethos of community and persistence has endured in the face of relocation, uncertainty, and struggle. As these artists look toward the future, they benefit from a rich legacy of artistic experimentation, community activism, and intergenerational exchange fostered at AAMARP.

The ICA/Boston is very proud to present the first museum survey of AAMARP, which highlights the diversity of approaches long championed by AAMARP artists and positions Boston as a key nodal point in the regional histories of the Black Arts movement that scholars are charting today. While the ICA's history and the history of AAMARP have periodically overlapped (AAMARP affiliated artists Ellen Banks, Chandler, Reginald L. Jackson, Kofi Kayiga, Marcia Lloyd, Vusumuzi Maduna [f.k.a. Dennis Didley], Bryan McFarlane, Rudolph Robinson, and Don West all showed their work in ICA exhibitions in the 1980s and '90s), an exhibition of this breadth and depth is certainly overdue.

We are grateful to Jeffrey De Blois, Mannion Family Curator, for advocating for this project, and for his unwavering commitment to situating local art, culture, and history within a global context at ICA/Boston. Jeff was ably assisted by Curatorial Assistant Meghan Clare Considine, an invaluable thought partner in every aspect of this project's development. For their generosity in helping realize this exhibition and publication, we greatly appreciate the lenders to the exhibition, The Kristen and Kent Lucken Fund for Photography, and Wagner Foundation, as well as the ICA board and staff.

Finally, for the opportunity to celebrate and share this extraordinary exhibition with our audiences, we thank all members of AAMARP, including those who are no longer with us, for trusting and partnering with us on this exhibition and publication. Our special thanks go to the current members, whose collaborative spirit and insight remain indispensable: Gloretta Baynes, Jeff Chandler, Marlon Forrester, L'Merchie Frazier, Ricardo Gomez, Reginald L. Jackson, Shea Justice, Kofi Kayiga, Khalid Kodi, Bryan McFarlane, Hakim Raquib, Susan Thompson, and Don West. We are honored to offer this exhibition as a testament to the meaningful, living legacy of the African American Master Artists-in-Residence Program, and to align mutually held values about inclusivity and community between our museum and the program.

NORA BURNETT ABRAMS, PhD
Ellen Matilda Poss Director

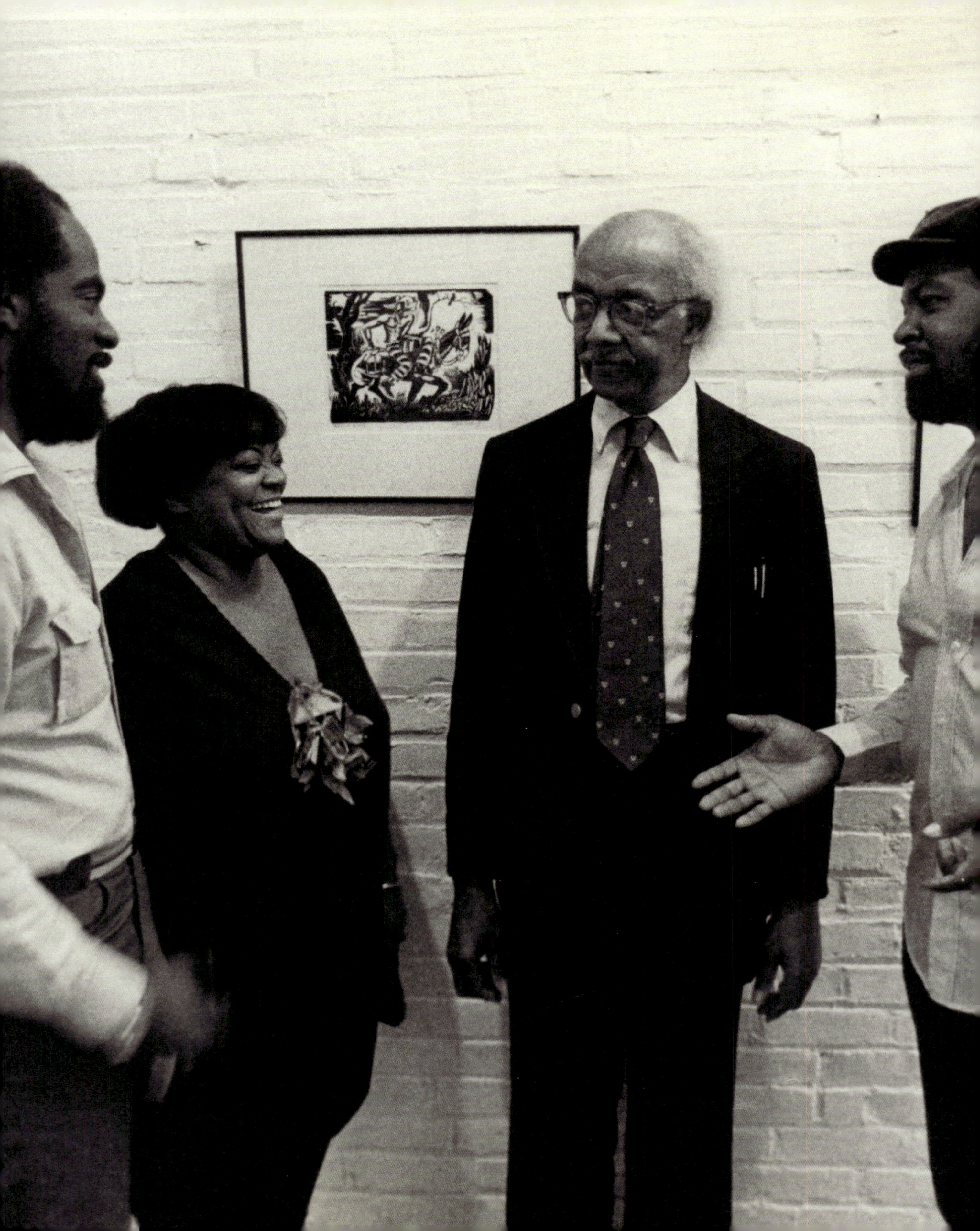

Preface

The African American Master Artists-in-Residence Program (AAMARP), driven for nearly fifty years by the imperative to value creative endeavors as intimately related to a unique, self-conscious community, arose from a very particular set of conditions. The Black Arts movement, borne of the widescale turbulence of the 1960s, and empowered by the realization that Black potential was frustrated at every turn, set the stage for powerful new forms of expression. Rooted as it was in earlier notions of Black genius posited by W.E.B. Du Bois and Alain Locke—which stressed cultivating Black creativity as a commonwealth that had not been recognized for its brilliance and inventiveness—this movement provided the scaffolding needed internally to imagine the possibility of a Black artist community. Externally, it laid the foundation within the larger framework of Northeastern University wherein supporting an entity such as AAMARP was viewed as progressive and responsive to broader changes.

At the same time, powerful political currents were arising. In the United States, newspapers reported daily on new political alignments like the Black Panther Party and the Student Nonviolent Coordinating Committee. Outside the U.S., long-standing colonial arrangements were collapsing, and what would come to be called the African diaspora was taking shape. African American artists expressed solidarity with Black artists throughout the Caribbean, the Americas, and across continental Africa. In the spirit of this swirling and evolving Black universe, AAMARP came to embody the ideal of a distinctive artistic arrangement that offered, without being unduly prescriptive, the opportunity for many artists to form a supportive community infused with a collaborative ethos representative of the African diaspora.

In Boston, Dr. Elma Lewis, an artistic visionary and institution builder, established the National Center of Afro-American Artists (NCAAA), a Black-focused arts institution. The Museum of Fine Arts (MFA) promised to help Dr. Lewis realize her dream, which was announced as a collaborative effort in 1969. Shortly thereafter, Dana C. Chandler Jr., a young artist attuned to the national Black arts scene, wrote, "A Proposal to Eradicate Institutional Racism at the Boston Museum of Fine Arts" (1970). The confluence of the MFA and NCAAA collaboration and the gravity of Chandler's accusatory letter led the MFA to commit to presenting the exhibition *Afro-American Artists: New York and Boston* (1970), the first of nearly a dozen shows co-organized by the MFA and NCAAA. Over time, these exhibitions created an appreciation for the contributions of Black artists, making it easier for a mainstream institution like Northeastern to support an experimental entity such as AAMARP. It is highly doubtful that such an embrace would have been possible without the work that brought Chandler to prominence as a forceful voice for Black artists during the early 1970s.

AAMARP evolved out of these historical conditions. Given the opportunity, Chandler made AAMARP a community center where multiple generations of artists addressed issues of growing concern. This openness to community endeared him widely and enhanced the ease with which his supporters within the university would be able to sustain the conditions that made the formal establishment of AAMARP possible in 1977. Throughout its history, however, AAMARP has had a complicated relationship with Northeastern. On one hand, it has burnished the university's standing in its surrounding community. On the other hand, AAMARP has had to continually fight for its existence and negotiate issues of access. Even as aspects of AAMARP's relationship with Northeastern remain opaque, what is decidedly clear is that it remains an active community of highly productive artists drawn from throughout the African diaspora eager to engage the public in dialogue and discovery.

—EDMUND BARRY GAITHER

AAMARP IS FOR EVERYONE

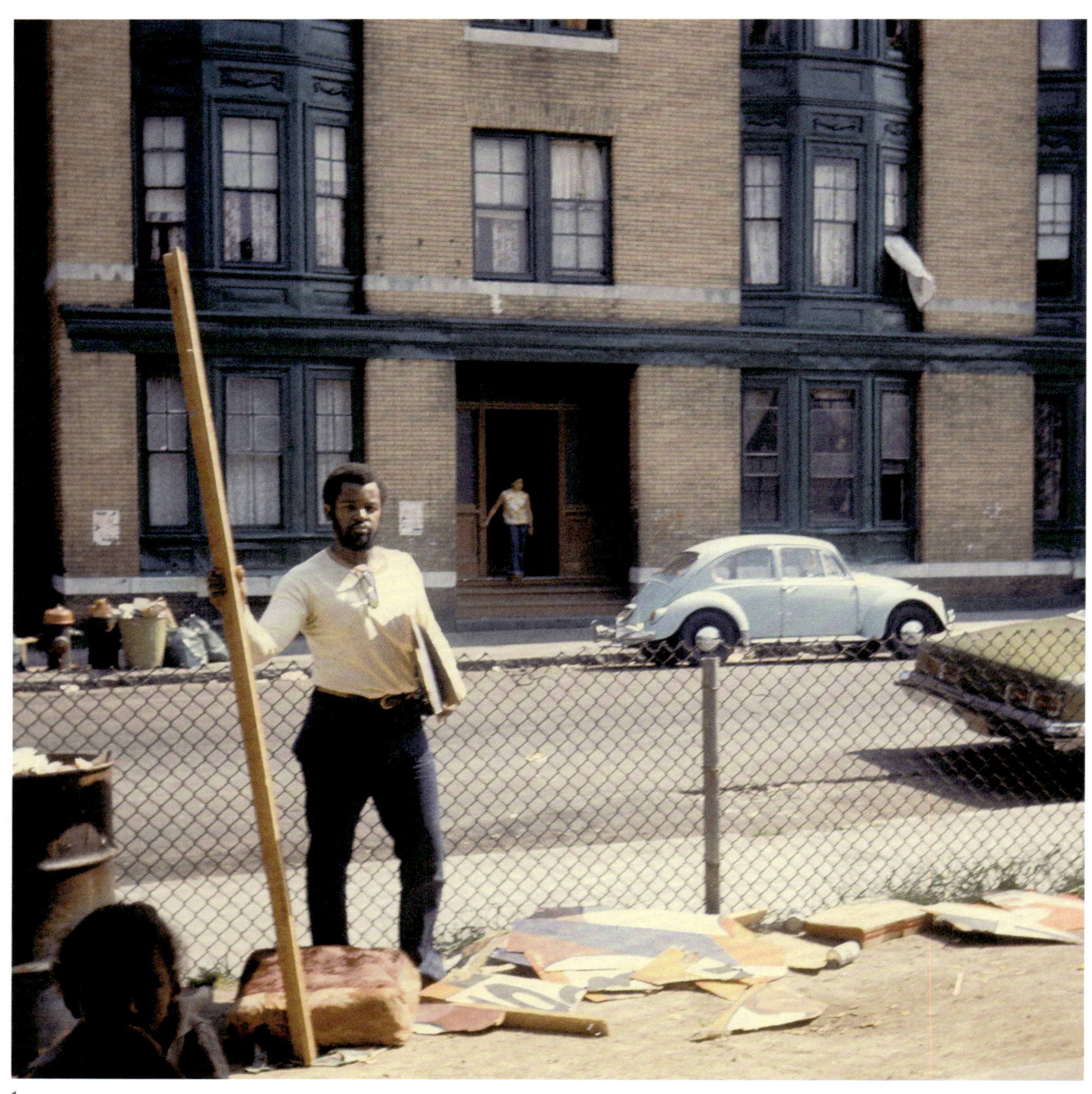

1

JEFFREY DE BLOIS

TAKE IT ALL

Nothing about this story should come as a surprise. In August 1973, artist, educator, and activist Dana C. Chandler Jr. returned from a family vacation to find his studio on West Brookline Street in Boston's South End ransacked. Many of his artworks, materials, and personal belongings were stolen.[1] Paintings and works on paper were scattered around the neighborhood, many ripped to pieces, others scattered around a nearby playground in a makeshift display of contempt for the artist. The intruders turned on the water in the building's basement and left it running, destroying more artworks stored there. The perpetrators were never apprehended by Boston police. This was not the first time Chandler's studio was looted, or that his work was vandalized. It would also not be the last.[2]

Chandler appeared in the April 1970 special issue of *Time* magazine ("Black America 1970"), where the tagline describes him as "Young and Angry."[3] Three years earlier, during the so-called long, hot summer of 1967, Chandler witnessed Boston police brutalizing the Mothers for Adequate Welfare (MAW), a group established to demand better welfare conditions. On June 1, MAW staged a sit-in at the Grove Hall Welfare Office on Blue Hill Avenue where they shut the doors and chained themselves in. The following day, the community in the predominantly Black neighborhoods of Roxbury and Dorchester took to the streets in response and the unrest lasted for three days before it was suppressed by the National Guard.[4] After Chandler witnessed these events,

on the heels of his graduation from Massachusetts College of Art and Design, his work adopted a new political urgency and a social realist style, with racism as a "central and persistent theme," according to curator Edmund Barry Gaither.[5] "This was my reactionary phase," Chandler later wrote, "when most of my paintings would describe bluntly and in realistic detail the depravity and brutality of some whites upon the bodies and minds of African-Americans."[6] Chandler was brashly outspoken and highly visible—"too damned radical"[7]— which made him a target in Boston, a city he describes as, "very hostile to Black people."[8]

In the *Time* photograph, Chandler appears in front of his painting *Fred Hampton's Door* (1970) memorializing the assassination of the titular deputy chairman of the Black Panther Party by Chicago police in 1969, at the age of twenty-one. The police fired first through the closed bedroom door where Hampton slept alongside Deborah Johnson, who was eight and a half months pregnant with their child, before shooting him two more times execution style in the head. Chandler responded by depicting a section of red door emblazoned with a green nameplate with Hampton's name misspelled and a white star inside a blue square with text that reads "U.S.A. Government Approved '69." When *Fred Hampton's Door* was presented at Expo '74 in Spokane, Washington, the painting was stolen and never recovered.[9]

Chandler recognized the radical potency of *Fred Hampton's Door*, and when it went missing, he recreated it, this time on a door he found in the wreckage of the

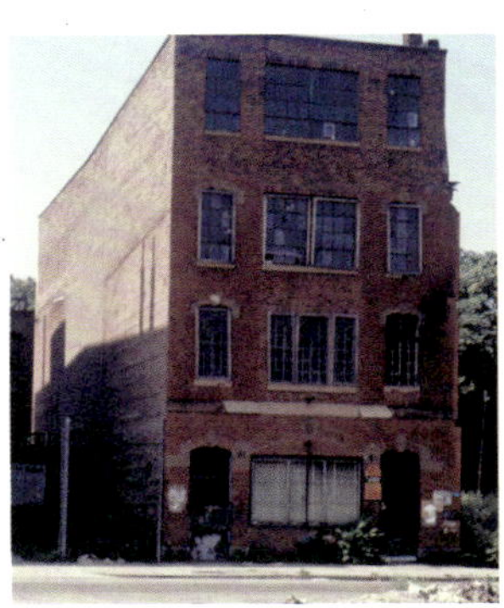

1. Dana C. Chandler Jr. with paintings in playground near ransacked studio, 1973

2. Chandler's studio at 115 West Brookline Street, n.d.

3. Chandler's studio basement ransacked, 1973

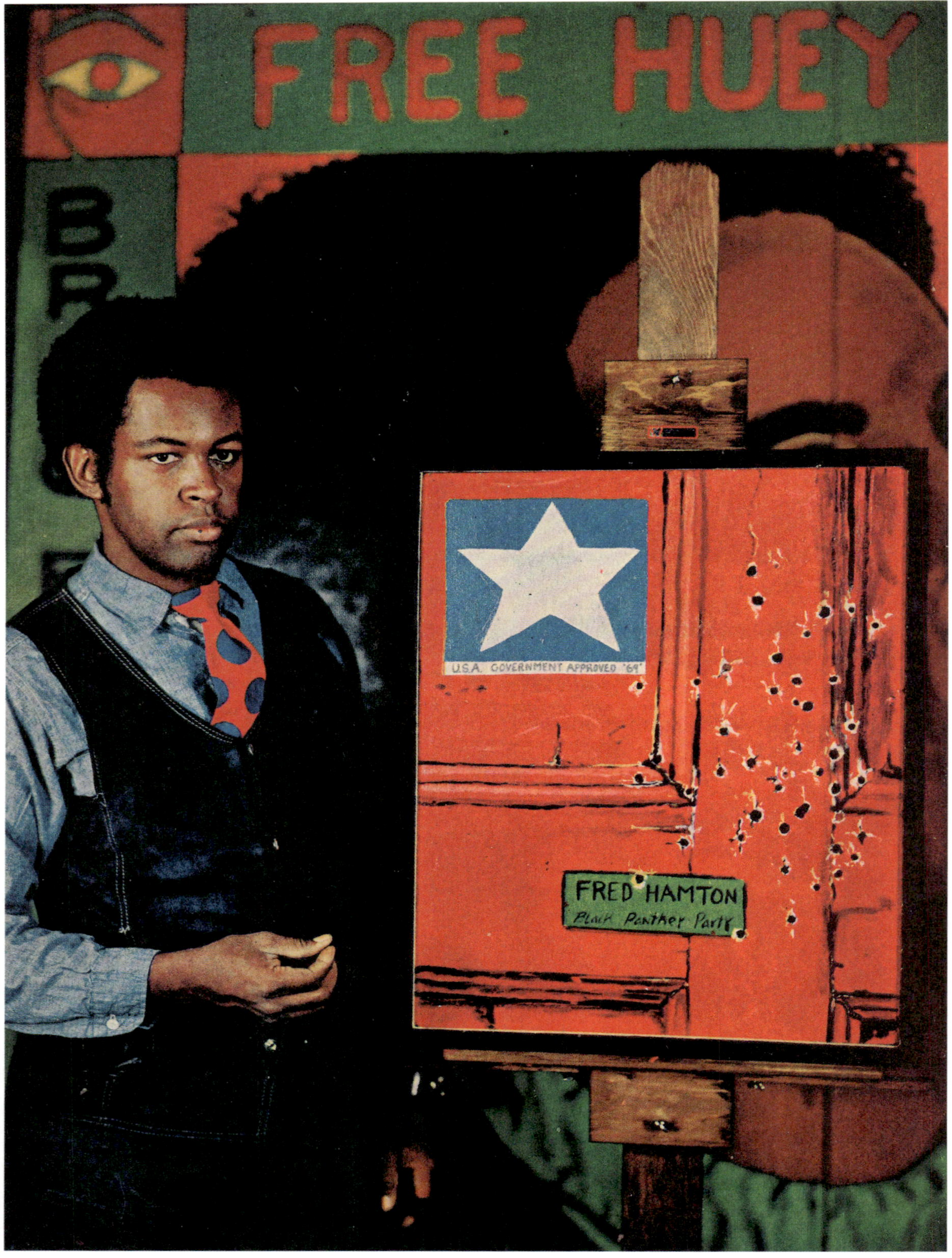

4. Chandler pictured in *Time* magazine with *Fred Hampton's Door* (1970), April 1970

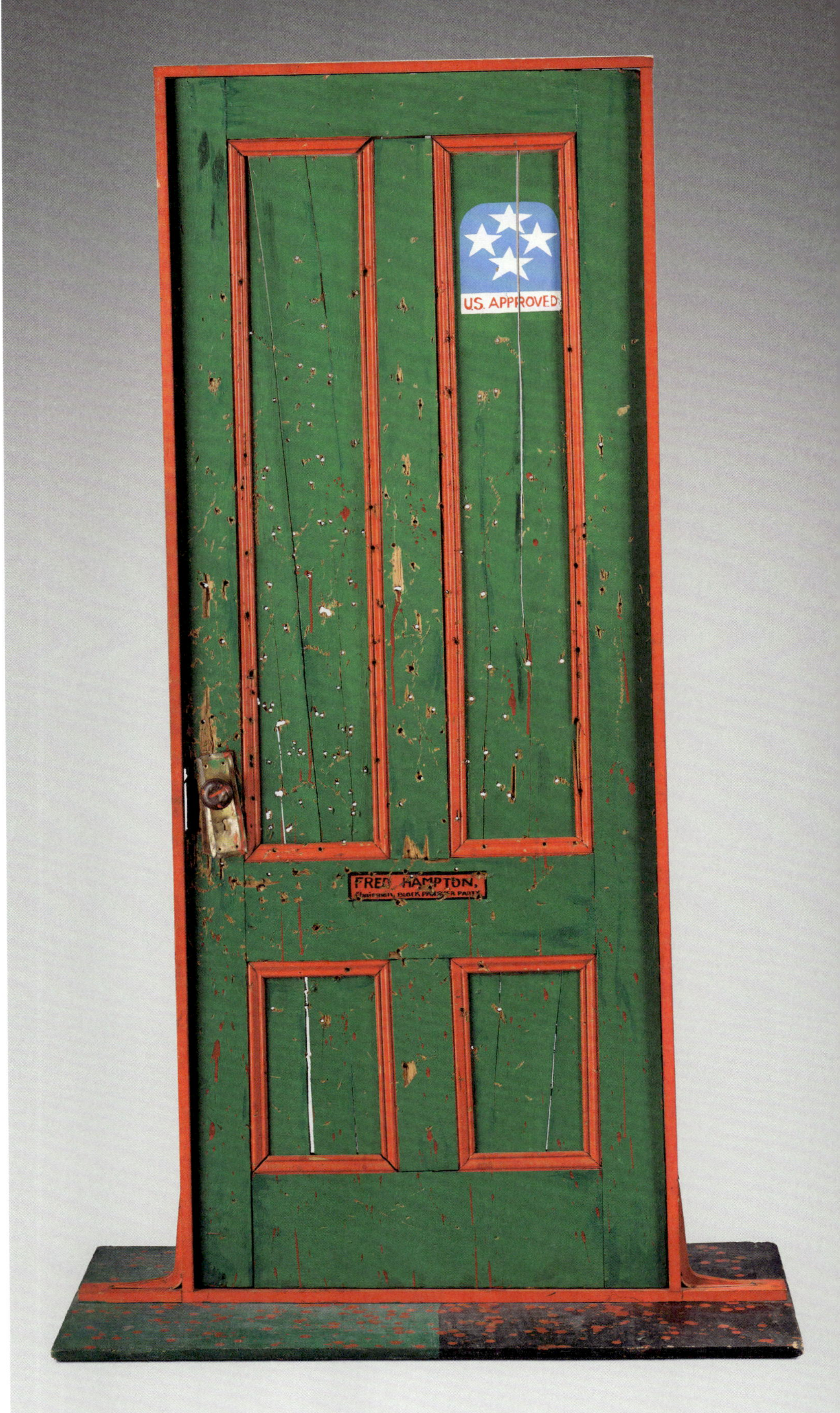

5. Dana C. Chandler Jr., *Fred Hampton's Door 2*, 1974. Acrylic paint on wood. 80 × 48 × 23½ inches (203.2 × 121.9 × 59.7 cm). Museum of Fine Arts, Boston; William Francis Warden Fund, The Heritage Fund for a Diverse Collection, and Gallery Instructor 50th Anniversary Fund

houses being torn down in his community. In *Fred Hampton's Door 2* (1974), the references are even more overt. The door and its base are painted red, black, and green, the colors of the Universal Negro Improvement Association, a Pan-African organization founded in 1914 by Marcus Garvey. This painted door is riddled with real bullet holes, as if to drag the painting from the realm of representation into the everyday life-or-death struggles of Black Americans. *Fred Hampton's Door 2* aligns with Chandler's imperative at the time that Black artists, "should deal with the social problems that black people are having in this racist society, so that there will be an accurate record of our progress from an oppressed to a free people."[10] Chandler's *Black Man Break Free of the Sucking, Mutherfucking White Egg* (1974), a print in which a clenched Black fist punches through a white egg, expresses this sentiment forcefully, even as his murals around Boston at the time—including *Knowledge Is Power–Stay In School* (1972), formerly painted on the side of a store on Washington Street in Roxbury in what is now Nubian Square—influenced a generation of artists from that community through its empowering message of social uplift and its visibility in the community.

After Chandler's studio was destroyed, he salvaged what he could and was approached by Dean Gregory T. Ricks of Northeastern University, who offered Chandler storage space at the African American Institute on campus in exchange for teaching a class. When Ricks noticed that Chandler had filled the space floor to ceiling with his work, he offered to show Chandler a space nearby on campus, where they were joined by Ramona H. Edelin, chairperson of what was then the Afro-American Studies Department, and Northeastern's executive vice president Kenneth G. Ryder, who would soon become the university's president. When they showed Chandler the unused second floor of a former clothing factory at 11 Leon Street—approximately 32,000 square feet of loft space with twelve-foot ceilings still filled with Singer sewing machines and fabric offcuts—the awestruck artist asked them how much of the space they would let him use.

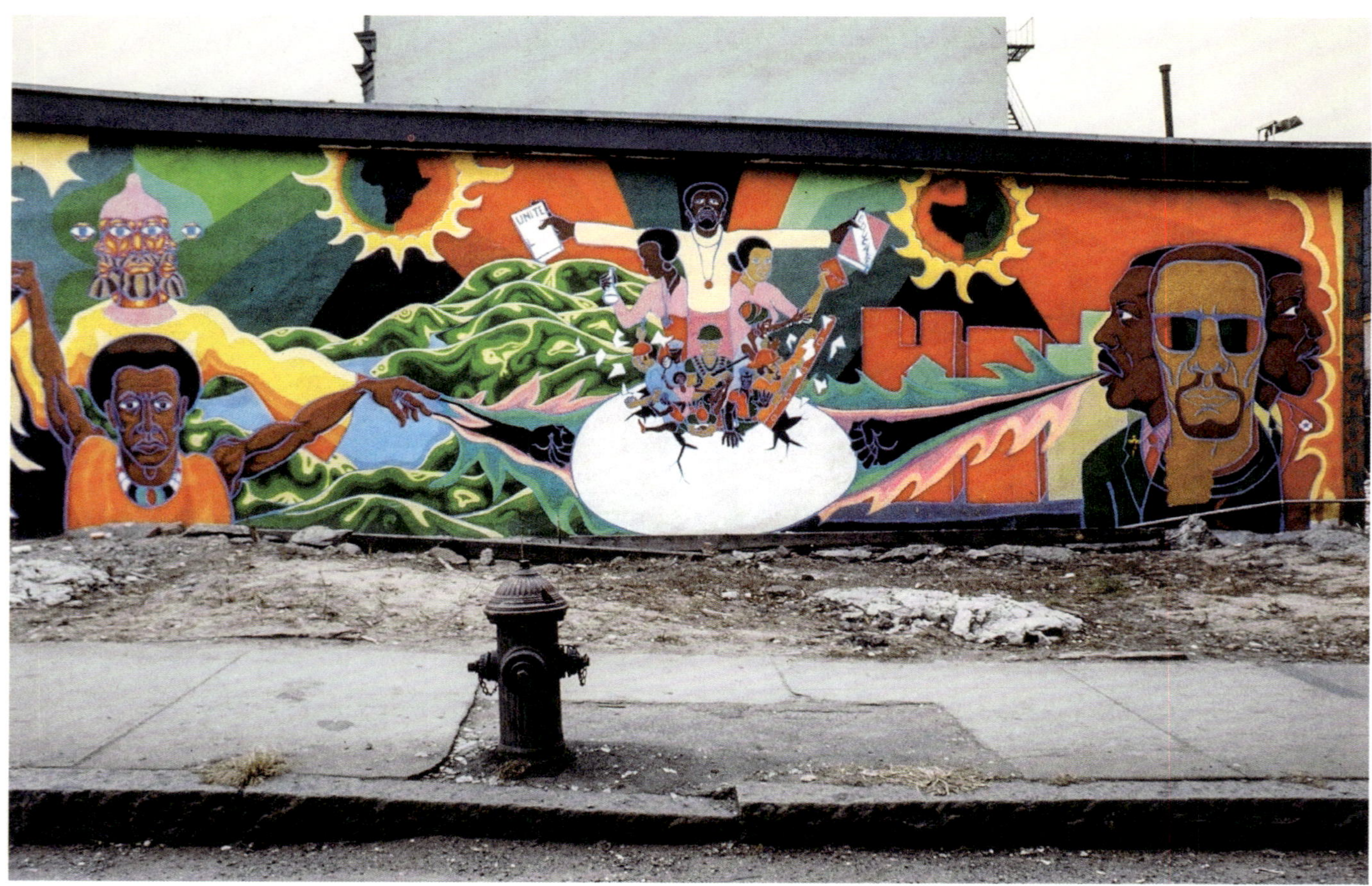

6

6. Dana C. Chandler Jr., *Knowledge Is Power–Stay In School*, 1972. Dudley Square, now Nubian Square, no longer extant

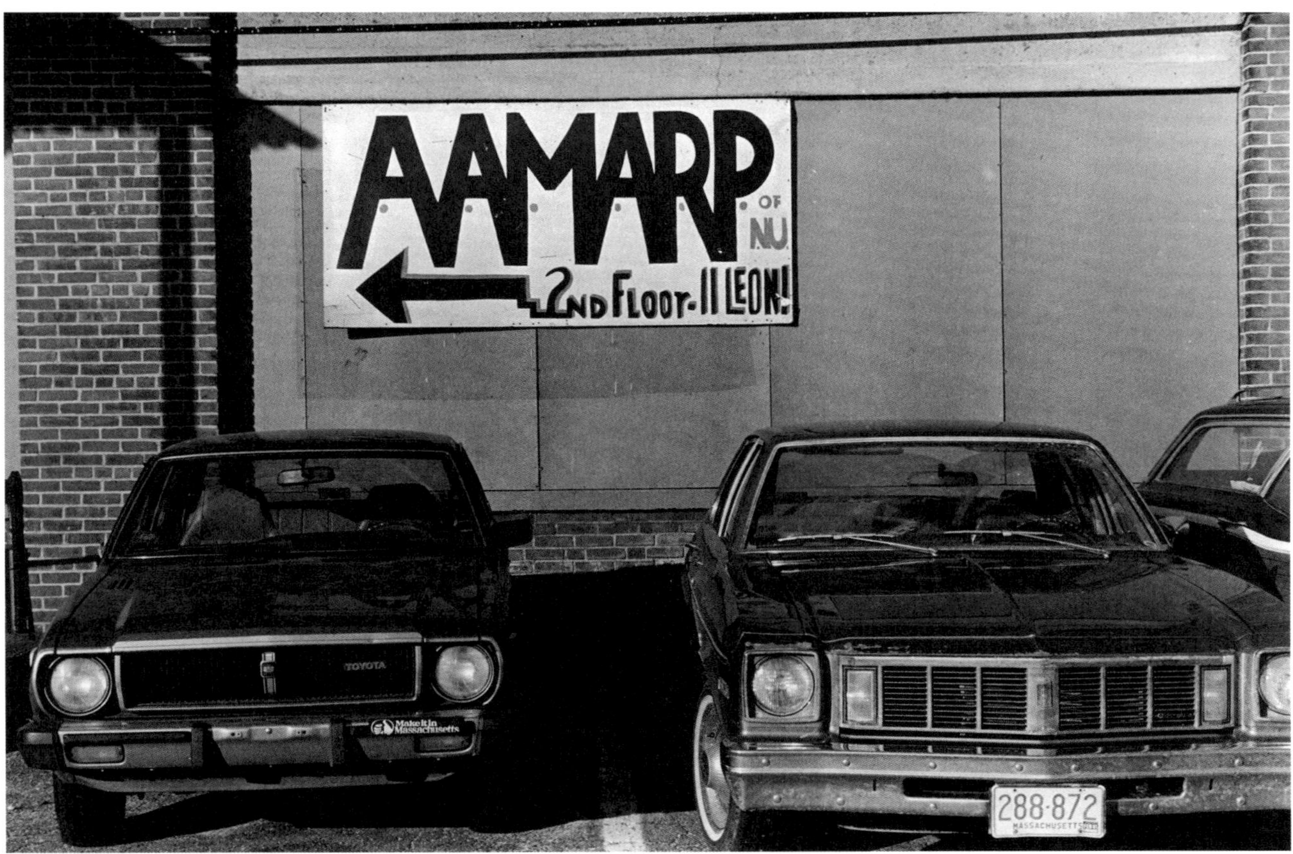

7

"How much do you need?" he recalls them asking. "I'll take it all."[11]

Chandler, ever savvy and realizing the opportunity he was being presented with, began to articulate immediately his idea to create a unique space for Boston's African American artistic community. Even going back to 1969, Chandler proselytized, "[Black people] must organize ourselves," influenced in part by the directive outlined by writer Larry Neal: "The Black Arts movement is radically opposed to any concept of the artist that alienates him from his community."[12] Chandler's "dream space," as he described it, included large studios for artists (including himself), galleries for staging exhibitions, spaces for dance and theatrical performances, poetry readings, and more, and always free and open to all, especially the Northeastern community. Ryder, who Chandler describes as an ally, was persuaded, as were Ricks and Edelin. As artist Napoleon Jones-Henderson

describes it, "Dana, in his own inimitable way, had sequestered a whole building."[13]

Jones-Henderson, a member of the influential artist collective AfriCOBRA who moved to Roxbury in 1974, was raised on the south side of Chicago in proximity to the South Side Community Arts Center and knew the incredible value of spaces for artists situated in the community. With the encouragement of Jones-Henderson and others, Chandler endeavored to create a community minded visual arts complex around a loose knit group of artists conceived as a collective. By 1977, three years after he moved into 11 Leon Street, Chandler had garnered the support of President Ryder and Northeastern, including a substantial budget, for his vision of an artist-run, on-campus complex. What he decided to call it infused it with purpose and ambition: the African American Master Artists-in-Residence Program.

7. Original AAMARP location
at 11 Leon Street, c. 1977

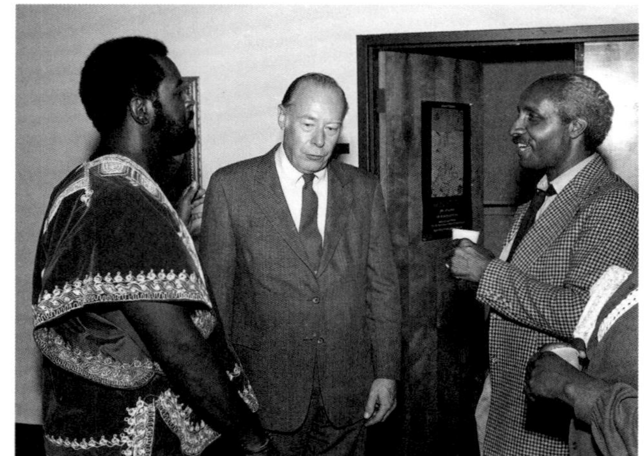

8

THE DREAM AND THE REALITY

The African American Master Artists-in-Residence Program, or AAMARP as it is commonly referred to, was one of the first in-residence programs for Black artists in the United States. Chandler outlined his vision for a program devoted to providing a "living focus" on "the diverse dynamics of African American aesthetics."[14] He selected an initial group of artists, including some of the area's major African American artists, "with an eye towards a diversity of visual arts disciplines and aesthetics, and proven professionalism."[15] Many of the artists explored similar themes as Chandler, especially Pan-Africanism, Black self-determination, and racism, though not exclusively. While he appeared dogmatic to some, he supported artists working in all media, with all manner of approaches at AAMARP, including those whose work did not deal explicitly with social problems facing Black people. As Chandler said, "I wasn't interested in having clones of myself at all. I wanted the work created at AAMARP to be extremely eclectic."[16]

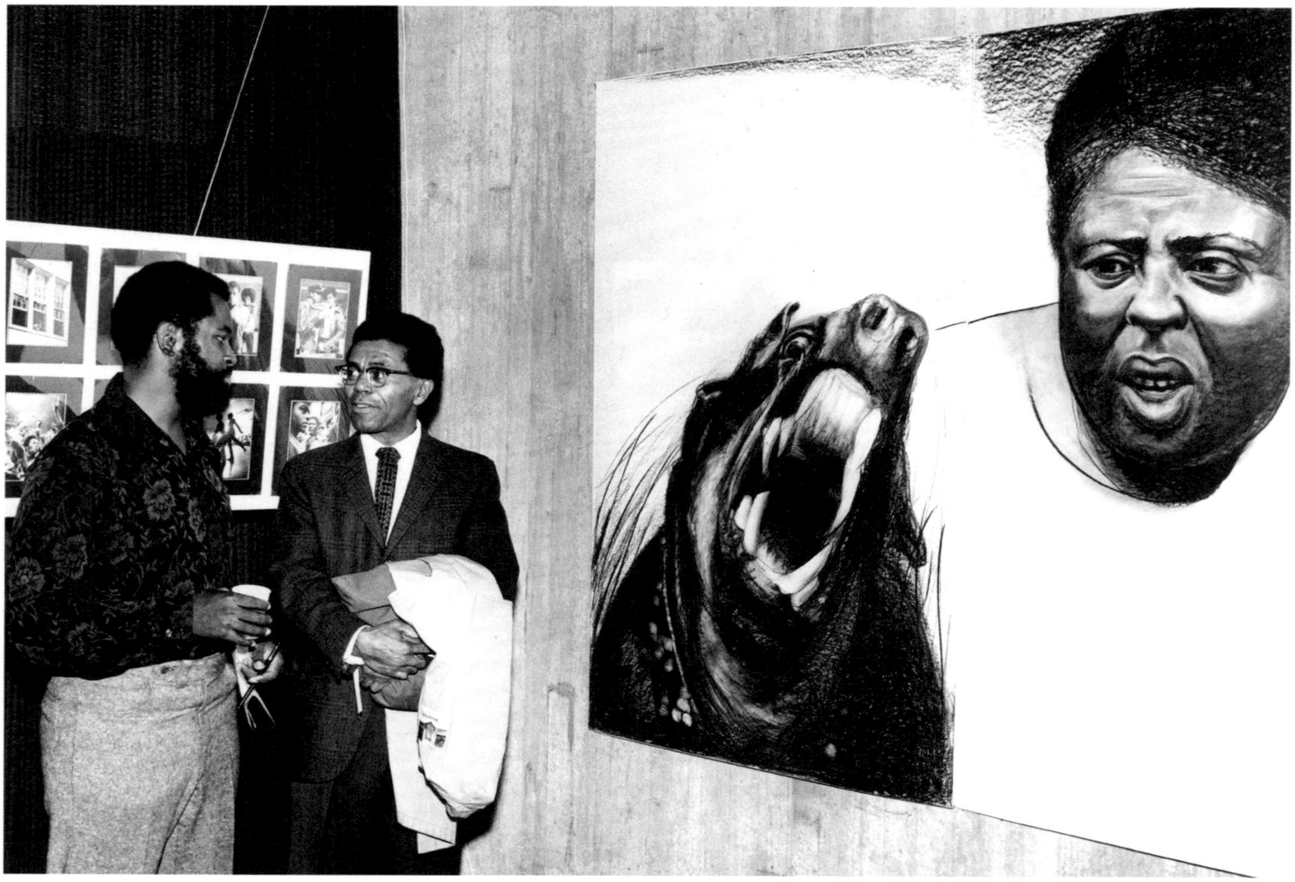

9

8. Left to right: Dana Chandler, Northeastern president Kenneth G. Ryder, and Milton Derr, 1980

9. Left to right: Dana Chandler and Calvin Burnett at Boston City Hall with *Fannie Lou Hamer* (1977), 1977

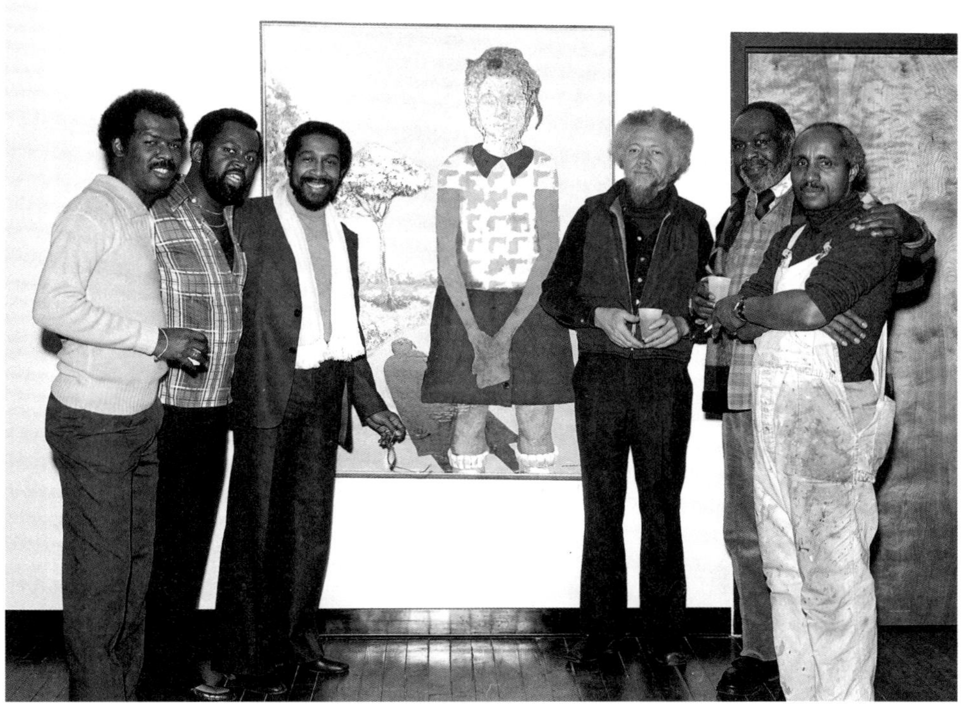

10. Left to right: Arnold Hurley, Dana Chandler, Barkley L. Hendricks, Benny Andrews, James Reuben Reed, and Milton Derr at Benny Andrews's AAMARP exhibition opening, 1980, with *Down These Mean Roads* (1972)

10

The loft space on the expansive second floor of 11 Leon Street was configured to include ten large studios, an L-shaped gallery, and a multipurpose room for community use. Each artist was given a three-year, rent-free lease (with options to renew), "thus enabling the artists to produce works at a level of intensity none has ever been able to attain."[17] And now, thanks to the studios, at a much larger scale. According to Chandler, the enormous freedom enjoyed by AAMARP artists, "was to become the dream and the reality."[18] In return, the artists would be present in their studios, accessible to students, and active participants and representatives of the program. Most importantly, because Chandler interfaced with Northeastern and acted as an administrator for the program, the artists could focus almost exclusively on their work, "to create at the level that they could actually create."[19]

While it may seem bombastic that Chandler used the term "master" in the program's name, it was in reverence for an older generation of established artists and educators he invited into the fold from the very beginning. Likewise, summoning the term master is aspirational in this context, grounded in an ethos of community, mentorship, artistic interaction, and exchange Chandler cultivated at AAMARP for each member to push others toward mastery of their respective media and to share skills, resources, and materials. Chandler carried forward sentiments artist Elizabeth Catlett outlined in her influential talk at the 1970 Conference on the Functional Aspects of Black Art via telephone when she said: "We should learn all the techniques we can, make ourselves as professional as possible, so that we are prepared to be the best of functioning artists."[20] This was especially important in some sense for a program housed within a university. For Chandler's image of the program, it was necessary that the artists were professional, making significant contributions to art history, and that they were tenured educators affiliated with the city's universities. In this regard, established artists and educators, such as Ellen Banks, Calvin Burnett, Milton Derr, and John Wilson, lent the program legitimacy through their involvement and provided shining examples of a level of mastery to be aspired to by younger artists. For Chandler, these artists were historical touchstones, who had mastered their respective crafts, and whose credentials and relationships connected the program to some of the most important artists of their generation, including Benny Andrews, Romare Bearden, Robert Blackburn, Elizabeth Catlett, Jeff Donaldson, Barkley L. Hendricks, and Charles White, to name a few. In the late 1970s, Chandler brought in artist James Reuben Reed, an "extremely erudite mentor," as codirector.[21] A generation older than Chandler, Reed was another gifted artist, a cofounder of the Boston Negro Artists' Association (now the Boston African American Artists Association), and a professor and later dean of Northeastern's Criminal Justice program.

Between 1977 and 1985, the dream and the reality were aligned. There was a vibrant spirit of inclusivity that extended to the exhibition program at that time, which Chandler described as "nondiscriminatory," offering a model that many museums aspire to still. More and more artists joined the fold, many as affiliates rather than residents. The range of activities at AAMARP during this period extended well beyond exhibitions to include dance performances; poetry readings; artist talks; workshops; awards ceremonies; and student group visits from daycare centers, Boston Public Schools, and the city's universities, who toured the complex regularly.[22] And that's just scratching the surface. The range of activities at AAMARP in a relatively short period of time is staggering and all encompassing.

Chandler routinely designed flyers for AAMARP programs, had them printed at Northeastern's print shop, and hand-delivered them on campus and around the community, to barber shops, beauty parlors, bars, churches, and nearby housing projects. Chandler, a master of self-promotion, always included flourishes like, "Bring Someone With You! Please Tell All Your Friends." A flyer Chandler made later read, "AAMARP Is For Everyone," and he meant it. Knowing that the success of the program depended on people from the community showing up—whether from Northeastern or otherwise—his flyers and exhibition announcements always insisted that AAMARP is "Free and open to the public at ALL times," including to children, tour groups, and anyone who walked through the doors at 11 Leon Street. By all accounts, the community showed up, again and again, and in large numbers. Chandler's vision of a visual arts complex was fulfilled through creating a "hospitable environment" for Black art to prosper.[23] From Northeastern's point of view, AAMARP brought an "immediate enrichment of cultural life" at the university.[24]

THE FUTURE IS TENTATIVE

In late 1984, Chandler and the other artists were notified that Northeastern was planning to renovate 11 Leon Street. While this would temporarily displace the artists and disrupt their programming, Northeastern promised to relocate the program and to address their concerns about the building as part of the renovation. By June of 1985, the artists were informed that their move was imminent, and on Friday, August 16, the artists moved to a building Northeastern rented from Wentworth School of Technology at 590 Huntington Avenue (a.k.a. 590), across the street from Massachusetts College of Art and Design. Before the move, Chandler wrote a memoran-

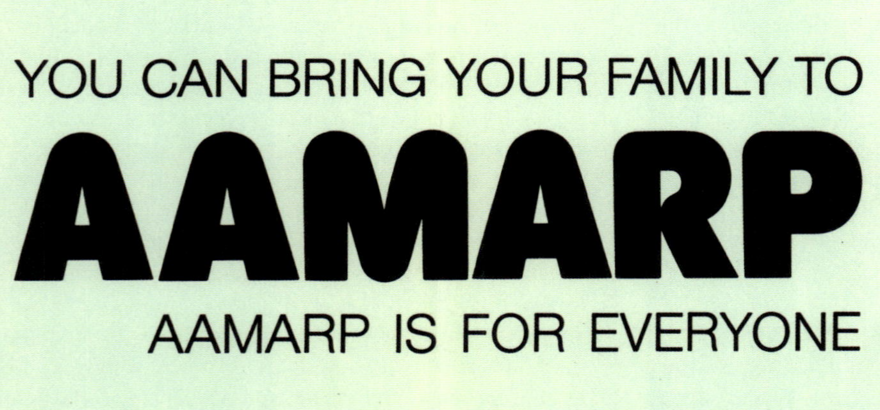

11. "AAMARP Is for Everyone" poster, c. late 1970s

11

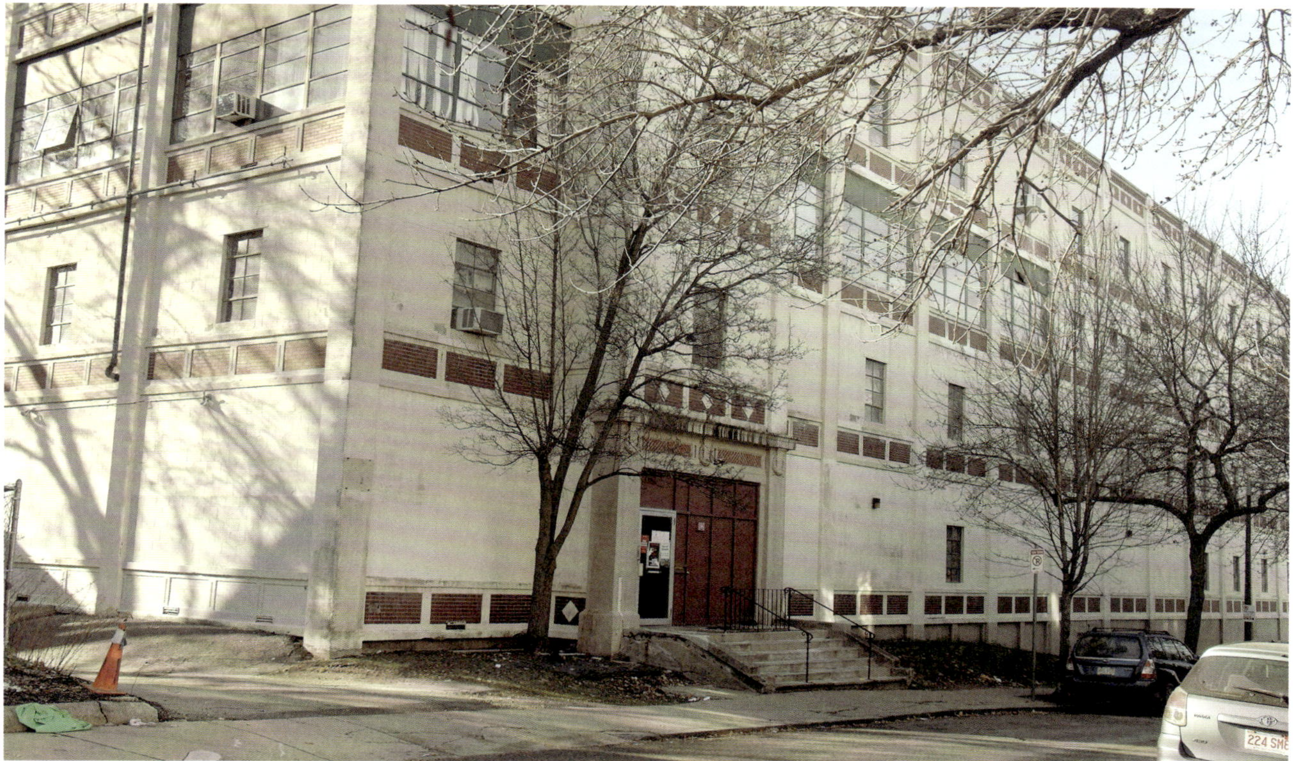

12

dum to the artists indicating that, "our new move is charged up with great new responsibilities and challenges."[25] He encouraged them to take the privileges AAMARP afforded seriously, saying: "AAMARP artists should be seen and heard of everywhere, especially if we wish AAMARP to exist long past our own personal participation."[26] He again implored them to foreground professionalism, both within the program in the context of the university, and beyond, by seeking exhibition opportunities outside of the program and participating in more "seminars, forums, organizations, panels, lecture series and the like than ever before."[27]

Despite Northeastern's assurances, as Chandler recalls: "[I] went to sleep every night knowing that the next day I would have to wake up and figure out what to do to keep someone from destroying my program."[28] While he still describes President Ryder as an ally, Chandler was always aware that others at the university did not support his program, and were displeased by his direct access to the university's president. The move to 590 would portend the growing instability of the program.

This instability is related in part to the program's unfixed administrative status within Northeastern.

Despite a long relationship with the African American Studies Department as an affiliate program, AAMARP was moved several times, including to the Division of Fine Arts in the College of Liberal Arts, joining the art, theatre, and dance departments. Previously, Chandler had successfully lobbied for AAMARP to be a department at Northeastern, rather than a program, in their official designation. "Programs," Chandler wrote in a memorandum to Director of the Division of Fine Arts Sergei Tschernisch after learning a decision had been made to redesignate AAMARP as a program without his input, "are built on soft money, are not institutions, are not solid, have no weight, and little power, generally speaking."[29] When AAMARP became a department, "the community felt less threatened, more assured that a cultural 'institution' they had watched grow from an idea in [Chandler's] mind to a solid physical structure, growing, improving, maturing, would last."[30] "What's in a name?" he continued: "In our community it is what you are called that determines how you are viewed; in fact who you are."[31]

The contents of the artists' studios at 11 Leon Street were placed in storage until 590 could be made to accommodate them. Even then, "a series of little cubicles went

12. AAMARP at 76 Atherton Street as it appears in *Painting the Back of the Hill*, a feature documentary currently in development about AAMARP and its artists

up, with very low ceilings in spaces not really intended for artists' use. The space was without windows for ventilation and natural light."[32] Despite the circumstances, the artists persisted in their work until 1988, when the renovations at 11 Leon Street—renamed Ryder Hall after the university's president—were complete. The university, however, did not keep its promise to return the whole program to campus. Only half of the artists were allowed to return to Ryder Hall, now an impressive facility next to the newly constructed Ruggles subway station on the MBTA's Orange Line. The other half of the artists remained in the less than favorable conditions at 590, even as new artists continued to join the program.

The year 1989 marked the end of Ryder's tenure as president, one of the program's most powerful champions. While there were many who did not believe that Northeastern's investment in AAMARP was worthwhile, there were still others like Ryder who understood its importance in the context of the university (in identifying the university as a patron of the arts), the local arts community (as providing "a genuine base of operations for black artists"), and beyond.[33] Still others at the university, including the new president John A. "Jack" Curry—who was executive vice president under Ryder—decided that Ryder Hall was needed for other purposes. AAMARP would have to "evacuate" 11 Leon Street again, just as the lease at 590 expired and was not renewed by Wentworth. The program, never fully reintegrated after the first move, was disrupted and unhoused again, and in search of a new home.

In 1990, the university began negotiations to acquire the former home of the Wireless Specialty Apparatus Company, a major manufacturer of commercial and military radio equipment, at 76 Atherton Street in Jamaica Plain. Given the university's history of real estate development in Boston's predominantly Black communities, "the idea of Northeastern moving up to Jamaica Plain did not sit well with the Jamaica Plain community."[34] When Northeastern proposed that the building would be the new permanent home for AAMARP, the acquisition became more palatable for the community. The artists were invited to participate in the negotiations, and the enthusiasm for AAMARP from the community was evident. After a year of negotiations, the Jamaica Plain Zoning Board approved the acquisition of the building zoned for use by the program and a warehouse for Northeastern's bookstore. Despite this development, it would be years before Northeastern made the space hospitable for the program. Even still, the artists occupied the third and fourth floors of the building and finished work on the individual studio spaces themselves. At 76 Atherton Street, the artists in the program were united for the first time in five years, though now they found themselves nearly two miles away from Northeastern's campus.

This wholeness was short lived. In 1991 Northeastern's provost Michael Baer informed Chandler that AAMARP's budget was being drastically reduced as part of university-wide belt tightening. Further, the university "could not fund the promised renovations of studio spaces and galleries" at 76 Atherton Street committed to by President

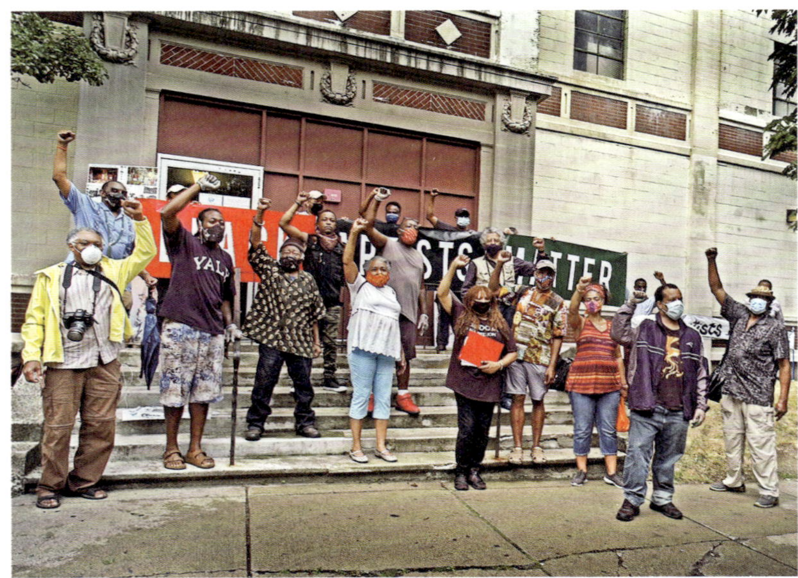

13. AAMARP artists and supporters protesting the lockout of their 76 Atherton Street building by Northeastern in 2020

13

Curry and other officials. Despite Chandler's appeals, and even his meticulous attempts to negotiate budgetary decreases line by line, the programmatic reductions moved forward. There was no longer a robust budget with which to return AAMARP's program to its earlier fullness. Even with a new dedicated building, the artists were on their own and largely untethered from Northeastern, far from campus and the community they cultivated there.

Two years later the program was further decimated. All staff positions as well as 80 percent of all program monies were removed by the university. As of June 30, 1993, Chandler was removed as director. He lamented this event as "the end of AAMARP" as part of a twenty-five-page *Urban Newsletter Art Piece* responding to Provost Baer's public statement about his disappointment that there wasn't "greater interaction" between AAMARP and the university.[35] The *Urban Newsletter* is a collage-based work aimed to counteract this claim by presenting, at length and in exhaustive detail, the many interactions of which the provost said there were "virtually none." Even as the program was underfunded and segregated from Northeastern's campus, they always endeavored to serve the university community however possible.

Following these catastrophic events and the public fallout, well respected artist and critic Edward Strickland was given the role of director. Strickland attempted to bolster AAMARP's claims for continuing interactions with the Northeastern community as a mode of survival, but largely without Chandler's aggrandizing flair for promotion. While Strickland worked to build the program back up to its overseers at Northeastern, "the artists went underground" at the same time.[36] They continued to make impressive work, adding new artists to the fold as others transitioned out, just as exhibitions were more intermittent and self-funded, and fewer programs and visitors were hosted at the building. What came into sharp focus at this time is the program's expansive definition of community. This always included operating as a safe haven for Boston-based activist work, and now included the individual artists' connections to Brazil, China, Ghana, Jamaica, Pakistan, and Sudan. In each instance, meaningful points of contact and exchange were pursued by these artists, just as others focused more intently on community partnerships in Boston. AAMARP's community became more international in reach, just as its activities became decentered and less beholden to the building itself as a community center.

After years of relative quiet, and many years after Chandler had retired and moved to New Mexico, the thirteen active members of the AAMARP collective received a letter from Northeastern's Facilities Department in 2018 ordering them to vacate 76 Atherton Street because of what the university described as "safety and security concerns."[37] Even though Northeastern owns the building, they cited code violations as the reason behind the eviction, violations for which they blamed the artists. Mayor Marty Walsh stepped in to facilitate conversations between Northeastern and the collective, aimed, according to Walsh's press secretary, at "strengthening the AAMARP program's future at Northeastern."[38] As a response, the artists "said the university has not made a good faith effort over the years to work with them to improve the building and has instead intentionally distanced itself from the collective."[39] Regardless, the relationship between AAMARP and the university remains tenuous. As artist Hakim Raquib said amid the tumult of 1993, "the future is tentative."[40] This sentiment continues today, as Northeastern controls the artists' access to the building, denying them free entry by way of key access, and only making the space available when a security guard is on duty during weekday hours. For several collective members who teach at area universities and high schools, this severely limits their studio access, which means they must at times work clandestinely.

Despite these less than favorable circumstances, the artists persist at 76 Atherton Street. The events of 1993 did not spell the end of AAMARP. The artists pursue good faith negotiations with the university to try to ensure the program's survival. Several longtime participants, now more advanced in age, work diligently to safeguard the legacy so that a younger generation of Boston artists struggling to afford studio space can join the collective. As Chandler now believes: "Northeastern never understood what they had in AAMARP, and I'm pretty sure they still don't."[41] According to longtime AAMARP artist L'Merchie Frazier, "we have a mission to preserve and conserve our own aesthetic," continuing Chandler's mandate for the program nearly fifty years ago.[42] What is abundantly clear is that artists working at AAMARP created a vast body of historically significant artworks, the depth of which is finally coming into focus. While the future of the program may still be "tentative," especially as so-called diversity initiatives are under aggressive attack nationwide, now is the time to bring "the dream and the reality" of AAMARP into better alignment. It is imperative to reinvest in Chandler's original vision of an artist-run alternative art space, one that is free and open to everyone, where Black art and culture, through a nondiscriminatory lens, can once again flourish.

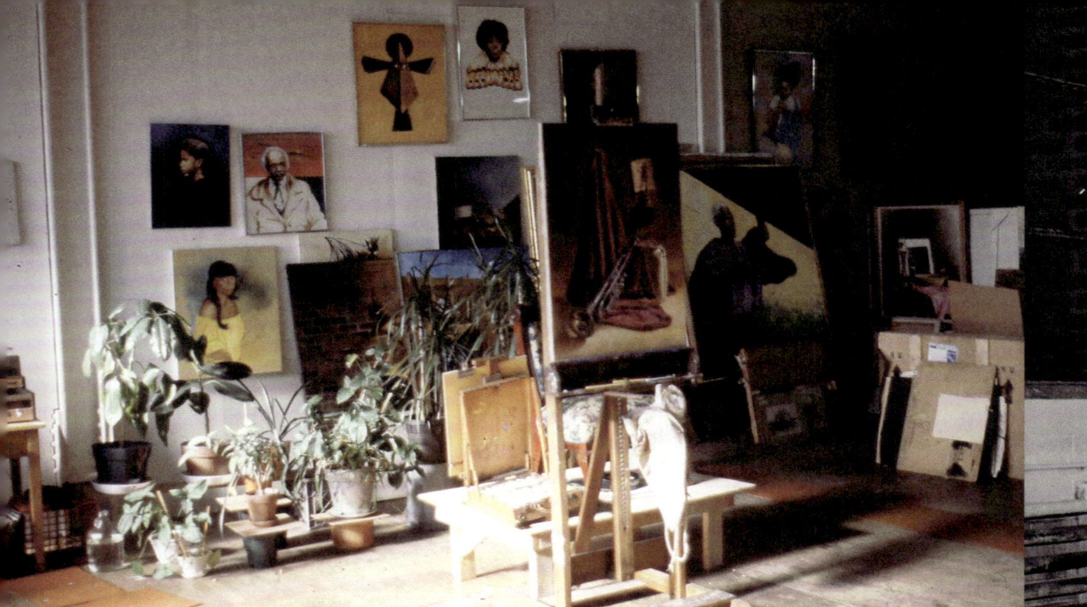

THE AFRICAN AMERICAN MASTER ARTISTS-IN-RESIDENCY PROGRAM OF NORTHEASTERN UNIVERSITY

AAMARP NEWS

JUNE 1980   AAMARP, 11 LEON ST., NORTHEASTERN UNIVERSITY   VOL. 1, NO. 1

Master Artist Milton Derr Has Major One Man Exhibition at AAMARP!

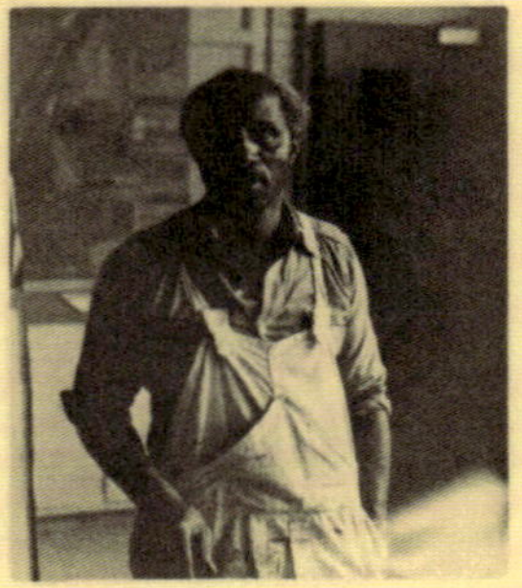

Milton Derr, the renowned African-American Master Artist-in-Residence at AAMARP, will be honored with the largest one-man exhibition of his paintings to date in the main gallery and corridor gallery at AAMARP.

Milton, who teaches at Tufts University and the Museum of Fine Arts Art School, has travelled extensively around the world and received some of his finest arts education in Japan, where he studied under some of Japan's best master printmakers. Mr. Derr also studied in Paris and was for a time a noted book illustrator. He has exhibited widely and won numerous awards for his work. You will find Mr. Derr's work in the collections of some of the more discerning art collectors here and abroad. Mr. Derr will be exhibiting a number of works created especially for this exhibition, along with those painted between 1975-1980.

There will be huge landscapes, numerous figurative pieces, and a number of significant historical "portraits". Mounted with these will be a series of portraits of local personalities. The public is invited to the show. Exhibition hours are 12 noon till 4 p.m. Saturday through Thursday. The opening is Friday, June 13th, 4-10 p.m. Admission is free at all times.

AAMARP Is an Award Winner!

AAMARP has been the recipient of a number of awards, including a Governor's citation and a State Senate citation. AAMARP has also been named "Critics Choice" five times by the *Boston Globe*, as well as an artistic breakthrough (*Boston Globe* 350 Magazine, May 18, 1980, p. 17) for its exhibitions. Come visit AAMARP and see why!

Master Artist and AAMARP Creator/Director Dana Chandler Wins Grants!

Artists Foundation and Simmons College Faculty Development Grants Received.

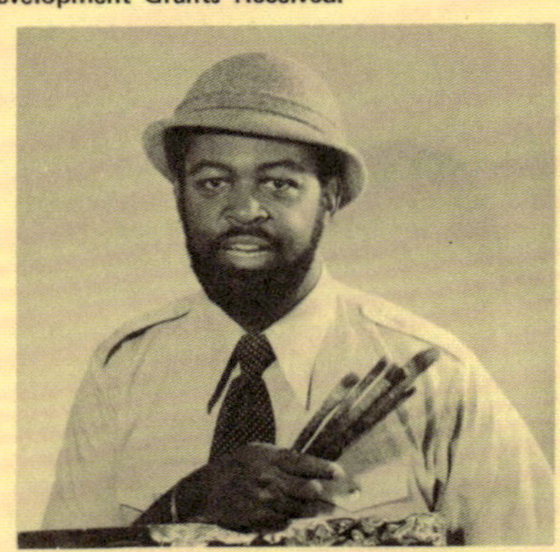

Professor Dana C. Chandler, Jr., of Roxbury is one of the ten recipients out of many hundreds of entries for the Artists Foundation grant for painting in Massachusetts. Chandler also received a Simmons College Faculty Development Grant for research in painting this month.

Professor Chandler, recipient of a Governor's citation and a State Senate citation for his work in the arts and the community in 1979, is Associate Professor (tenured) of Art/African-American Art History at Simmons College, Boston, and Creator-Director of the highly successful, award-winning African-American Master Artists-in-Residency Program (A.A.M.A.R.P.) at Northeastern University.

Professor Chandler's award-winning work may be seen in the Federal Reserve Bank of Boston's main gallery (first floor) through June, and in the inaugural exhibition "Art of the 70's" on view in the new home of the Museum of the National Center of Afro-American Artists (NCAAA) in Roxbury during June and July, 1980.

AAMARP Adopts New Summer Hours

AAMARP Hours Now 12 pm - 4 pm Daily July 7th Through September 1. Saturday Through Thursday.

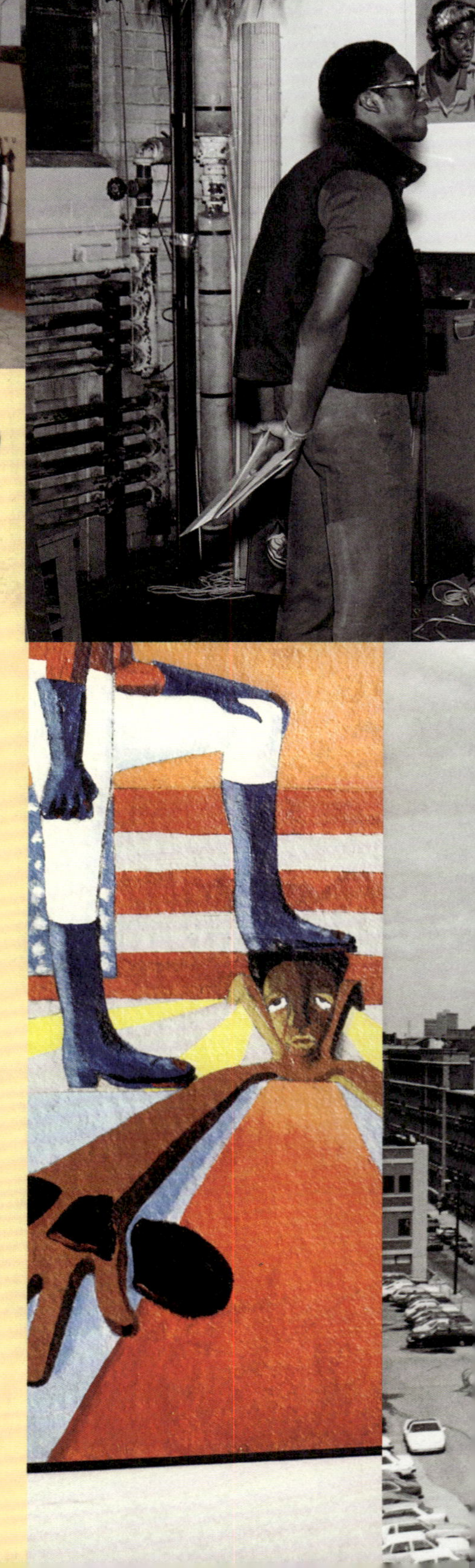

AAMARP IS THE BEST INFLATION FIGHTER IN TOWN! AAMARP EXHIBITIONS ARE FREE!

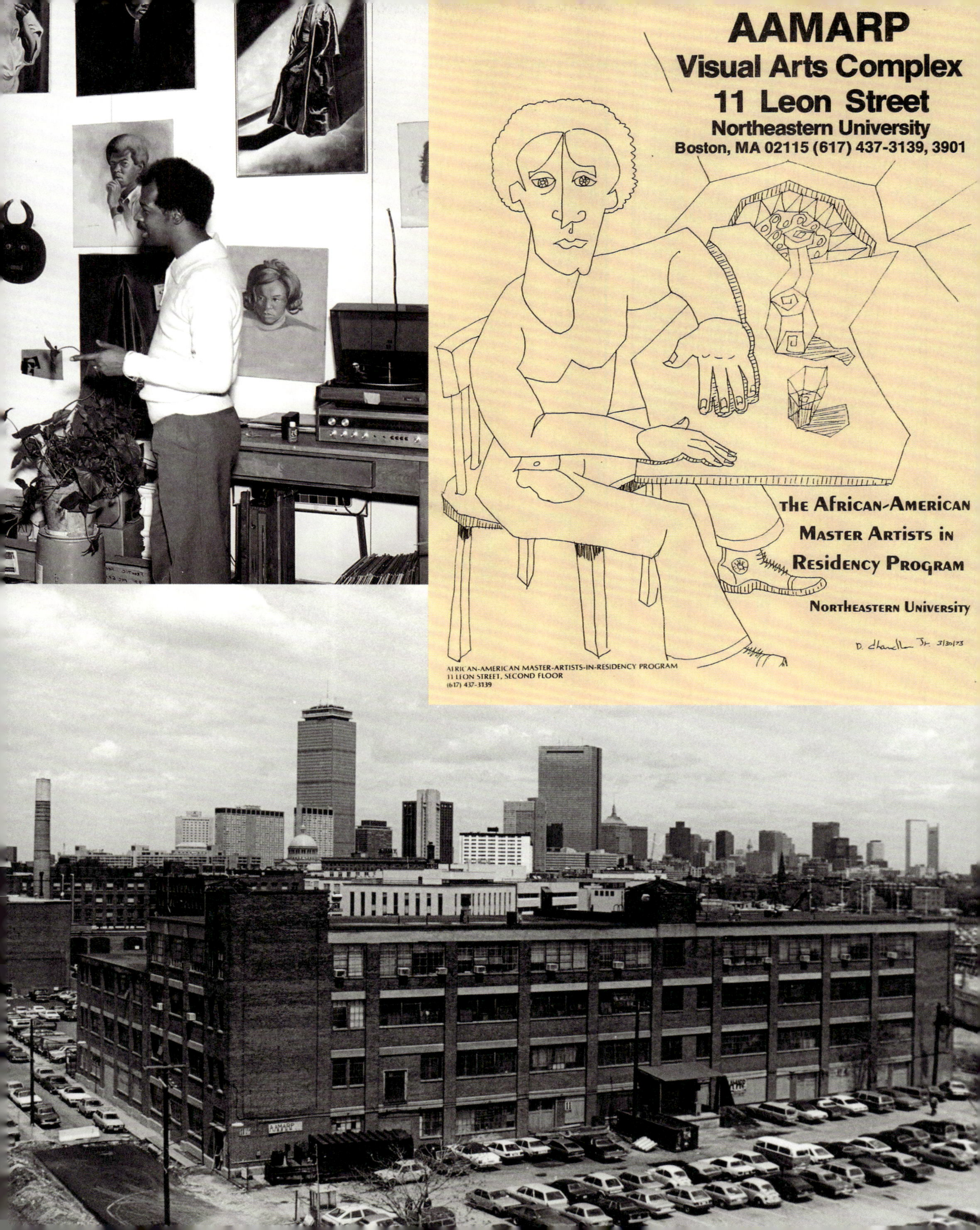
AAMARP
Visual Arts Complex
11 Leon Street
Northeastern University
Boston, MA 02115 (617) 437-3139, 3901
the African-American
Master Artists in
Residency Program
Northeastern University
AFRICAN-AMERICAN MASTER-ARTISTS-IN-RESIDENCY PROGRAM
11 LEON STREET, SECOND FLOOR
(617) 437-3139

AAMARP 1977–1992

Compiled by
MEGHAN CLARE CONSIDINE MCC
and JEFFREY DE BLOIS JDB

Artist reflections by
NAPOLEON JONES-HENDERSON, SUSAN THOMPSON, EKUA HOLMES, WEN-TI TSEN, REGINALD L. JACKSON, BRYAN MCFARLANE, RENÉE STOUT, HAKIM RAQUIB, AND RENE WESTBROOK

This chronology of the African American Master Artists-in-Residence Program is imperfect, pieced together from a variety of sources. It is constituted from information gleaned from a range of materials: archival documents, photographs, written statements, artworks, exhibition announcements, newsletters, memoranda, and artist recollections, among others. Some aspects of the program's early history are well documented in the records of Northeastern University Archives and Special Collections, while later moments are almost nonexistent in the official record. This imbalance is reflected in the chronology by counterbalancing the material history present in the archive with the looser, anecdotal history of recollections, and through a necessary two-part structure. The first part surveys a selected exhibition history of the program and key artists from 1977 to 1993, whereas the second is more elusive, following an indeterminate path into the present. At a certain point, when the host institution becomes openly hostile, the program's survival is understood best in moments that are difficult to narrate, illustrate, or know for certain (a certainty that so many chronologies demand). Likewise, some events in the history of AAMARP are intensely personal and beyond the scope of what can be captured here. This chronology is a first attempt to apprehend the unruly history of AAMARP, across three locations in Boston, and in shifting orientations to Northeastern University and its different administrations.

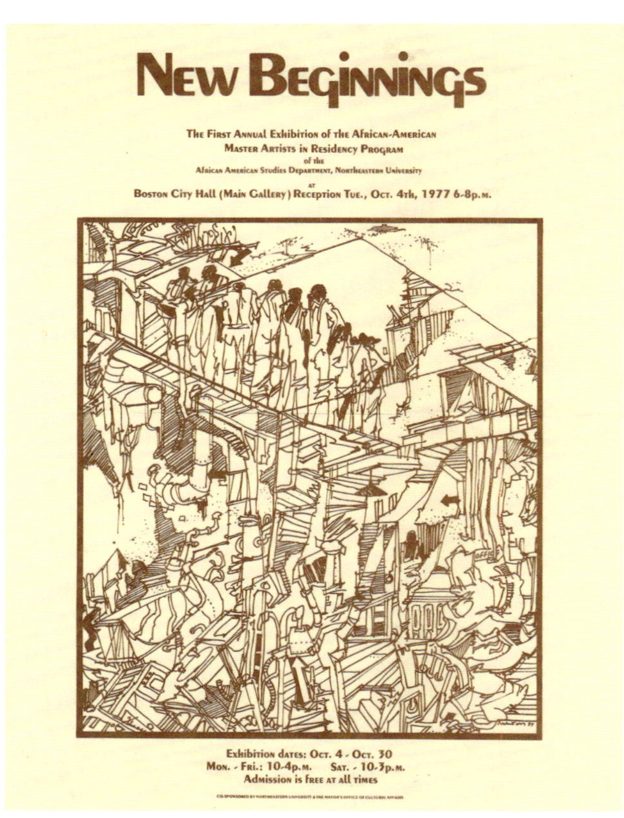

1

1. *New Beginnings* flyer featuring uncredited drawing by Milton Derr, 1977

AAMARP AT 11 LEON STREET

"I met Dana in Chicago at an NCA convention and then the CONFABA conference organized by my AfriCOBRA brother Jeff Donaldson. Shortly thereafter, meeting Calvin Burnett and his Massachusetts College of Art and Design (MassArt) students, I moved to Boston to teach weaving at MassArt. Upon arriving, I immediately looked up Dana in hopes of getting '*the lowdown*' on studio space.

Before AAMARP was established, with the assistance of Harriet Forte Kennedy, I was awarded an '*Artist-in-Residence*' grant from Massachusetts Arts Council at 11 Leon St. where Dana had his studio which subsequently became the AAMARP studios. During this residency Dana and I would discuss the needs of artists in Roxbury, reflecting on the studio space Dana met me in while in Chicago.

We spent a lot of time together and had many conversations about AAMARP before it came into existence. When it did kick off, it was a celebratory environment that surely was impregnated with the ethos of *community*. It was a place in which people from the whole diaspora seeped through when they came to Boston. Along with a few other places, AAMARP was a pivotal institution of cultural activity. AAMARP was in many ways an example of what could be, if one chose to do the work. That's my mantra: *Do the work*. AAMARP, and the artists there have all done the work, and are still doing the work, and it has blossomed out into the larger community, meaning the world. AAMARP is a place early on that encouraged aspiring artists because they were able to come through and mingle very freely with, 'successful,' artists. If success means we are connected to each other, if I can be some inspiration or encouragement, then I accept that, but this is not the end of it. AAMARP is like a well where everyone can come get a drink when they're thirsty." Napoleon Jones-Henderson

1977

New Beginnings

BOSTON CITY HALL

OCT 4–31

Ellen Banks, Calvin Burnett, Dana C. Chandler Jr., Milton Derr, Arnold Hurley, Stanley Pinckney, Rudolph Robinson, John Wilson, and guest artists

FIGS. 1–2

AAMARP's debut presentation was staged at the main gallery of Boston City Hall from October 4 to October 31, 1977. It is a testament to Dana C. Chandler Jr.'s tenacity that the group announced themselves as an intergenerational artist collective by staging a public exhibition before being formally recognized as such by their benefactor, Northeastern University. Although Chandler accused Northeastern of delaying a public announcement for over two years, the exhibition announcement still listed the university as a cosponsor. At City Hall, Calvin Burnett showed an ambitious, two-panel charcoal drawing titled *Fannie Lou Hamer* (p. 16, bottom) that had been

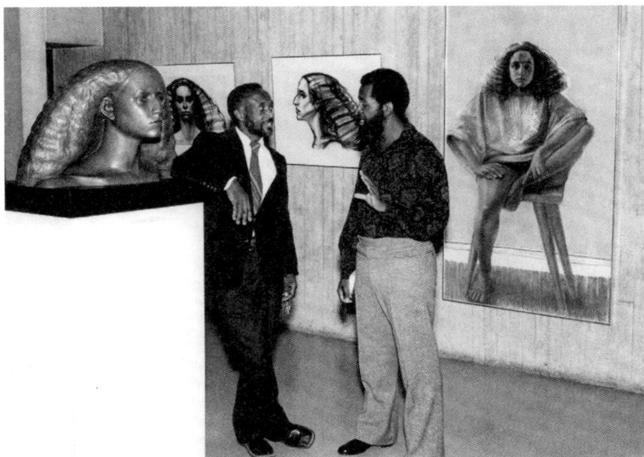

2

2. Left to right: John Wilson and Dana Chandler at Boston City Hall, 1977

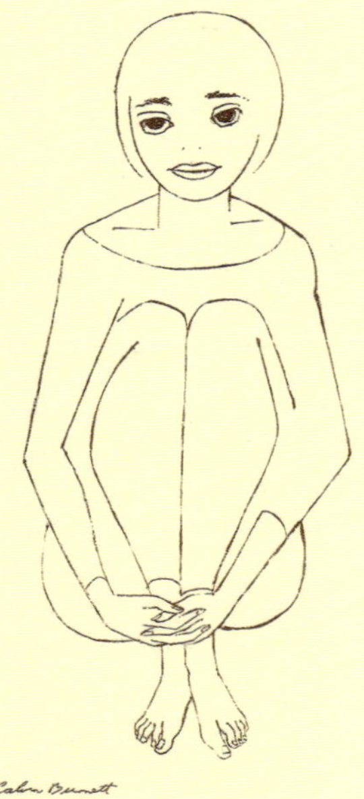

3

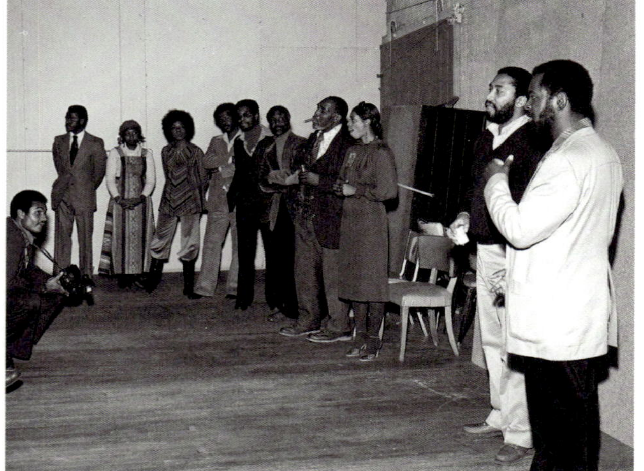

4

completed earlier that same year. The work engages with key iconography of the civil rights movement: the eponymous legendary voting rights activist, and the vicious, snarling attack dogs police forces notoriously set upon freedom fighters across the South. It was meaningful to present this imagery in Boston, which during this period was undergoing its own violent desegregation effort across the public school system. John Wilson exhibited a bronze bust and three drawings of his oldest granddaughter, Gabrielle. These deeply sensitive portrayals emphasized Gabrielle's natural curls and confident demeanor. The assembled artists testified to a key conviction of Chandler's that continues to characterize AAMARP to this day: "Talk to older artists and learn from them. They must be doing something right if they're still alive and eating. And pass on what you know about living to those younger than you. You may need their help one day."[1] **MCC**

1978

AAMARP Artists — Recent Works

NORTHEASTERN UNIVERSITY ART GALLERY, SECOND FLOOR, DODGE LIBRARY, 360 HUNTINGTON AVENUE, BOSTON

NOV 8–DEC 9

Ellen Banks, Calvin Burnett, Dana C. Chandler Jr., Milton Derr, Tyrone Geter, Arnold Hurley, Reginald L. Jackson, Stanley Pinckney, James Reuben Reed, Rudolph Robinson, Barbara Ward, John Wilson, Theresa-India Young

FIGS. 3–8

AAMARP's grand opening was celebrated on November 8, 1978, with open studios and galleries at 11 Leon Street and a presentation of recent works by affiliate artists at Northeastern University Art Gallery. *Recent Works*, the first annual AAMARP group exhibition, featured several new artists in addition to the core group first assembled for *New Beginnings*. These included: Tyrone Geter, a gifted draftsperson and painter who lived in Boston between 1976 and 1978 and later returned to the city; Stanley Pinckney, a textile artist working primarily with traditional resist dye techniques, who also painted a portrait of Negritude poet and politician Léopold Sédar

3. *AAMARP Artists—Recent Works* flyer featuring drawing by Calvin Burnett, 1978

4. AAMARP artists on stage in Dodge Library, 1978. Left to right, standing: Stanley Pinckney, Theresa-India Young, Ellen Banks, Arnold Hurley, Reginald L. Jackson, John Wilson, James Reuben Reed, Barbara Ward, Gregory Ricks, and Dana Chandler

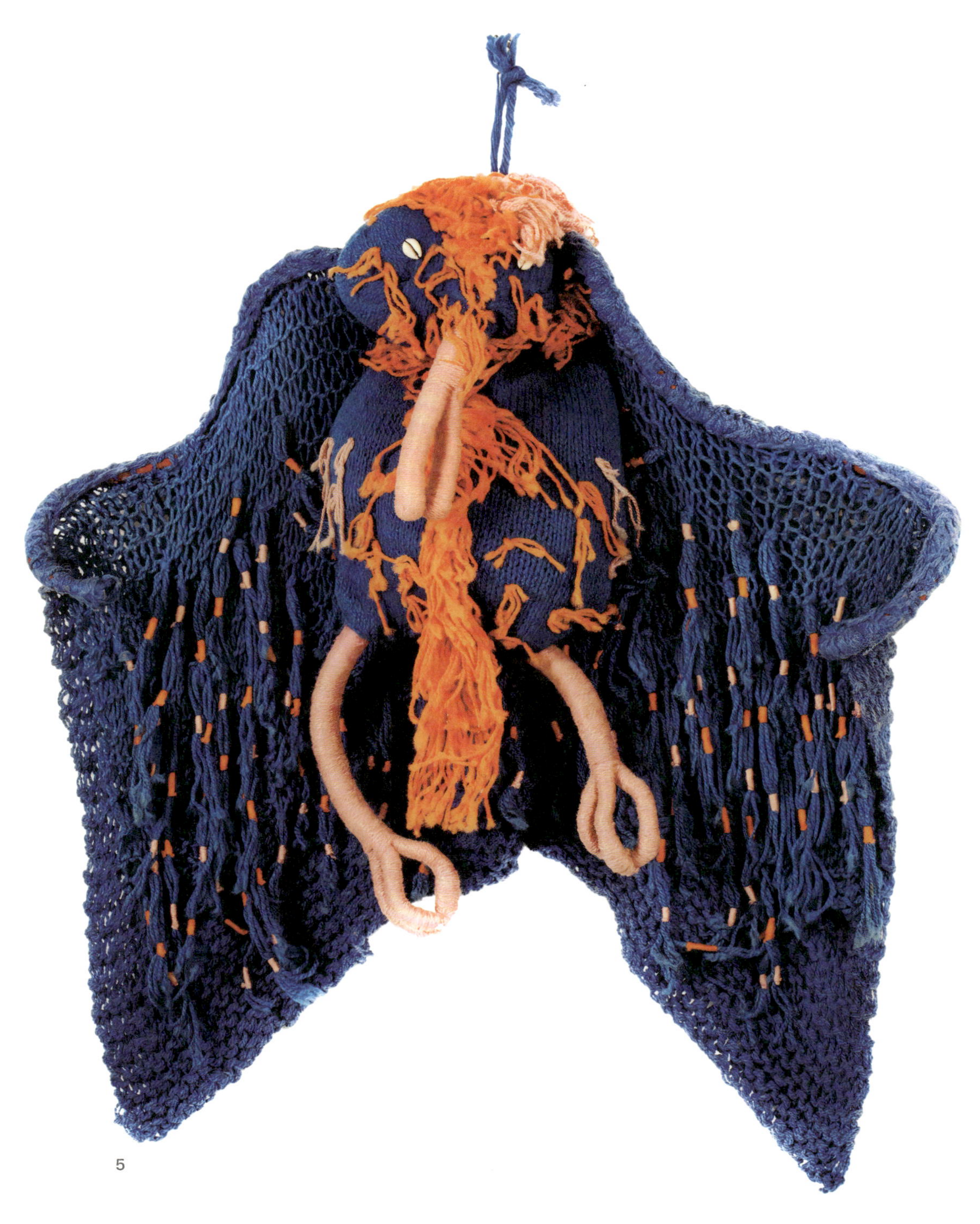

5. Theresa-India Young, *Blue Bird*, 1981. Cotton, silk, wool and synthetic yarns, and cowrie shell beads. Approximately 36 × 60 inches (91.4 × 152.4 cm)

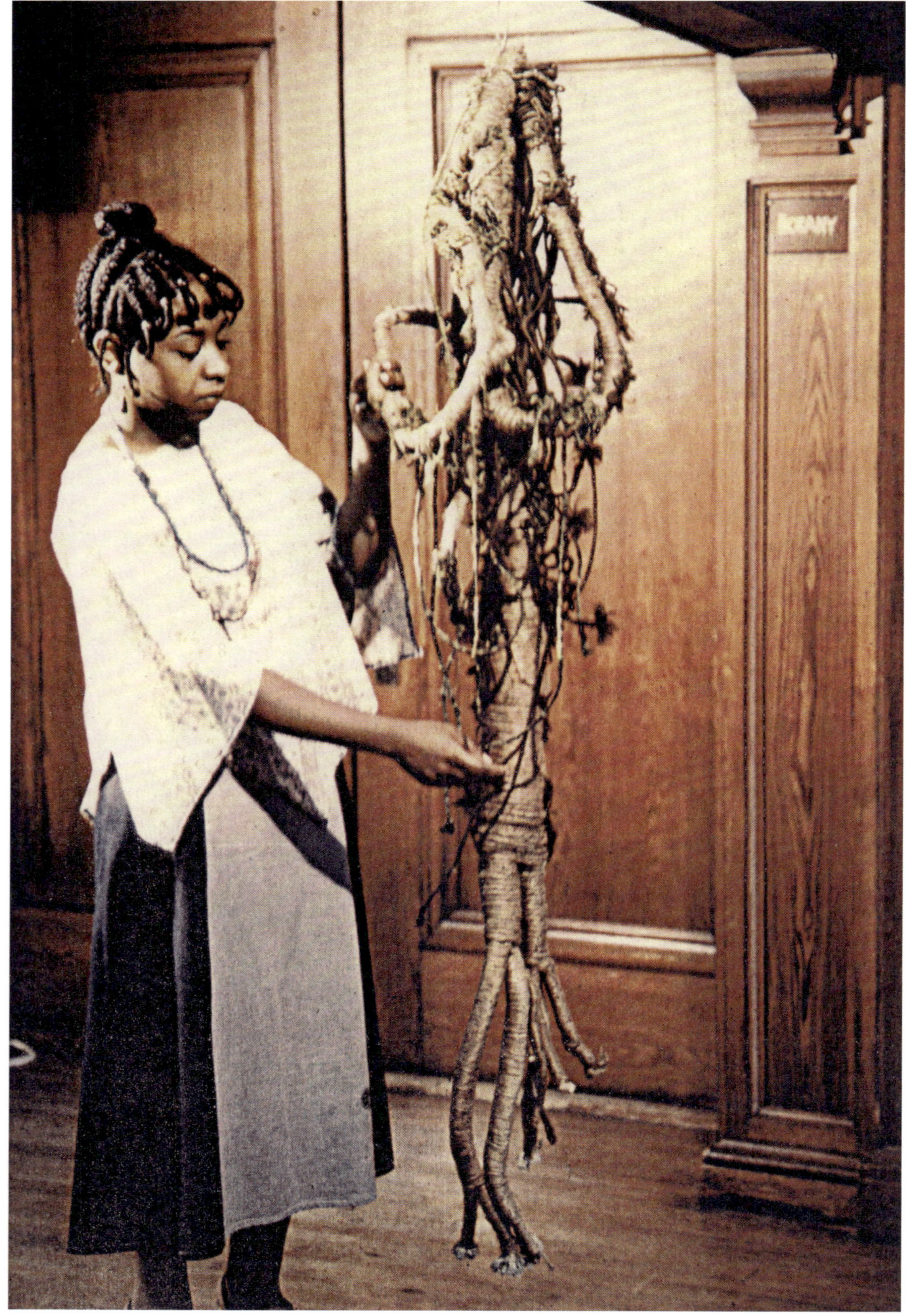

6. Theresa-India Young with
Tree Form, 1981

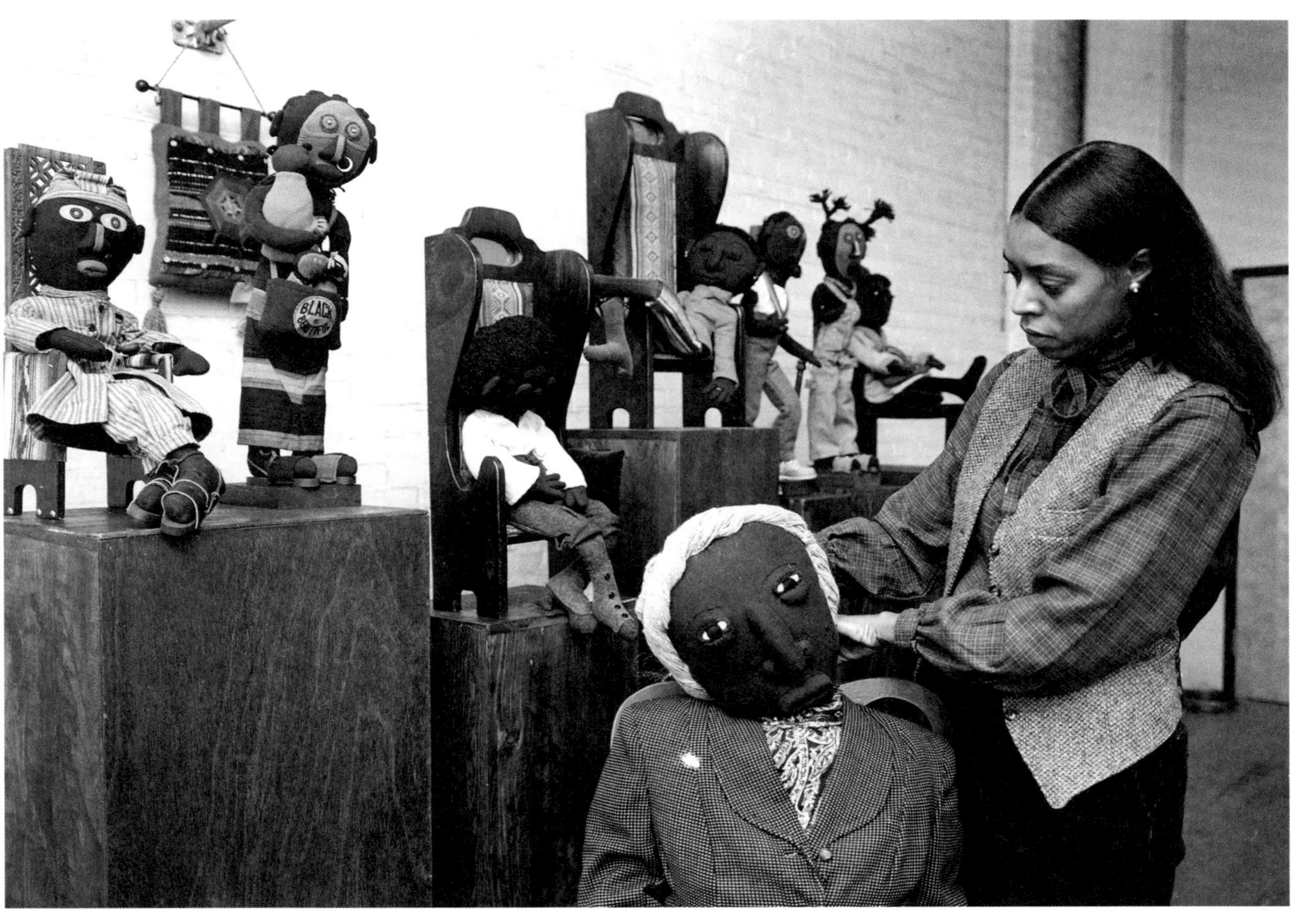

7

Senghor displayed in the presidential palace in Dakar; Barbara Ward, a self-taught artist and former dancer and choreographer who made figurative soft sculptures as a paean to her multiethnic and intergenerational community; and Theresa-India Young, whose fiber-based sculptures were often inspired by "tree forms and environments, particularly the colors and textures of mountainsides and aerial landscapes."[2] The innovative techniques of Ward and Young in particular are indicative of the material inventiveness of artists at AAMARP. Ward drew formal inspiration from African masks and incorporated fabric swatches from multiple cultures, often positioning her figurative sculptures (each with a distinct personality), as compelling expressions of third world feminist solidarity. As a child, Young learned basketry, finger weaving, and braiding from her grandmother, and later traveled throughout Africa to study traditional techniques. Valuing thrift and reuse, common household scraps such as grass, rope, hair, wire, and sticks frequently appeared in Young's richly textured fiber sculptures. *Recent Works* continued to lay the groundwork for the inaugural exhibition in the program's galleries the following year, a two-person exhibition of "new images" from AAMARP residents Geter and Arnold Hurley, a dynamic realist painter of portraits and still lifes. **JDB**

7. Barbara Ward staging soft sculptures in her studio, 1978

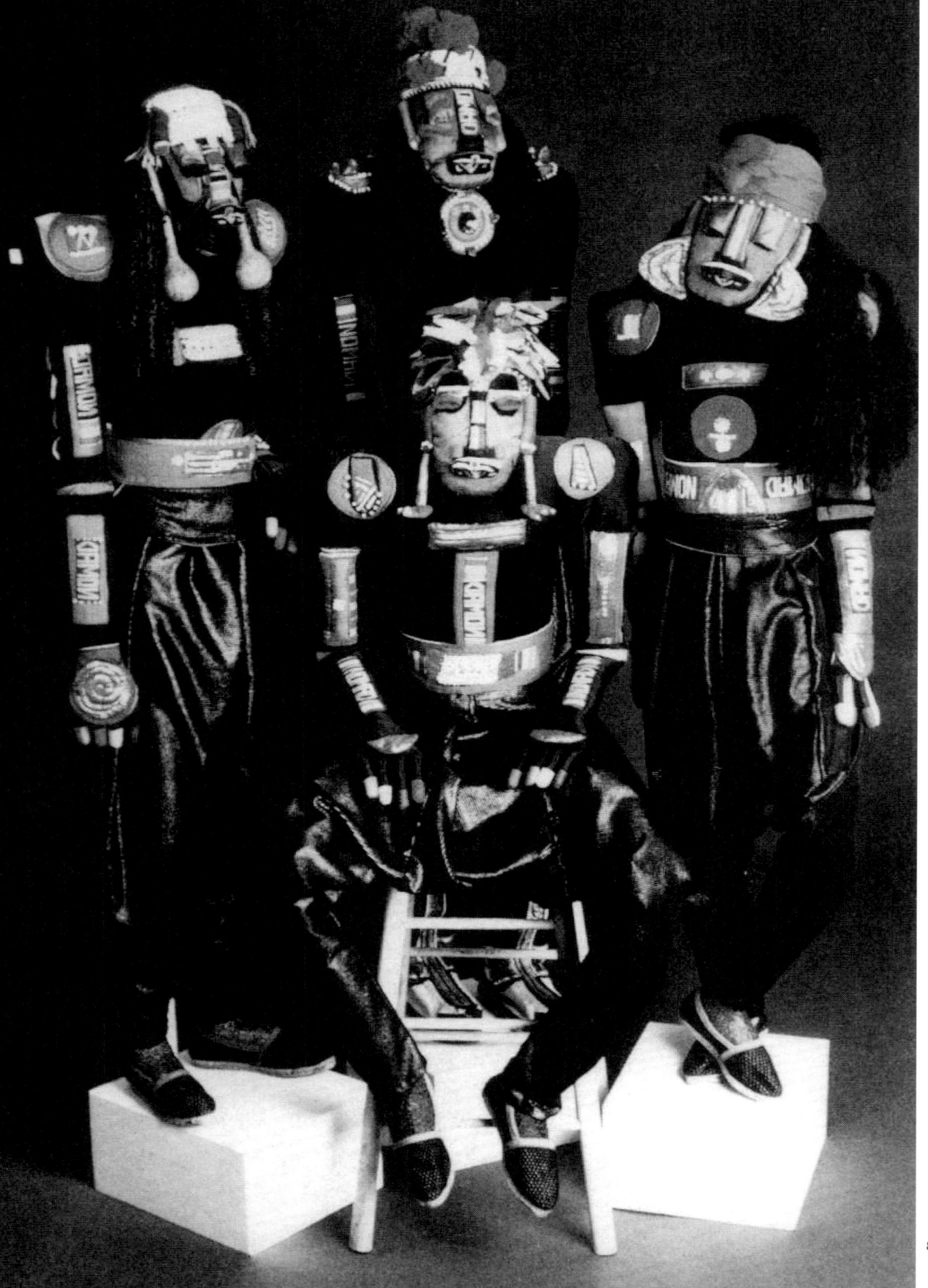

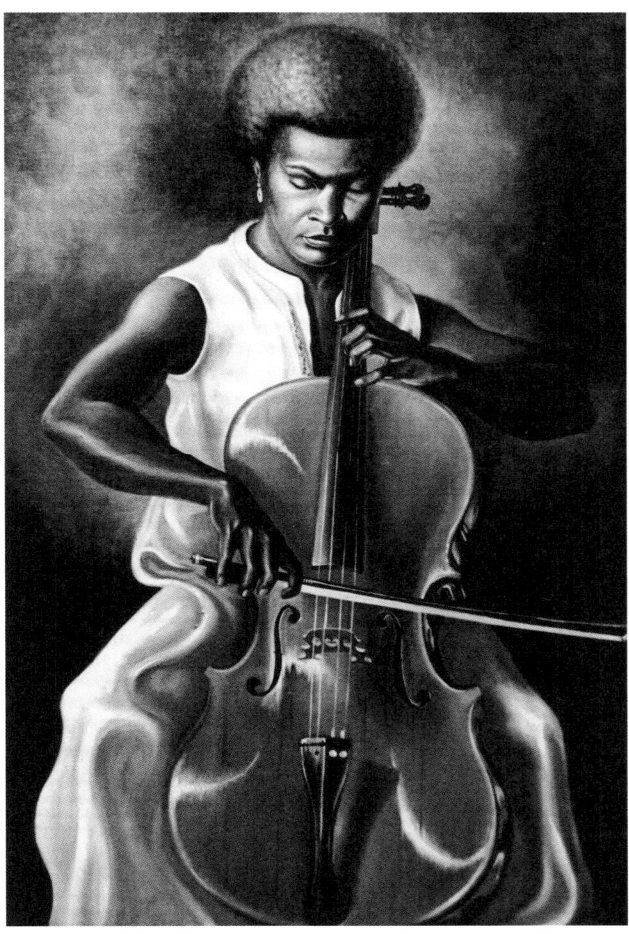

9

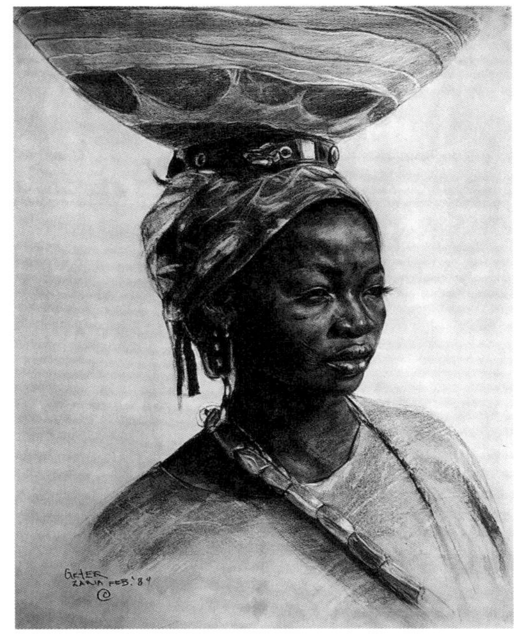

10

8. Barbara Ward, *New Race II*, 1987–88. Soft sculpture. Four parts, each approximately 67 × 22 × 24 inches (170.2 × 55.9 × 61 cm). Cambridge Public Library Archives and Special Collections

9. Arnold Hurley, *Betty*, 1979. Oil on canvas. 48 × 31 inches (121.9 × 78.7 cm)

10. Tyrone Geter, *Binta*, 1984. Graphite on paper. 22 × 18 inches (55.9 × 45.7 cm)

1979

Arnold Hurley and Tyrone Geter: New Images

AUG 19–SEPT 15

FIGS. 9–10

Hale Woodruff, Wilmer Jennings, and Allan Rohan Crite

THE MUSEUM OF THE NATIONAL CENTER OF AFRO-AMERICAN ARTISTS IN COOPERATION WITH AAMARP

SEPT 16–OCT 12

Nelson Stevens: Primal Force

OCT 14–NOV 10

Greater Boston Women's Exhibition

NOV 25–DEC 23

Elizabeth Ahern, Robin Barlow, Martha Bedrosian, S. J. Belton, Deborah Brown, Susan Hardy Brown, Cassandra Bryan, Elli Crocker, Lotus Do, Janie Driscoll, Kathleen Driscoll, Irene Fairley, Lee Farrington, Georgina Forbes, Martha Friedman, Carla Golembe, Ekua Holmes, Joyce Idelicato, Mela Lyman, Katherine McGlynn, C. T. McKee, J. L. McRath, Mary Grace Mellow, Denise Minter, Ann Northrup, Brenda Pinardi, Diane Rolnick, Heidi Rufeh, Emily Socolov, Priscilla Stadler, N. Stapen, Maria Termini, Susan Thompson, Johnetta Tinker, Ei T. Turchinetz, Irene Valincius, Martha Vitagliano, Barbara Ward, Elaine Wong, and Pacifica Ycaza

FIG. 11

During AAMARP's first years of exhibitions at 11 Leon Street, Chandler and others realized an ambitious, inclusive, and nondiscriminatory exhibition program. This began with what was planned to be the first of many annual exhibitions of women artists from the greater Boston area.[3] The exhibition included a large majority of artists not otherwise affiliated with the program, such as Ekua Holmes, an artist born and raised in Roxbury working primarily in collage; Susan Thompson, a textile-based artist and protégé of Allan Rohan Crite (an artist often referred to as the Dean of Black Artists in Boston); and Johnetta Tinker, who creates evocative works on paper and was a student of influential artist John T. Biggers.[4] Following the inaugural *Greater Boston Women's Exhibition*, *The Contemporary Arab World* (1980) presented objects from the collection of Edmond Moussally,[5] a professor of music at Roxbury Community College; a major exhibition of international child art was staged in 1981 from the collection of Al Hurwitz, coordinator of Visual and Related Arts for Newton Public Schools at the time; *Beyond These Walls* (1980–81) presented works from the Prison Art Project of Massachusetts; and *All Our Relations* (1983) featured works by Native American

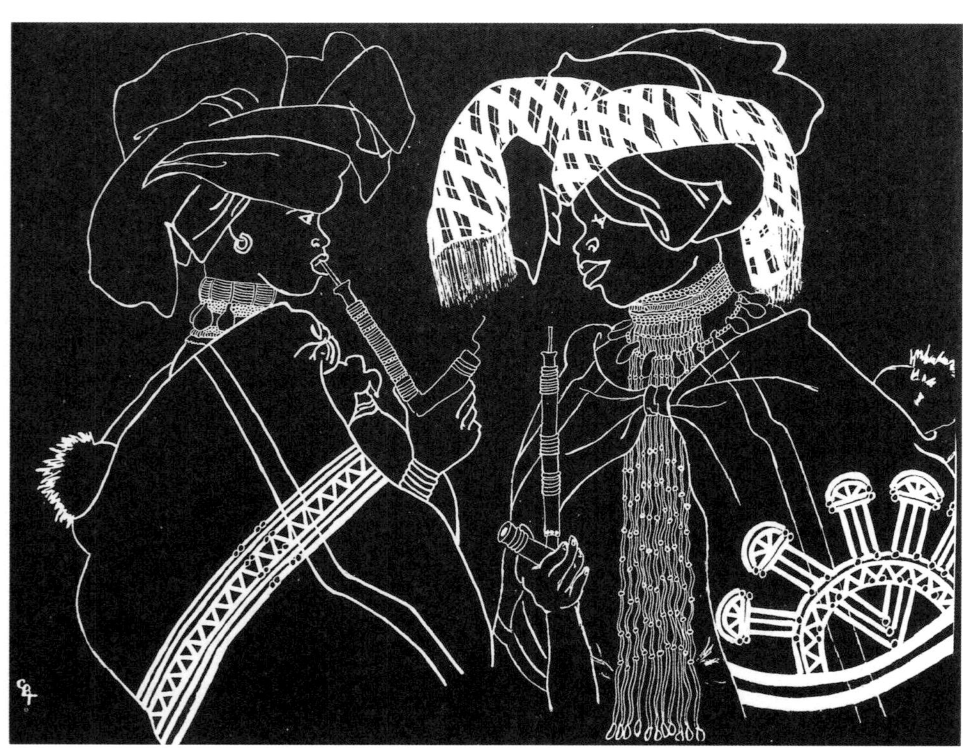

11. *Greater Boston Women's Exhibition* flyer featuring print by Cassandra Bryan, c. 1979

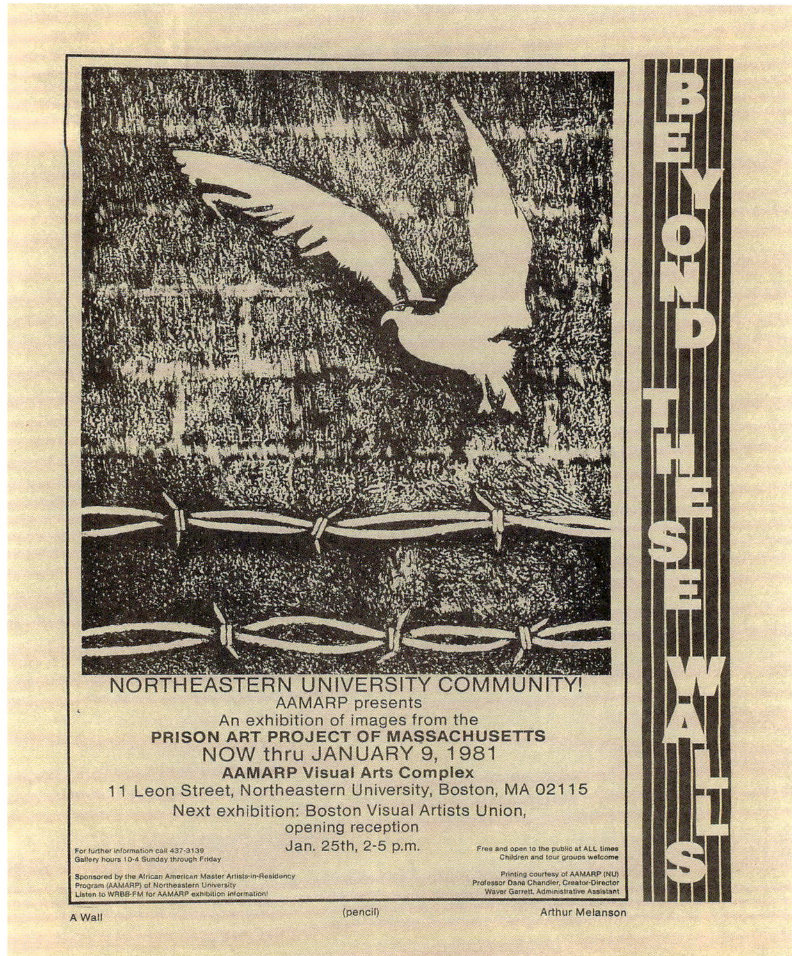

12

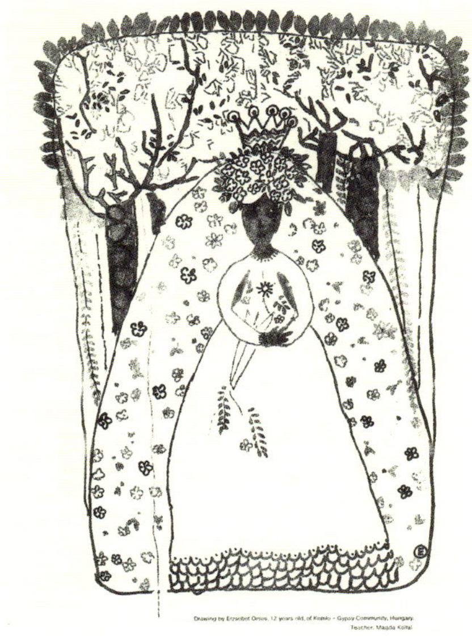

13

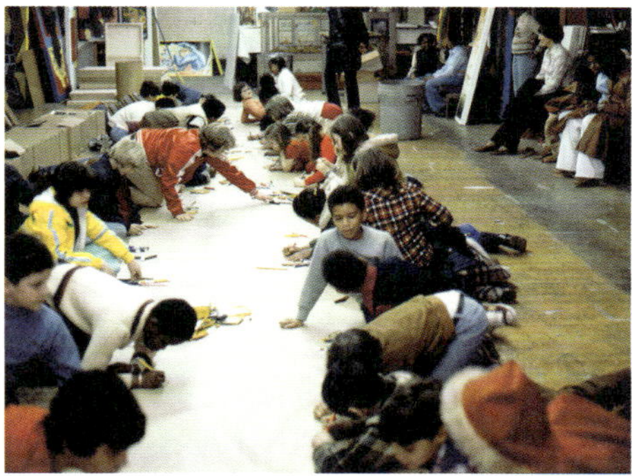

14

makers. Taken together, these five exhibitions provide a sense of the diversity of the exhibition program during AAMARP's first years at 11 Leon Street, and are a model of inclusivity that museums aspire to still.   **JDB**

"Being an AAMARP artist has been the highlight of my artistic career. The studio space means that I have a place to work, and a place to show my work, and that I have been in the company of master artists. To me, it made all the difference in the world to be in that atmosphere, where on a regular basis I could see great works of art from my contemporaries. I think that has helped push me ahead as an artist and has helped me to fine-tune my skills as an artist. Dana always encouraged me, always. When he invited me into the program, I was just starting out as an artist. I had been working with Allan Rohan Crite, but my career was new. Everything was new to me. Dana invited me in, and that's when I first said "I gotta do this." I didn't want to disappoint Dana and Allan. I had to try to prove that I am an artist. I used to work all night, until 2:00 or 3:00 in the morning, after making sure everything was good at home. Because that's what I had to do. Dana would always comment on a piece. He would say, "Good work, keep it up." That meant everything to me because of his mastery, because he was so prolific. To get that encouragement from him was a big deal and I sincerely appreciated it."
Susan Thompson

12. *Beyond These Walls* flyer featuring Arthur Melanson's drawing *A Wall*, 1981

13. *International Child Art* flyer featuring drawing by Erzsebet Orsos, 1981

14. Children's collaborative art project at AAMARP, c. 1980

1980

Benny Andrews

JAN 6–FEB 9

FIGS. 15–16

Benny Andrews's solo exhibition at AAMARP was curated by Chandler himself, who was a longtime acolyte, and featured roughly fifty works in oil, acrylic, and pen and ink. Despite having already been the subject of solo shows at the Studio Museum in Harlem, the High Museum of Art, and the Wadsworth Athenaeum, Andrews especially valued staging exhibitions in the context of community spaces like AAMARP, housed within universities, for the way he could engage "the future writers, the future curators." As he noted to Kay Bourne, arts editor of the local Black newspaper, the *Bay State Banner*: "My work is important to [students] at an impressionable time of life and they remember me."[6] The AAMARP exhibition featured *Nene* (1978), a collaged oil portrait of the artist's future wife Nene Humphrey leisurely resting against a tree at MacDowell, an artist retreat in New Hampshire where the pair met, as well as *American Gothic* (1971), which would later enter the collection of the Metropolitan Museum of Art. Predating Andrews's tenure as director of Visual Arts for the National Endowment for the Arts, he provided key mentorship to Chandler as he sought government grants to fund AAMARP in its early years. As a founder of the Black Emergency Cultural Coalition, which advocated for Black representation in New York's art museums, as well as for arts education programs for incarcerated individuals, Andrews's engagement with AAMARP illustrates a cosmopolitan network of support and exchange across regional centers of the Black Arts movement.   **MCC**

Calvin Burnett: Retrospective

FEB 17–MAR 14

FIG. 17

Milton Derr: 1975–80

JUNE 13–JULY 6

FIG. 18

In 1980, two of AAMARP's senior affiliated artists presented their work in extensive solo exhibitions in the program's galleries. The first was a retrospective of forty-plus years of work by Cambridge-born artist Calvin Burnett, who worked principally in painting and printmaking and taught at Massachusetts College of

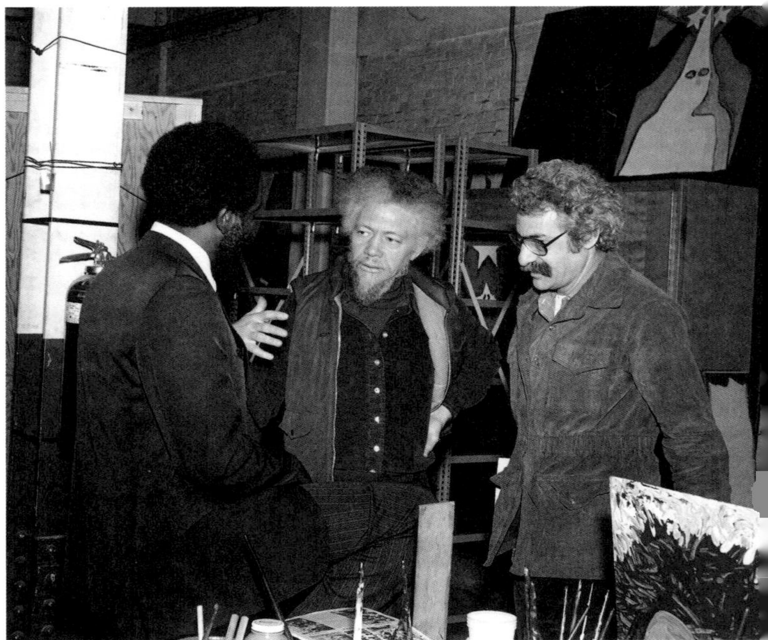

15

Art and Design for more than thirty years, where he was Chandler's instructor. Burnett depicted a range of subjects in his work, from scenes based on his experience working at the Boston Navy Yard in the early 1940s, to later depictions of African Americans who experienced anti-Black violence at the voting booth. The lithograph *Freedom Fighter for Operation Exodus* (1969) was inspired by a community-based response to segregation in Boston's public school system. Made to raise funds in support of these self-funded school desegregation efforts, *Freedom Fighter for Operation Exodus*, with its rich texture, portrays the head of a young African American person in profile, imbued with emotional intensity.

Milton Derr (formerly Milton Johnson), who taught for forty years at the School of the Museum of Fine Arts, Boston, presented works made between 1975 and 1980 at AAMARP. Derr's work was inspired by his interest in Asian cultures, especially the expressive linearity of Chinese landscape painting and Japanese screen paintings, as much as by Western traditions. Like other of his richly layered canvases, *Untitled* (c. 1980) is a two-part painting bursting with color. On the surface, *Untitled* seems like a straightforward depiction of a mother staring lovingly at her child. Even though they are at the center of the painting, they are secondary to dense

15. Left to right: Edmund Barry Gaither, Benny Andrews, and Arnold Trachtman, 1980

16. Benny Andrews, *Nene*, 1978. Oil and collage on canvas. 50½ × 35½ inches (128.3 × 90.2 cm), signed. The Andrews-Humphrey Family Foundation and Michael Rosenfeld Gallery LLC, New York

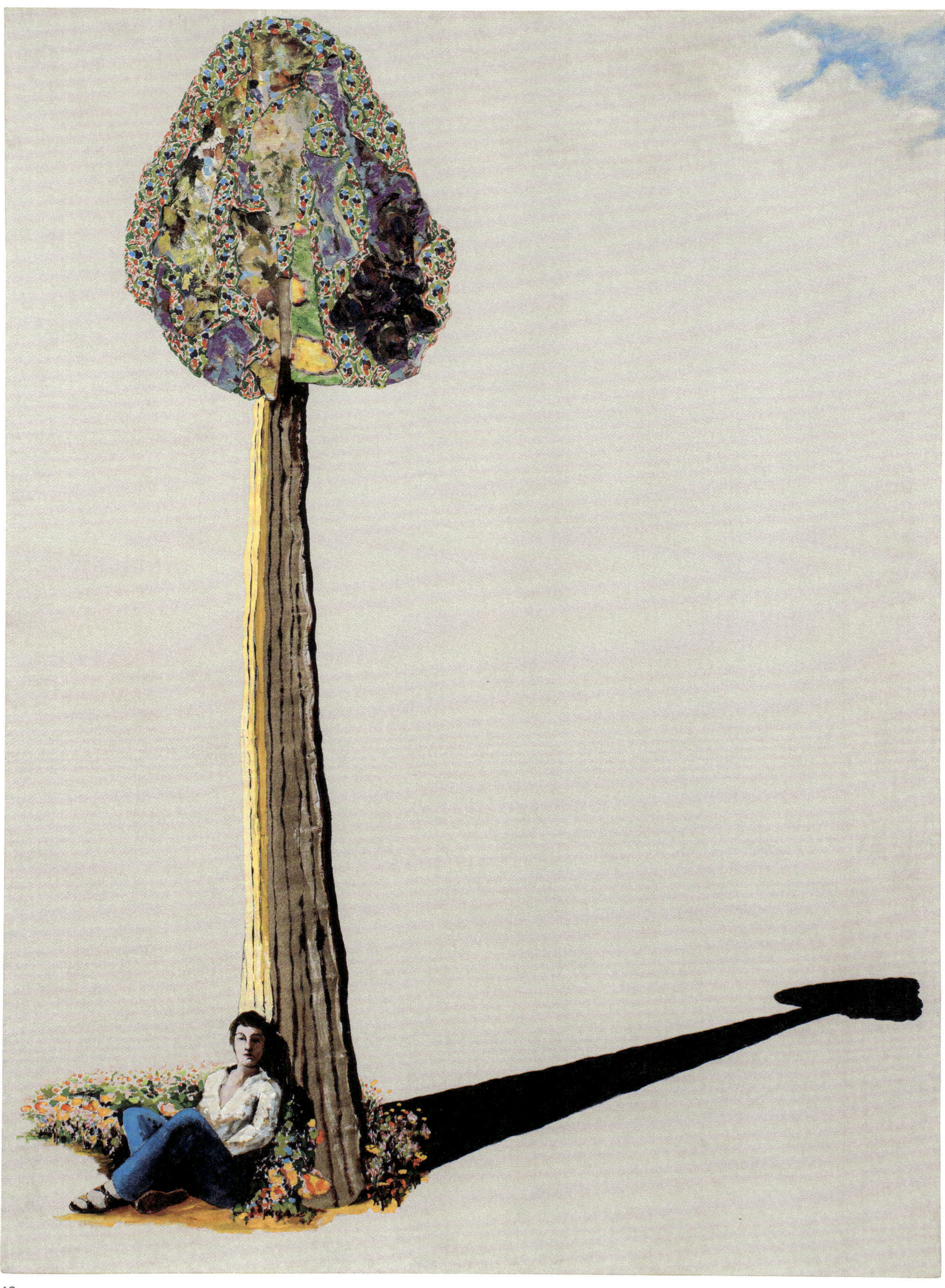

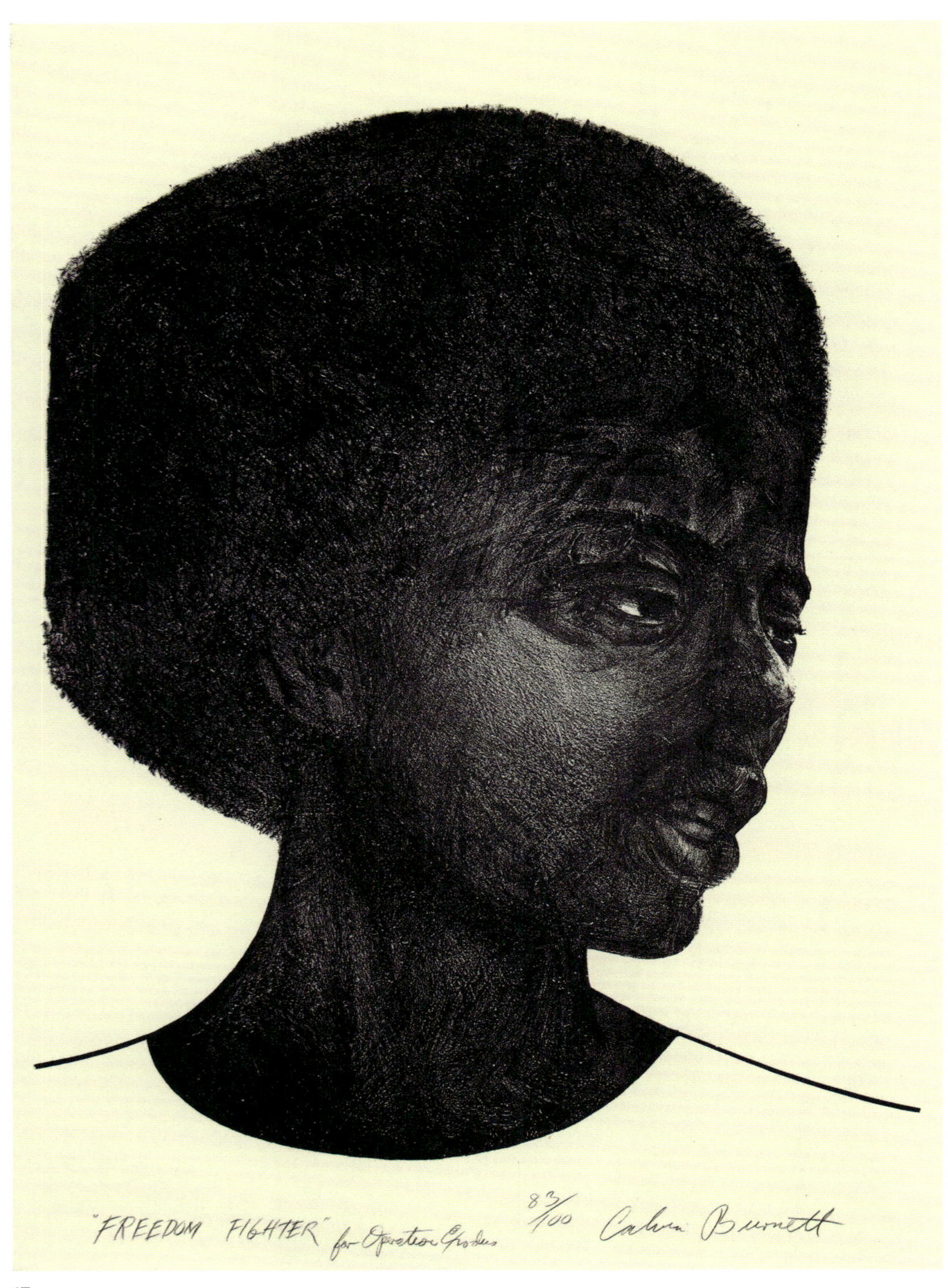

17

17. Calvin Burnett, *Freedom Fighter for Operation Exodus*, 1969. Lithograph. 30 × 24 inches (76.2 × 61 cm). Syracuse University Art Museum; Gift of Marvin A. Sackner

18. Milton Derr, *Untitled*, c. 1980. Oil on canvas. 48 × 35½ inches (121.9 × 90.2 cm)

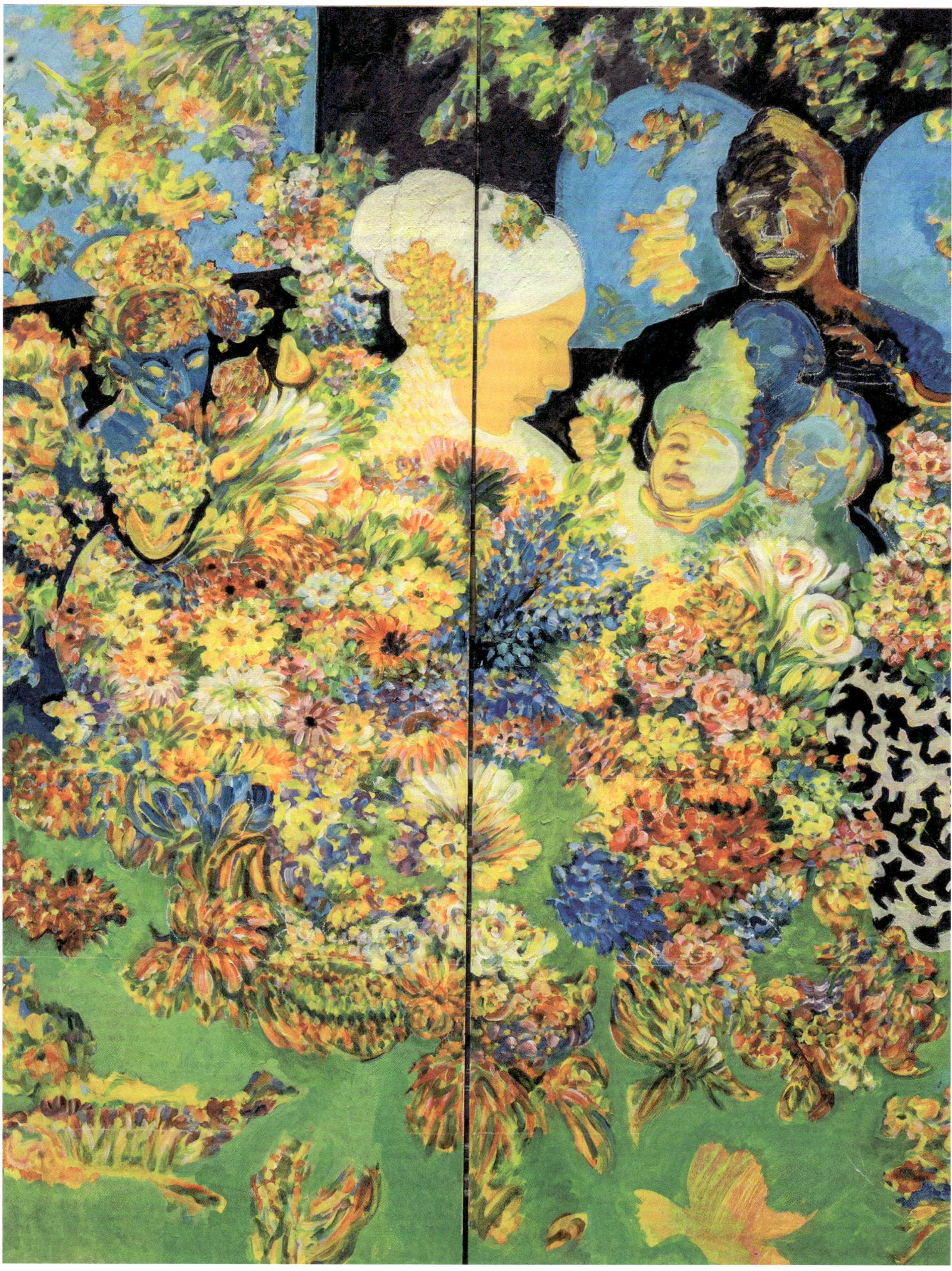

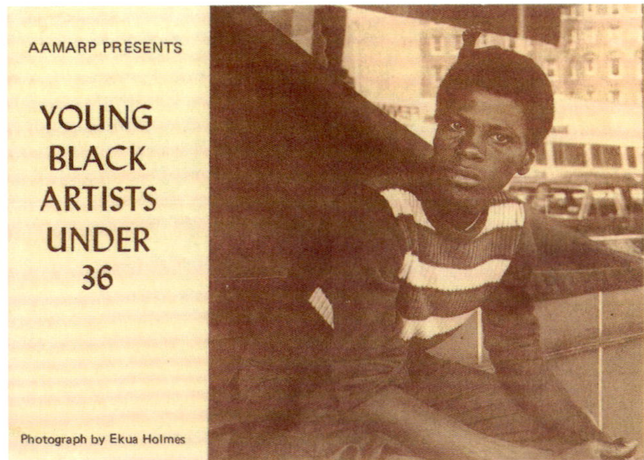

19

arrangements of flowers that nearly cover the entire surface of the painting. Derr depicts a shadowy man standing in the background, in a tender scene of motherly love nevertheless infused with the emotional complexity of parenting.   **JDB**

The Contemporary Arab World: The Edmond Moussally Collection
MAR 16–APR 18

Lila Oliver Asher: Printmaker
MAY 4–JUNE 6

Young Black Artists Under 36
OCT 5–NOV 9
FIG. 19

Beyond These Walls
DEC 22–JAN 9, 1981
FIG. 12

1981

A Major Exhibition of International Child Art from the Collection of Al Hurwitz
MAR 8–27

Dana C. Chandler Jr.: Upon My 40th Year (With Selected Memories)
APR 1–30
FIG. 20

In 1976, in relationship to his position as artist-in-residence in Northeastern's African American Studies Department, Dana Chandler (who also adopted the name Akin Duro) presented *If the shoe fits, hear it!*, a survey of nearly ten years of work presented at the University Art Gallery. The exhibition was accompanied by a richly illustrated, self-published catalogue with autobiographical text by Chandler, and featuring commentary from artists Benny Andrews and Romare Bearden, and others such as institution builder Elma Lewis and scholar Ramona H. Edelin. Five years later, in AAMARP's fourth year, and on the occasion of his fortieth birthday, Chandler presented his first solo exhibition at 11 Leon Street picking up from where the previous one left off. With his typical flair for publicity, he described the exhibition as his "strongest show ever," though not one he deemed safe for children. "The main thrust of the exhibition will focus on statements concerning the explosive growth of racism, the Klan, racially motivated murders and crime, drugs, black on black crime and race genocide," as he described it.[7] While that may be true, as any of the myriad photographs of Chandler posing in his AAMARP studio among his paintings and plants can attest, he worked tirelessly with a broad range of techniques and subjects as an image maker. Even as the many toxic incarnations of racism in America were his primary subject in caustic, often confrontational paintings, he also created countless images of Black uplift and Pan-Africanism, including public facing works throughout the city. For the Grove Hall branch of the Boston Public Library, for example, he made the monumental painting *The Role of Books in Black History* (1968–76, location unknown), which features figures such as Frederick Douglass, Sojourner Truth, Huey P. Newton, and Angela Davis, as well as his recurring symbols of the Pan-African man and a raised Black fist punching through a white egg.   **JDB**

Arnold Trachtman: Paintings 1976–81
MAY 3–31
FIGS. 21–22

With shared roots in the blue-collar city of Lynn and a mutual commitment to social realism, Dana Chandler and Marxist painter Arnold Trachtman had a profound respect for each other. Trachtman was one of a handful of non-Black artists working within AAMARP's orbit who were embraced for a commitment to community, interracial solidarity, and a sense of justice. Trachtman's

19. *Young Black Artists Under 36* flyer featuring photograph by Ekua Holmes, 1981

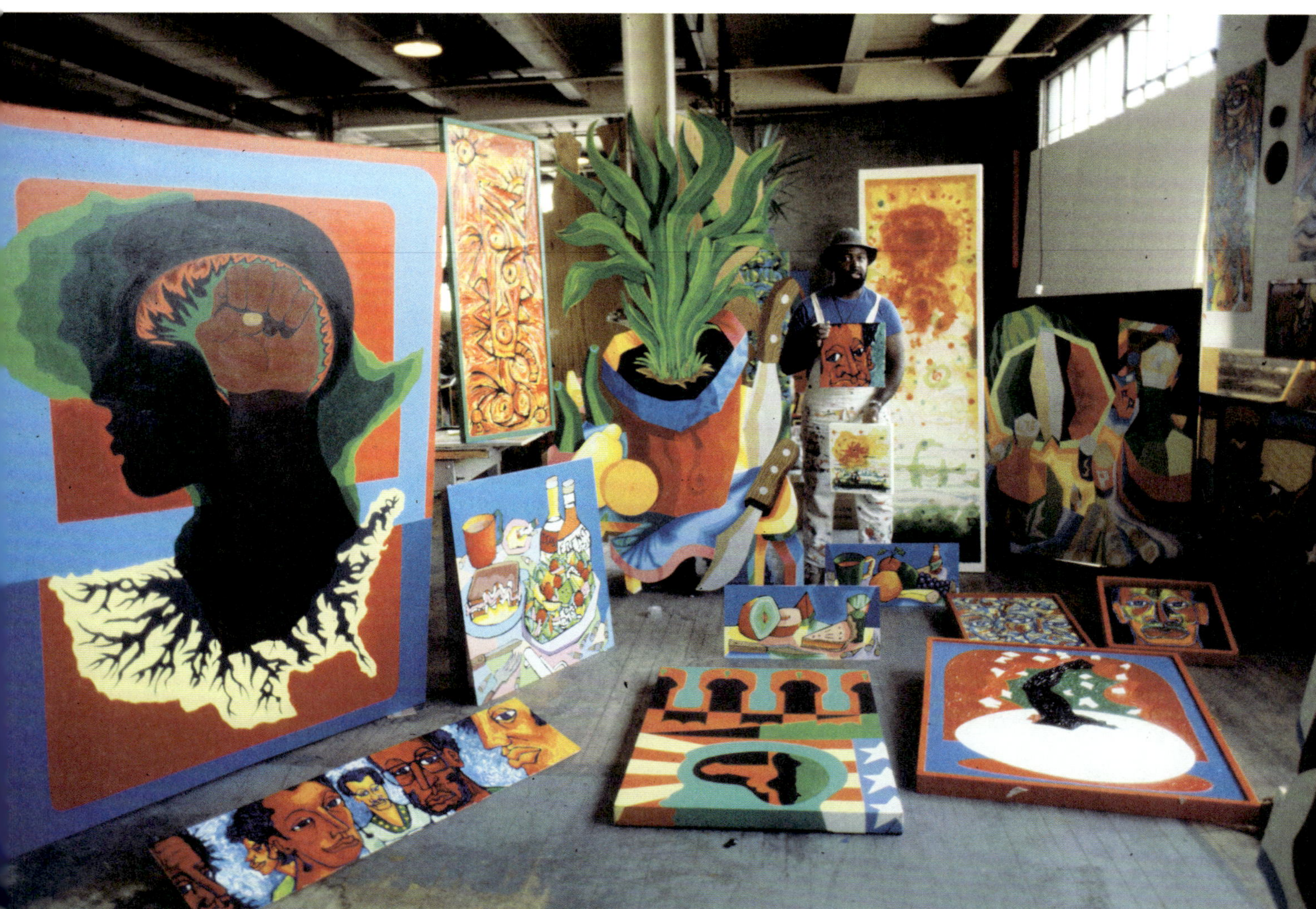

1982 solo exhibition at AAMARP featured *Spirit of '76 (Louise Day Hicks and Ted Landsmark)* (1979), which depicted an excruciating episode in Boston's still-raw school desegregation busing crisis. On April 5, 1976, Black attorney and civil rights activist Ted Landsmark was rushing into a meeting at City Hall when he was intercepted by a group of anti-bussing demonstrators exiting a rally hosted by Louise Day Hicks, a notorious local politician staunchly opposed to school integration. There, Landsmark was assaulted by white teenager Joseph Rakes with an American flag, an event rendered iconic through photojournalist Stanley Forman's lens in a widely circulated image titled *The Soiling of Old Glory*, that went on to win a 1977 Pulitzer Prize. Tensions were high in Boston during this period, and school desegregation faced significant resistance from white residents. Trachtman's painting captures this tumult in a vertiginous composition whose title invokes a bitter sense of irony on the occasion of the nation's bicentennial. Exhibiting this work at AAMARP was particularly meaningful; Chandler served as president of the Metropolitan Council for Educational Opportunity from 1977 to 1986, and regularly hosted school desegregation organizer meetings at AAMARP. **MCC**

20. Dana Chandler in his
studio, c. 1974

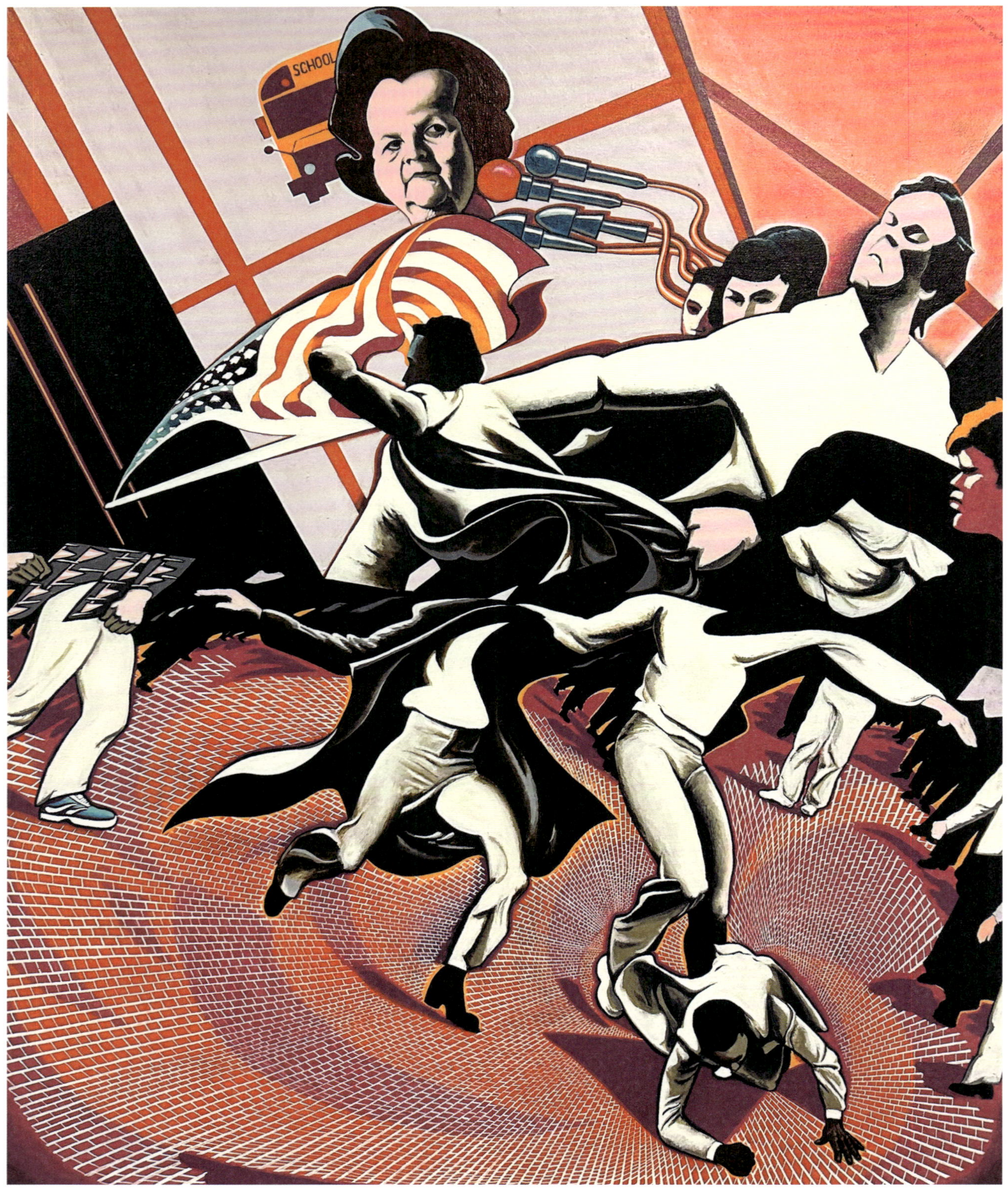

21

21. Arnold Trachtman, *Spirit of '76 (Louise Day Hicks and Ted Landsmark)*, 1979. Acrylic on canvas. 77 × 64 inches (195.6 × 162.6 cm)

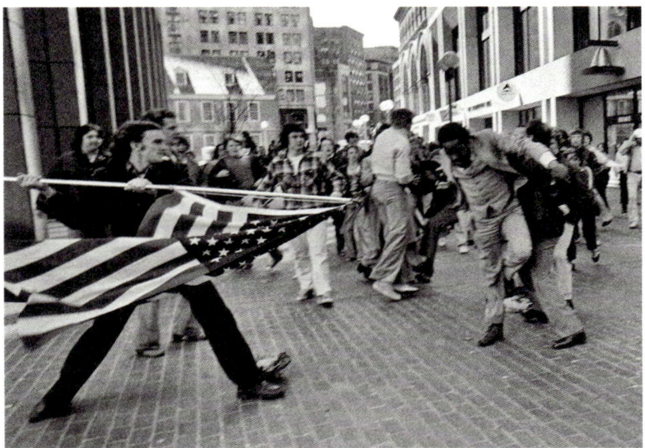

22

Dennis Didley

JUNE 3–30

FIGS. 23–24

Dennis Didley pursued a synthesis of traditional African forms in expressive sculptures constructed of found wood, though he maintained that the belief systems that gave rise to such forms "were not mine."[8] Didley would later adopt the name Vusumuzi Maduna, bestowed on him by a group of South Africans. For the artist, the name Vusumuzi in particular—which he took to mean "builder of culture" from isiZulu—was indicative of how he viewed his artistic identity and cultural role. In addition to his involvement with AAMARP, he was also cofounder and director of the Harriet Tubman Gallery in Boston from 1977–1988, a key node in Boston's Black institutional infrastructure where many AAMARP artists presented their work. *La Diablesse as Sentinel* (1987–88) is indicative of Maduna's signature style. The lithe, suggestive feminine figure stands sentinel-like, as per the title, her red painted body an embodiment of the titular temptress from Caribbean folklore. *La diablesse* is said to have been an enslaved woman who traded her soul to the devil in exchange for eternal beauty, her hideous face hidden by a wide-brimmed hat. The head of Maduna's figure is concealed through abstraction, represented as a raw piece of wood emblazoned with the burnished form of a snake. A dark, mask-like face appears to emerge instead from her pelvic area, with glowing green eyes and hair made of rope, surrounded by nails hammered into her body as in *nkisi nkondi*, power figures of the Kongo peoples of Central Africa. The exploration of African forms in Maduna's works was an attempt to connect to his roots,

even as, for curator Edmund Barry Gaither, "the Africa which they suggest is tomorrow's Africa; it is the Africa of the quiet, reflective moment."[9] **JDB**

New African Company and New England Black Playwrights Forum

OCT 31–NOV 2

FIG. 25

The New African Company was founded by James Spruill (then-host of WGBH-TV's *Say Brother*) and Gustave Johnson in 1968 with the motto of "Theatre for the People." A Black nationalist ethos characterized the company from the beginning, as Spruill relayed to the *Boston Globe*'s theatre critic in 1968: "there must be a black theater for the black community, our own voices in our own playwrights, and the more black rage the better."[10] Identifying a shared value system, in March 1980 Dana Chandler formally invited the New African Company to become AAMARP's first resident theatre company. Until at least 1983, the ensemble staged productions and workshops in the multipurpose room at 11 Leon Street that were meant to "create an understanding of the theatre as a potential image-maker for the Black community."[11] Workshop topics included directing, stage movement, dance, arts administration, improvisational acting, and playwriting. Community members had the opportunity to become apprentices to theatre artists and were even invited to join the company after demonstrating a certain proficiency and commitment. In October 1980, the New England Black Playwright Forum was hosted by AAMARP. Under the banner of "A Vision for the Eighties," the three-day convening brought major figures including Alice Childress, sonia sanchez, and Brenda Walcott to present new and recent work. Partnerships

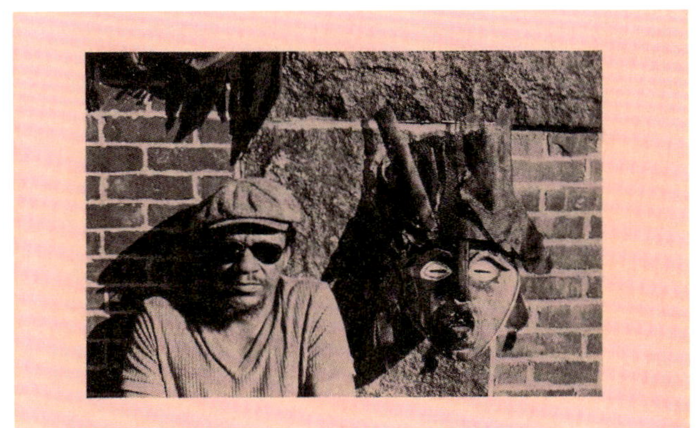

23

22. Stanley Forman, *The Soiling of Old Glory*, 1976

23. Dennis Didley (Vusumuzi Maduna) flyer, 1981

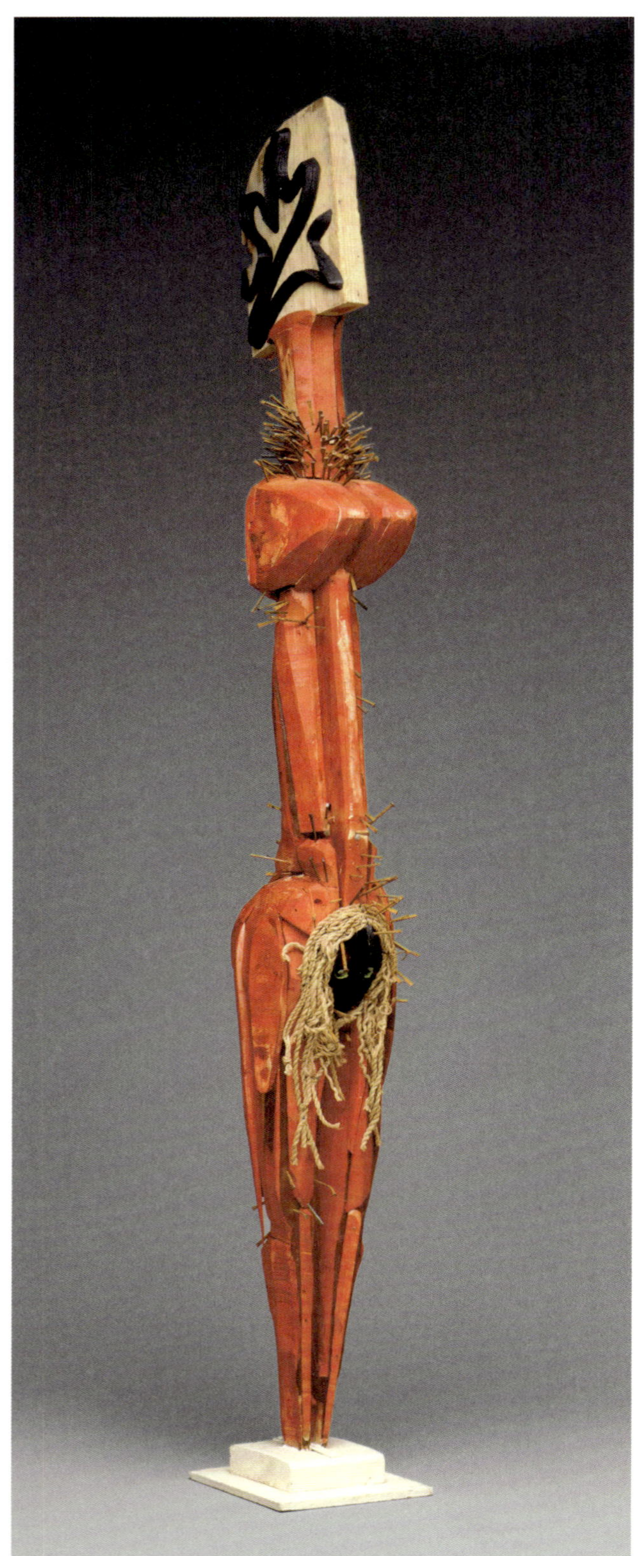

such as these are emblematic of the historic interdisciplinary nature of AAMARP's programmatic offerings. They also demonstrate AAMARP as an important meeting place, where key figures of the Black Arts movement congregated as they travelled to Boston.   **MCC**

1982

Five Women

MAR 3–31

Lotus Do, Valerie Jayne, Weeta Lopes, Susan Thompson, Johnetta Tinker

Two Artists: Michael Jones and Bryan McFarlane

JULY 2–AUG 31

Wen-ti Tsen

SEPT 5–OCT 8

FIGS. 26–28

Chandler met Cambridge-based, Chinese American artist Wen-ti Tsen when curator Nyna Polumbaum and photojournalist Ted Polumbaum, assembled eight artists to paint a guerrilla-style mural calling attention to the situation in Chile after the coup in 1973. Chandler recognized in Tsen an affinity with his own way of confronting issues overtly in social realist paintings. In 1968, Tsen's contract to teach at School of the Museum of Fine Arts, Boston was not renewed due to his political activities, and coupled with the election of Richard Nixon as presi-

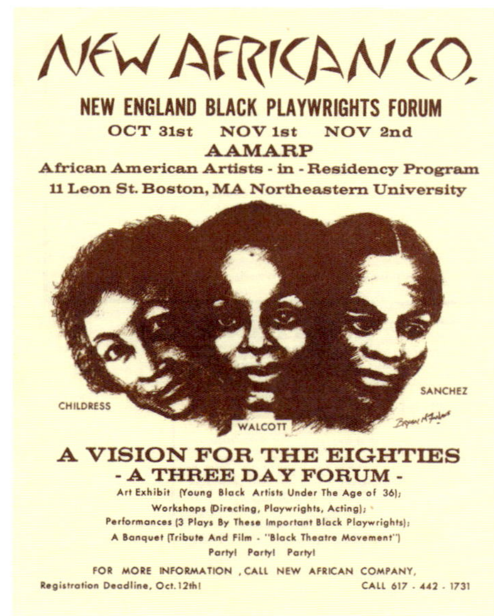

24. Vusumuzi Maduna, *La Diablesse as Sentinel*, 1987–88. Wood and mixed media. 82¼ × 10¼ × 10½ inches (208.9 × 25 × 26.7 cm)

25. New African Company flyer featuring drawing by Bryan McFarlane, 1980

dent, he decided to move to Lebanon where he continued his involvement in the global progressive movement. There, he painted *Peaceable Kingdom* (1971), a hinged, two-part work with double doors that open to reveal a triptych, and which he later presented at AAMARP. The closed front includes several images composited together, including a murder suspect of three civil rights workers in Mississippi, a child in the arms of a member of Concerned Citizens Against Pornography, and a 1970 Cadillac Coupe DeVille, among other imagery. At the center is an iconic image that remains when the panels are opened: a captured and wounded Vietcong soldier with a pained look on his face. On either side of the opened panels are U.S. soldiers holding the now split body of the Vietcong soldier. At the center, Tsen painted a version of Edward Hicks's *The Peaceable Kingdom* (1826). Tsen's appropriation of Hicks's image of harmony, which includes a scene of members of the Lenni-Lenape tribe meeting William Penn during the Treaty of Shackamaxon, becomes the backdrop for Tsen's meditation of the complicated dynamics of everyday life in America that continued largely unabated during the Vietnam War. **JDB**

"I left China in 1949 when I was thirteen for France and later London where I went to art school. My family moved to Boston when my brother was hired at Northeastern and I followed some years later. In Boston I attended the School of the Museum of Fine Arts, who gave me a scholarship that allowed me to travel the world for two years. I returned to Boston where, because of the political nature of many of my artworks, I lost my teaching contract. I left Boston again in 1969 after Nixon was elected, and spent the next years in Beirut, Lebanon, making artworks against the Vietnam War, like *Peaceable Kingdom*. Back in Boston in 1972, the atmosphere was totally different. There was widespread collaboration, and because my work was overtly political I connected with other progressive artists. This is how I met Dana Chandler and eventually became one of several collaborators on a guerilla style temporary mural staged for one day in Boston Common. Meetings and painting sessions were hosted at AAMARP, and a few years later Chandler encouraged me to show my work there. After that exhibition I did not have much further connection with the program. I later understood how meaningful that moment was, of everyone searching for a way to work together toward common causes, because soon after people separated into different identity-based groups who advocated for a more limited set of interests." Wen-ti Tsen

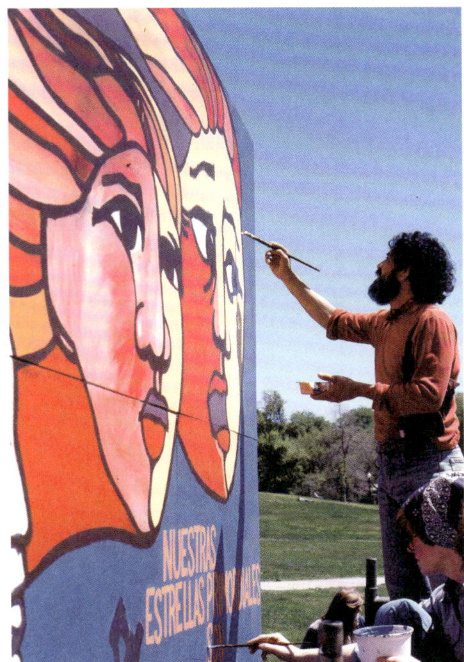

26

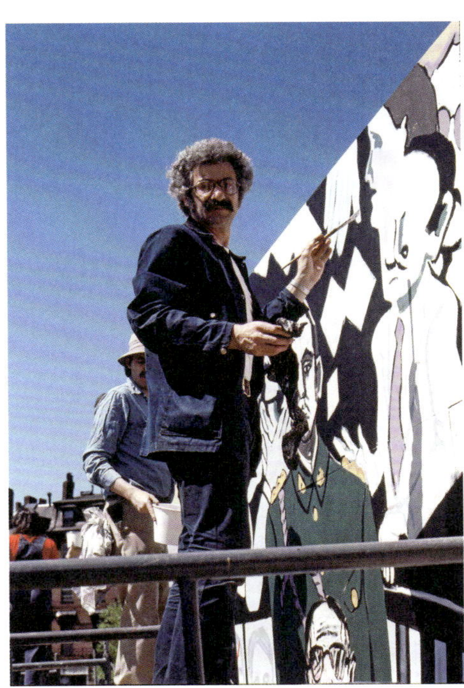

27

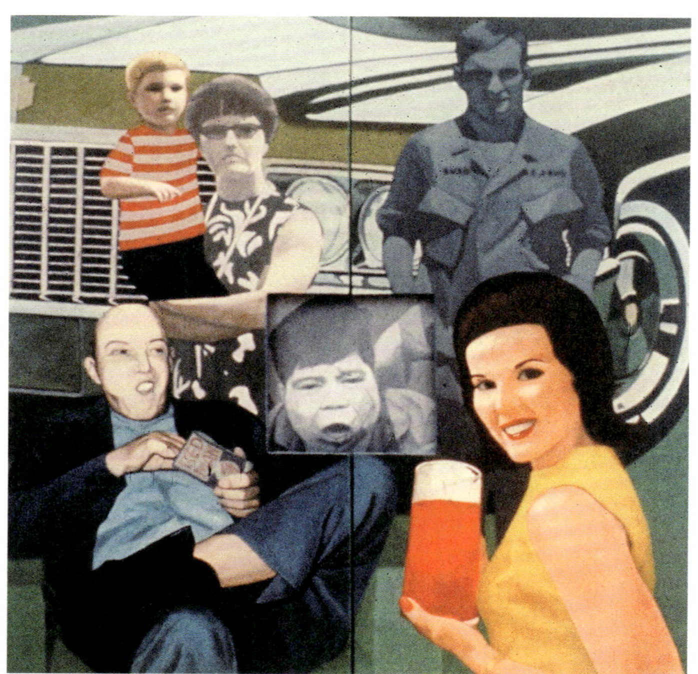

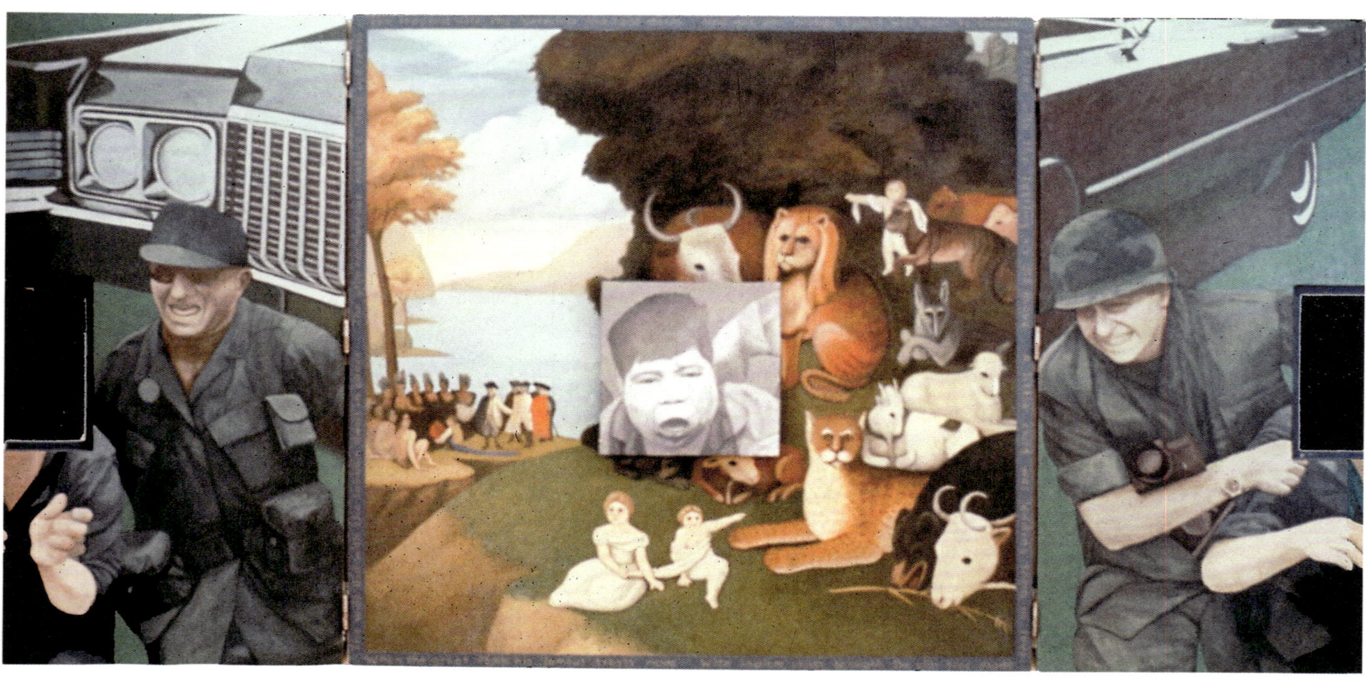

28. Wen-ti Tsen, *Peaceable Kingdom* (closed and open), 1971. Oil on canvas. 60 × 60 inches (152.4 × 152.4 cm) (closed); 60 × 120 inches (152.4 × 305 cm) (open)

Reginald L. Jackson: Axé

FIGS. 29–31

Photographer Reginald L. Jackson studied under
renowned photographer Walker Evans at Yale University,
where in 1968 he was a founding member of the Black
Workshop. The Black Workshop sought to illuminate
tacit antiblackness present in art and architecture curric-
ula and redirect training and practice toward serving
the needs of communities.[12] Later, Jackson traveled
across postindependence African nations documenting
cross-cultural influences and Pan-African celebrations,
including notably at FESTAC in Lagos, Nigeria, in 1977.
During this period Jackson shot the iconic photograph
Things Go Better?, which features three Ghanaian individuals in traditional dress strolling past a massive
Coca-Cola advertisement. Jackson and Chandler met
by happenstance in Ghana in 1970 and later Jackson
became Chandler's colleague at Simmons College (now
University).[13] Jackson soon joined the initial cohort of
AAMARP artists and today he leads the executive committee. Jackson's 1982 AAMARP exhibition *Axé* was
titled after the Afro-Brazilian Portuguese translation of
the word *àṣẹ* from the Yoruba language. It is a word of
affirmation and a key religious concept in Yoruba and
Candomblé worldviews referencing the life force flowing
through all things. African and African-derived religious
practices and syncretism are key themes for Jackson,
which crystallize in series such as Urban Ceremonial
Mask. In the late 1970s Jackson would stroll across
Boston with elder artist Allan Rohan Crite, documenting
sites of Black life in the city and overlaying them with
sacred African objects, such as the ivory Benin Ceremonial
Pendant that became an icon of Pan-Africanists globally
after FESTAC. **MCC**

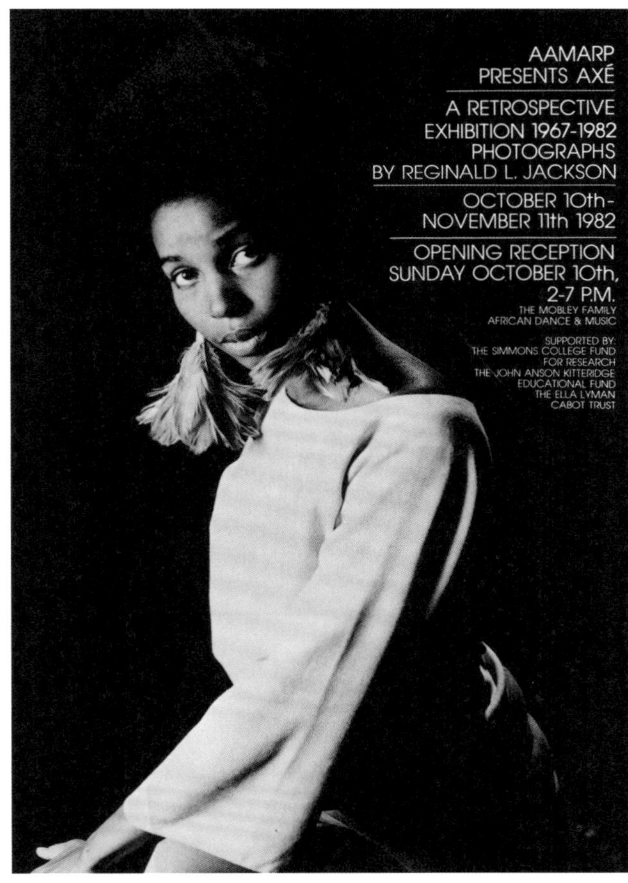

29

"In August 1970, on the first of many trips I would make
to West Africa, I met already legendary artist, Prof.
Dana C. Chandler Jr. walking down a dusty road in
Kaneshie in Accra, Ghana. Little did I know that four
years later I would be joining the faculty at Simmons
College where he taught, and we would become friends
and colleagues.

Dana's resourcefulness, quick wit, sense of community, and willingness to put it all on the line was
immediately apparent as we navigated and negotiated
as a group of faculty and staff, mostly of African
descent, with the Simmons administration and beyond,
to make sure our students and community were
treated fairly.

29. *Reginald L. Jackson: Axé*
flyer, c. 1982

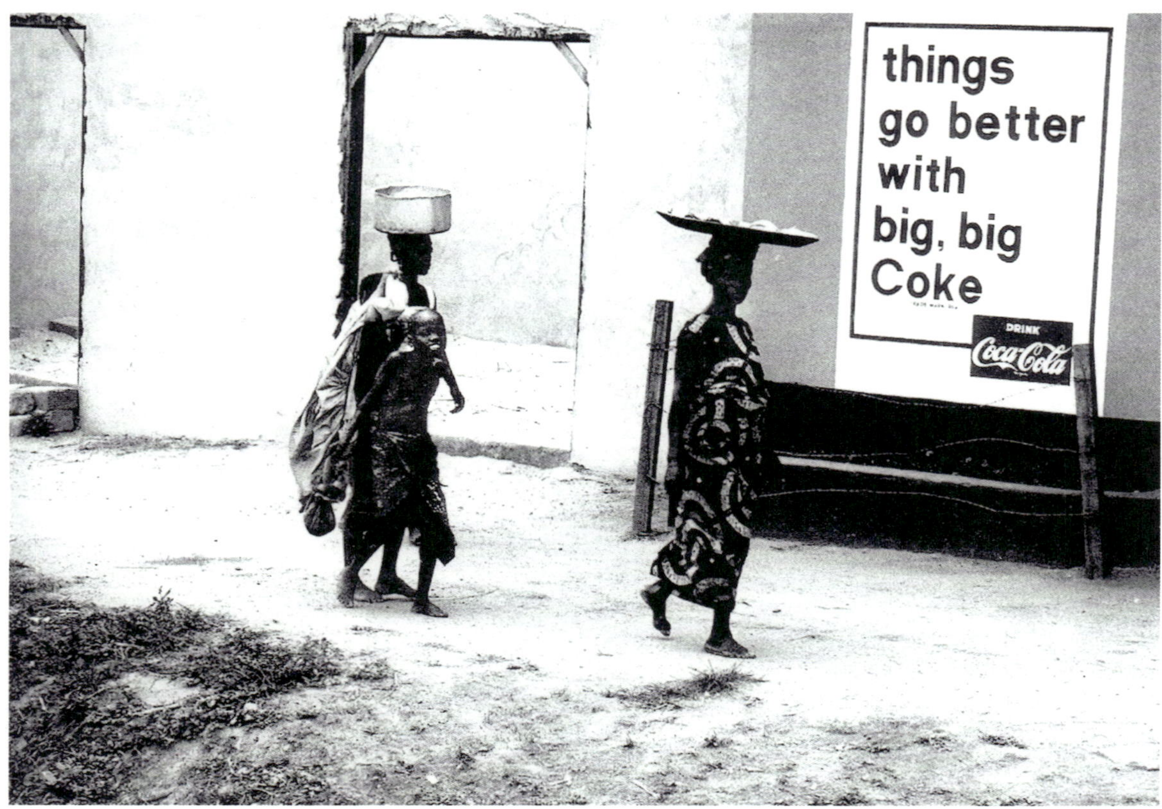

30

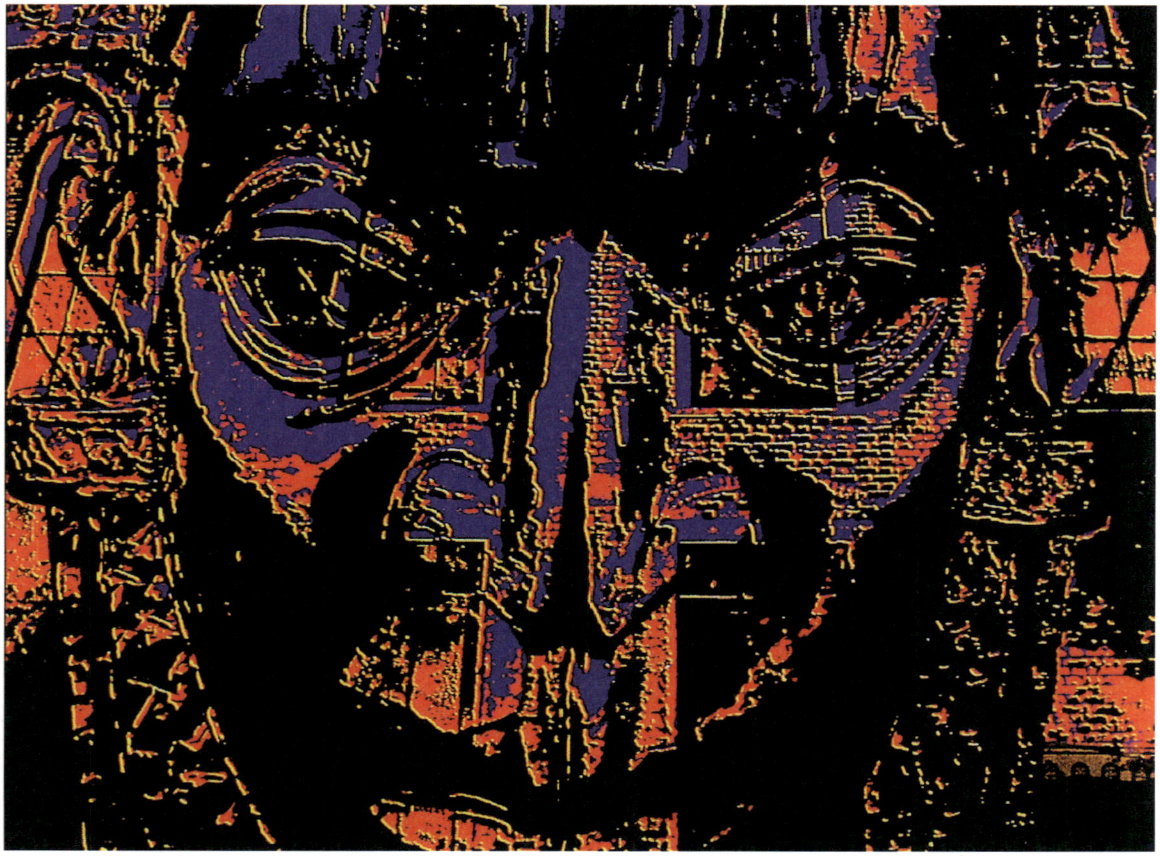

31

As part of the first cohort of African American artists at AAMARP, in 1977, Dana asked me to become a board member of METCO (Metropolitan Council for Educational Opportunity), which Dana led and met in his large studio at 11 Leon Street on the Northeastern University campus. I also was introduced to a cadre of amazing artists in Boston and eventually the legendary National Conference of Artists, the oldest group of artists meeting continuously annually nationally, through Dana.

In addition to being an educator, prolific visual artist, and community worker, Dana was a remarkable marketing genius who never seemed to run out of ideas or energy. He was an expert at promotion for self and for others, knowing how best to get ideas across both verbally and of course visually, to a wide spectrum of the art world.

Always encouraging to younger artists and students, Dana will be remembered as a fearless revolutionary artist who advocated for the elevation of African American art to its rightful place, and who not only made thought provoking art but also provided the means for others to do so. May he now rest among many of our esteemed colleagues and others who have taken their place among the ancestors, assured that his legacy will inspire others to do the same.

As they say amongst the Akan in Ghana, 'Ayekoo!' Job well done Dana."   Reginald L. Jackson, PhD

All Our Relations: Native American Art, North and South

ORGANIZED BY ROBERT P. PINEDO, CHIRICAHUA APACHE

NOV 14–DEC 19

1983

AAMARP at the Fed: Fifth Annual AAMARP exhibition

FEDERAL RESERVE BANK OF BOSTON,

JAN 10–FEB 18

Ellen Banks, Calvin Burnett, Dana C. Chandler Jr., Robin Chandler, Milton Derr, Arnold Hurley, Reginald L. Jackson, Michael Jones, Bryan McFarlane, James Reuben Reed, Rudolph Robinson, Barbara Ward, John Wilson, and Theresa-India Young, with special guest artists Marcia Lloyd and Bill Travis

Ellen Banks

EXACT DATES UNKNOWN

FIGS. 32–33

In an undated artist statement, Ellen Banks asks: "Given the political/social pressures toward Black Awareness, how can a Black Painter of good conscience work in the abstract?"[14] The question was urgent. Chandler admired Banks and demonstrated that by including her in his initial cohort of master artists. But Chandler was also emblematic of a strand of politically engaged Black artists of this period who were openly hostile toward abstract practices. As art historian and curator Lowery Stokes Sims has described it, the prevailing dogma was that "if an artist was black, then he or she did black art, and their mission was to cast the black image against stereotypes and create images of an idealized black nation."[15] Banks balked at such an expectation, noting that to conform to the tendency would be an "intellectual and emotional . . . failure" and that the "Black Community is not well served by failure."[16] It was under this shadow that Banks, who was trained in both painting and piano, created a remarkable body of geometric abstractions derived from the

30. Reginald L. Jackson, *Things Go Better?*, c. 1970. Gelatin silver print. 27 × 18 inches (68.6 × 45.7 cm)

31. Reginald L. Jackson, *African Meetinghouse*, 1976–77. From the series Urban Ceremonial Mask. Chromogenic color print. 22½ × 18½ inches (57.1 × 47 cm)

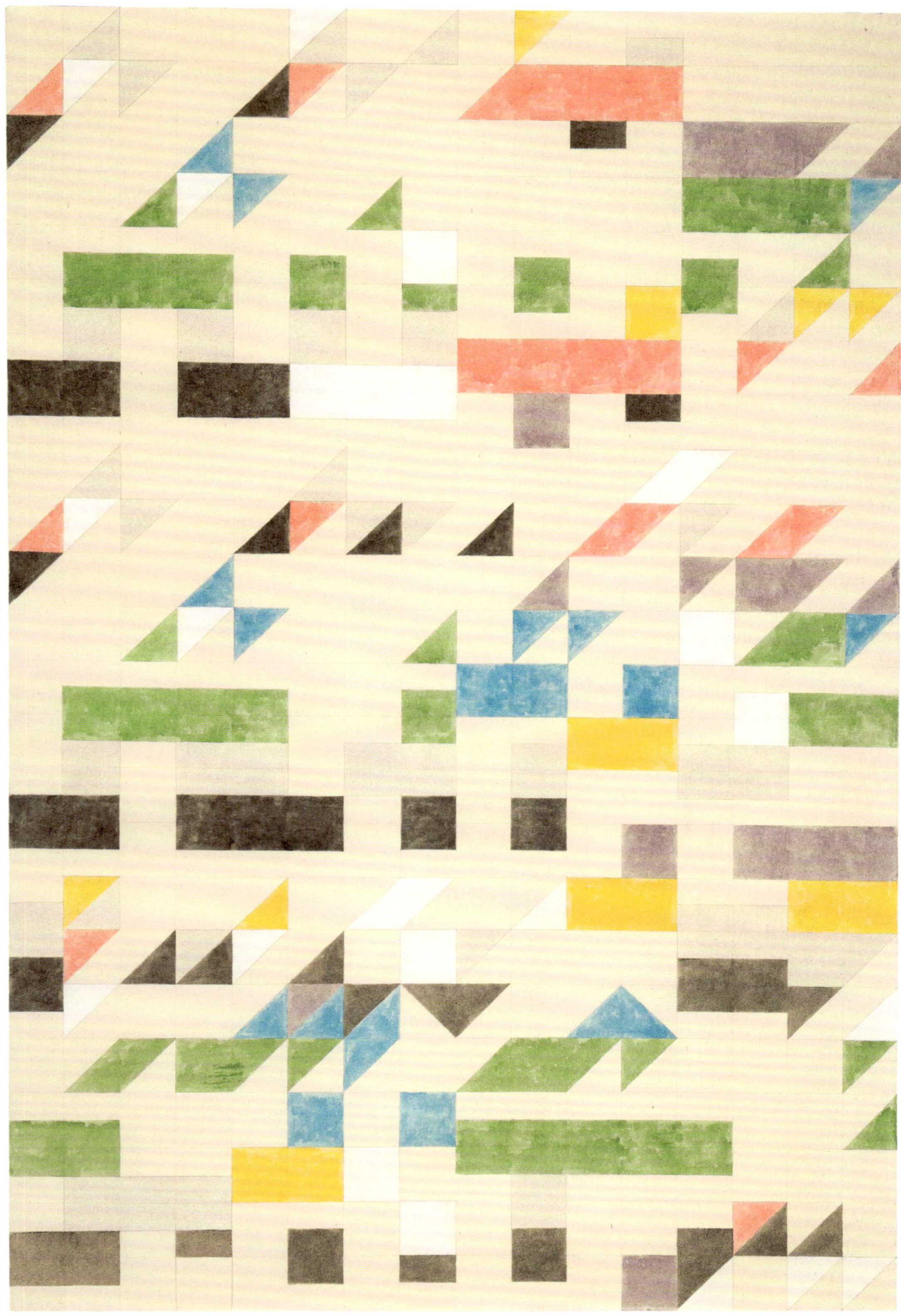

32. Ellen Banks, *Scott Joplin*, 1982. Acrylic on canvas. 72½ × 48½ inches (184.2 × 123.2 cm). Addison Gallery of American Art, Phillips Academy, Andover, MA; Museum purchase

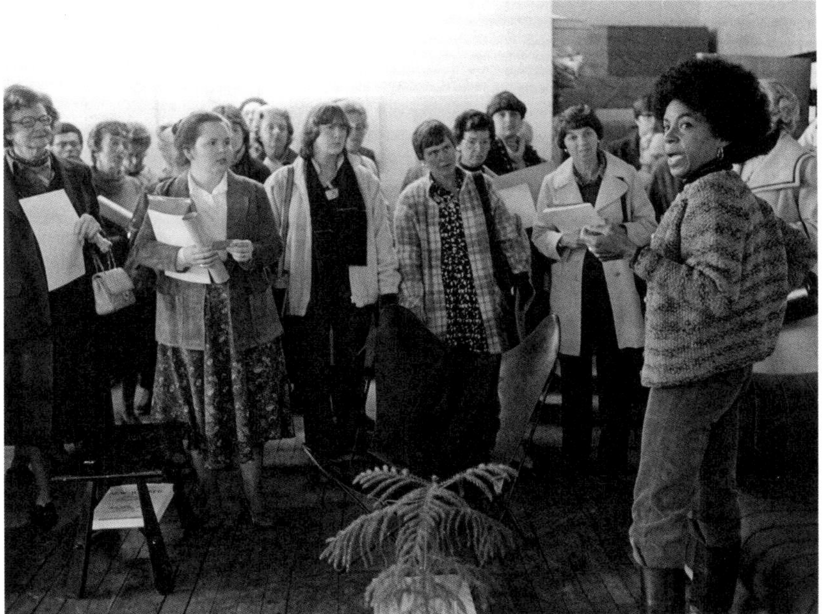

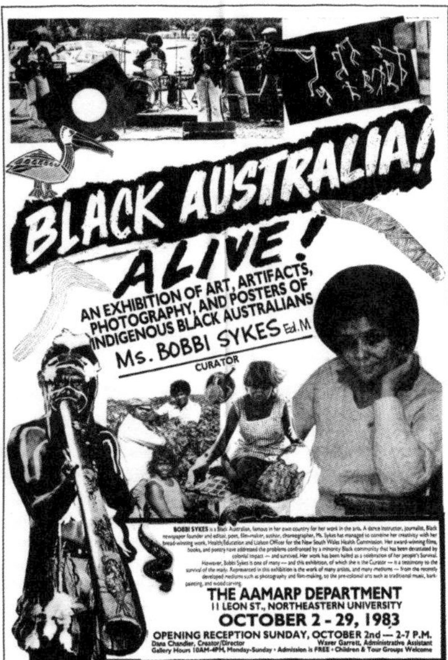

formal properties of musical scores. From Bach's cantatas and adagios to single measures of Thelonious Monk's jazz compositions, to the playful ragtime tunes of Scott Joplin, Banks developed an elaborate and synesthetic personal language wherein certain colors corresponded to certain pitches, and shapes corresponded to different durations and tempos. Rather than expressionist or gestural abstractions inspired by improvisatory performance practices, Banks found freedom and generative creativity in developing a meticulous system that used the written musical score as a scaffold on which to build. **MCC**

Black Australia! Alive!

AN EXHIBITION OF ART, ARTIFACTS, PHOTOGRAPHY, AND POSTERS OF INDIGENOUS BLACK AUSTRALIANS, ORGANIZED BY BOBBI SYKES

OCT 2–29

FIG. 34

Prominent Black Australian activist, feminist, and poet Roberta "Bobbi" Sykes spent the early 1980s in Cambridge, Massachusetts, where she was invited to pursue doctoral studies at Harvard University.[17] During this period, she organized *Black Australia! Alive!* at AAMARP, a multidisciplinary presentation of art, artifacts, posters, and photographs both made by and featuring Black Indigenous Australians. Sykes was not herself Indigenous but felt strong solidarity with the Aboriginal community due to her own experiences of virulent anti-Black racism during her youth in North Queensland. She would become deeply involved with, and indeed a face of, the Aboriginal rights movement centralized in Redfern, a suburb of Sydney. In 1972, she served as founding executive secretary of the Aboriginal Tent Embassy, a permanent protest for Indigenous land rights sited outside of the Parliament House in Canberra. As coeditor of the radical journal *Koori-bina* (1976–79), Sykes translated the principles of Black Power for an Australian audience, articulating the transnational movement through the lens of Indigenous cultural politics.[18] These experiences earned her a place at Harvard, where she was lauded as the first Black Australian student in the institution's history. Given Sykes's commitments, it is not unexpected that she found her way to AAMARP. *Black Australia! Alive!* serves as a testament to both Sykes's investments in education, cultural pride, and solidarity, as well as the longstanding internationalist and inclusive ethos of AAMARP. **MCC**

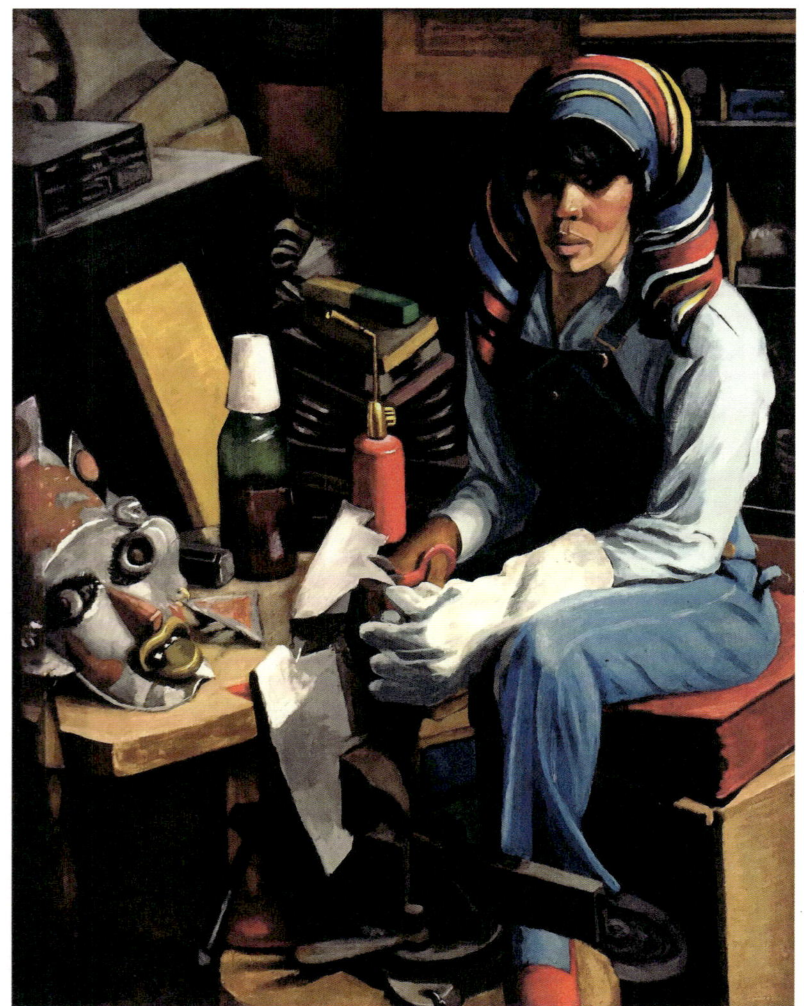

35

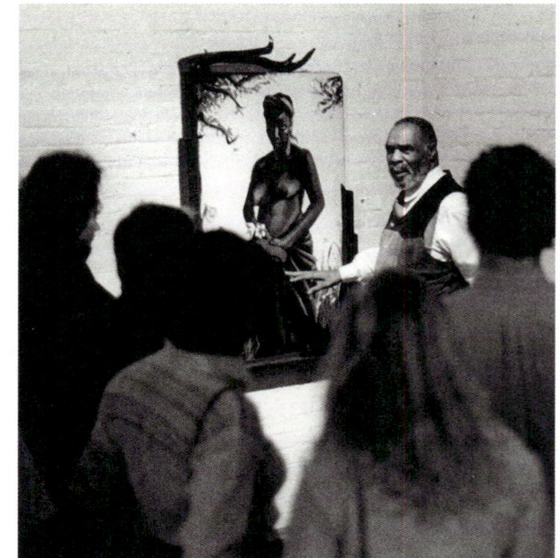

36

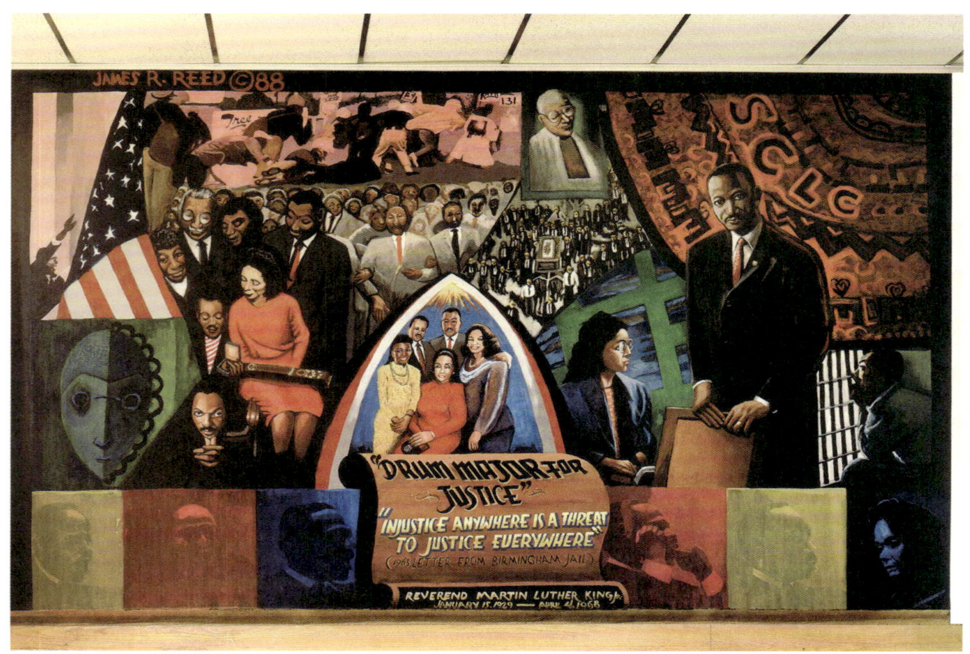

37

35. James Reuben Reed, *The Mask Maker (Portrait of Susan Thompson)*, 1983. Acrylic on canvas. Approximately 42 × 28 inches (107 × 71 cm). The Museum of the National Center of Afro-American Artists

36. James Reuben Reed with group at AAMARP, 1984

37. James Reuben Reed, *Drum Major for Justice*, 1988. 12 × 18 feet (3.7 × 5.5 m). Martin Luther King Jr. Towers, 280 Martin Luther King Boulevard, Roxbury, MA

1984

Irish and Black Stereotypes in Boston

JAN 7–31

Exchange

**AAMARP GALLERIES AND THE COPLEY SOCIETY OF BOSTON AT
158 NEWBURY STREET**

FEB 4–29

David Aronson, Ellen Banks, Jason Berger, Alfred Braconier, Calvin Burnett, Dana C. Chandler Jr., Robin Chandler, Robert Cormier, Milton Derr, Robert Douglas Hunter, Arnold Hurley, Reginald L. Jackson, Michael Jones, Mary Kaye, Jack Kramer, Bryan McFarlane, Thomas O'Hara, Arthur Polansky, Paul Rahilly, James Reuben Reed, Rudolph Robinson, Susan Thompson, Barbara Ward, John Wilson, and David Zaig, featuring a slide lecture, "The Spiral of Afro-American Art," presented by Edmund Barry Gaither

James Reuben Reed: A Tribute to Black Women

OCT 7–31

FIGS. 35–37

The 1950 winner of the prestigious Atlanta University Purchase Prize, James Reuben Reed was a skilled figurative painter who moved to the Boston area in the 1940s and later became a major mentor to Dana Chandler. In the early years of AAMARP the pair served as codirectors. In spring 1980 Reed resigned as codirector to focus on his recent appointment as assistant dean of Northeastern's College of Criminal Justice but remained artist in residence and a trusted advisor to Chandler. His 1984 exhibition *A Tribute to Black Women* featured over forty paintings, pastels, and drawings of dignified Black women. One of these paintings, which later entered the permanent collection of the Museum of the National Center of Afro-American Artists, is a sensitive portrait of fellow AAMARP artist Susan Thompson titled *The Mask Maker* (1983). Donning denim overalls, work gloves, and metalworking tools, the painting pictures Thompson as a skilled craftswoman and innovator of the arts of the African diaspora. *A Tribute to Black Women* adopted an experimental format and was framed as a "works-in-progress exhibition." Exhibition announcements encouraged visitors to "come watch the show grow!" emphasizing AAMARP as a studio space that encouraged organic connections between community members and resident artists. The exhibition was supported by the organization B.W.O.N.E. (Black Women of Natural Elegance) that was then chaired by Bernice Miller. *A Tribute to Black Women* coincided with a multiyear period of significant Black feminist organizing in Boston, led by the Combahee River Collective, following the horrific murders of eleven Black women and one white woman in Roxbury and Dorchester between January and May 1979.   **MCC**

1985

Bryan McFarlane

FEB 3–28

FIGS. 38–40

Before a dedicated solo exhibition in 1985, Bryan McFarlane had presented his paintings at AAMARP several times, including in a two-person exhibition with painter Michael Jones and in *Young Black Artists Under 36*. One year later he made *I Dream of African Souls* (1986) (presented at ICA/Boston the same year), an ambitious three-panel painting representative of McFarlane's work at the time. The bottom panel features a sleeping figure drawn in charcoal, perhaps dreaming, as the title suggests, of the African masks and ritual figure painted on the other panels. Another mask is sketched out hovering above the sleeping person, partially obscuring the delicately rendered huts that compose an African village. McFarlane's painting foregrounds that African sculptures are living subjects infused with agency that connect him to his childhood growing up in Jamaica, where African retentions are more present than in the United States. Indeed, McFarlane affixed a beautifully ornate strip of kente cloth given to him by his grandmother across the top panel, synthesizing the personal and the archetypal to address the complexity of his inner experience.   **JDB**

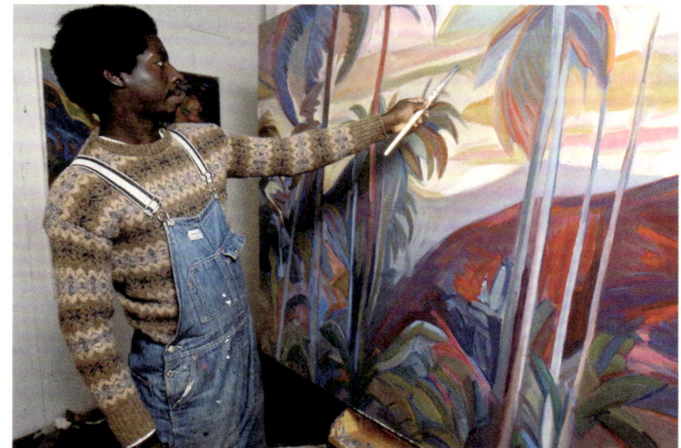

38. Bryan McFarlane in his studio, n.d.

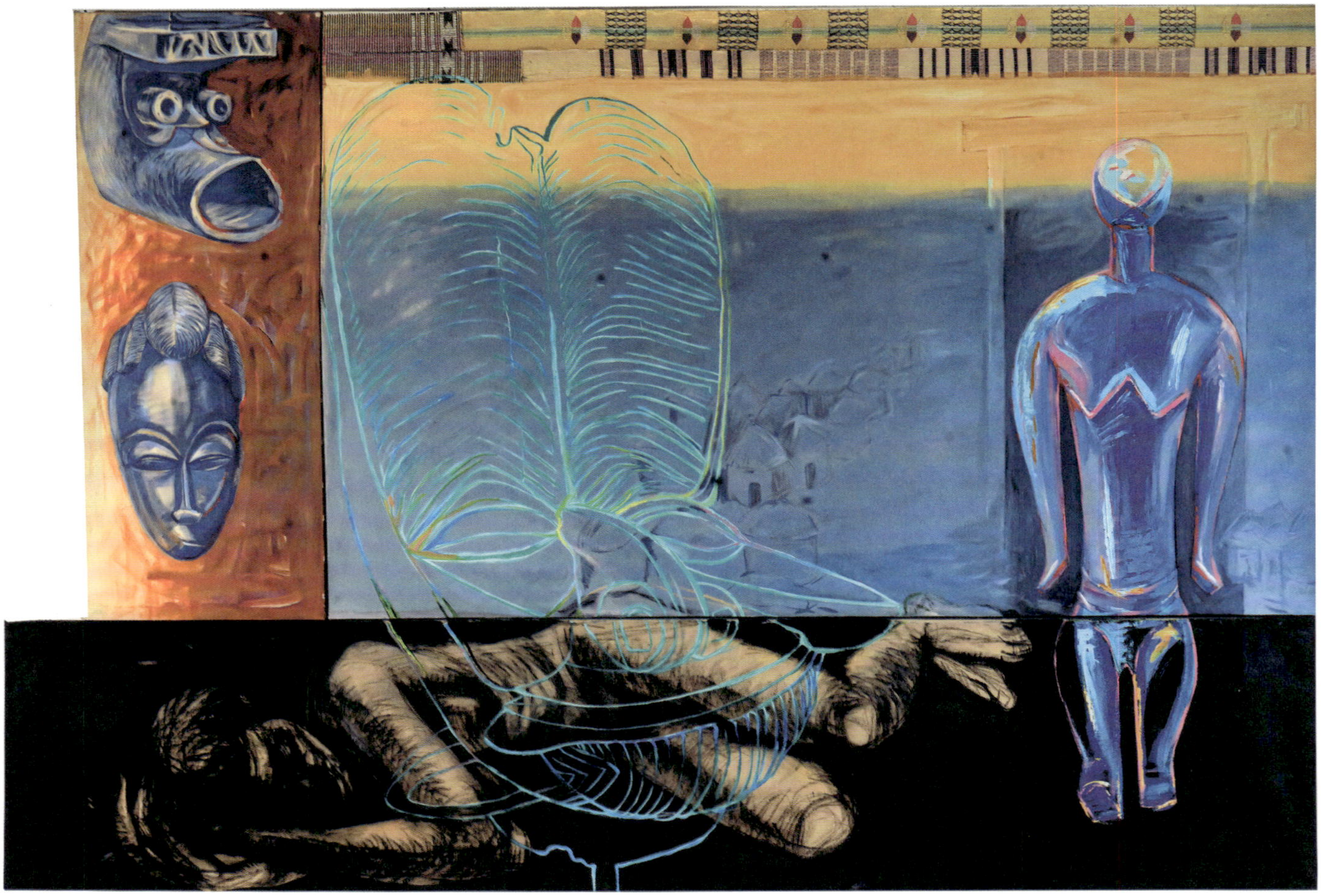

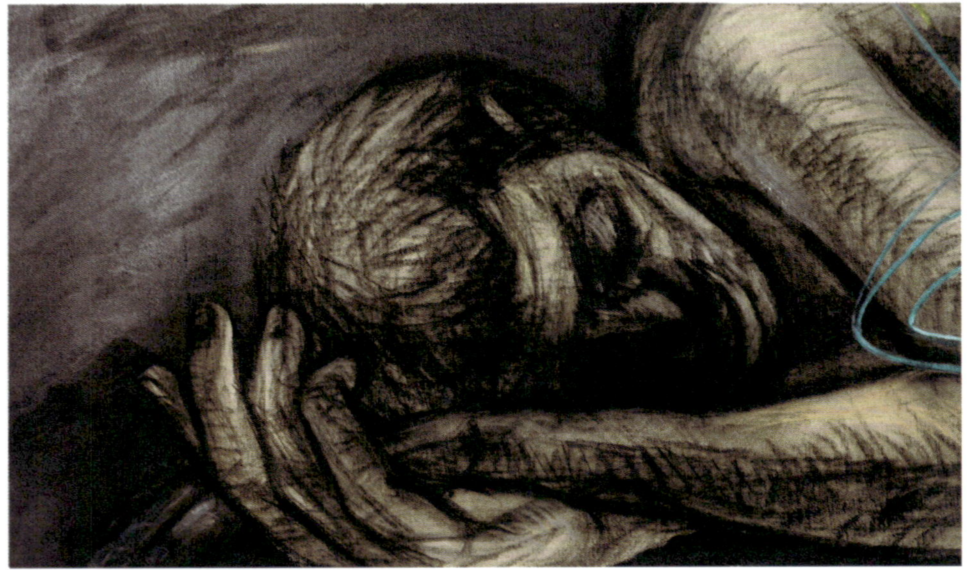

39

40

39. Bryan McFarlane, *I Dream of African Souls*, 1984. Oil on linen. 92 × 137 inches (233.7 × 348 cm)

40. McFarlane, *I Dream of African Souls* (detail), 1984

"I spent my formative years studying at the Edna Manley College of Art in Kingston. I taught there as I continued to engage in numerous activities throughout the Caribbean. I later studied at the Massachusetts College of Art and Design, where I became convinced that travel and broader cultural exposure were key components for my growth. AAMARP provided vital studio space to experiment and explore ideas rooted in the program's early Pan-Africanism.

African American art in Boston was flourishing fifty years ago thanks in part to AAMARP. Dana Chandler created a visionary institution which foregrounded art and aesthetics in our community, so much of which may have never come to light otherwise. My entire growth as a visual artist since the 1980s, along with countless others, was nurtured and encouraged at AAMARP. The program played an invaluable role in healing our communities of color, and greater Boston, whose population was severely isolated, racially divided, and culturally conservative. Some art institutions struggled to create a dignified and inclusive space as the city experienced brutal riots which tore communities apart. Even today, AAMARP remains a beacon and carries this possibility forward."

Bryan McFarlane

Allan Rohan Crite: Retrospective Exhibition

MAR 3–30

AAMARP: The Last Picture Show

MAY 19–JUNE 30

Ellen Banks, Calvin Burnett, Dana C. Chandler Jr., Robin Chandler, Milton Derr, Arnold Hurley, Reginald L. Jackson, Michael Jones, Marcia Lloyd, Bryan McFarlane, Renée Neblett, James Reuben Reed, Rudolph Robinson, Susan Thompson, Bill Travis, Rene Westbrook, John Wilson

FIG. 41

The Last Picture Show was the first of two exhibitions staged at contentious moments in AAMARP's history that both take their title from Peter Bogdanovich's 1971 film of the same name. Whereas the film is a coming-of-age drama set in northern Texas, this exhibition was organized by Chandler in protest of the program's disruption as part of the impending move of AAMARP out of 11 Leon Street during the building's renovation by Northeastern. In a memorandum, he encouraged artists to "please design one work around this issue," though the results of this request are uncertain.[19] Several artists included in the exhibition worked predominantly in genres that did not necessarily align with the political stakes of the appeal, such as landscape painter Marcia Lloyd who painted tranquil, unpeopled scenes at the Arnold Arboretum, or the Blue Hills as seen from a weather observation tower. For Lloyd, the landscape is an always-dynamic subject, whose various elements of light and space are beyond her control, stimulating her deep interest in light, color, atmosphere, and distance.[20] As the final exhibition in a consistent string at 11 Leon Street since 1979, *The Last Picture* show marked AAMARP's transition to a phase of compounding uncertainties.   **JDB**

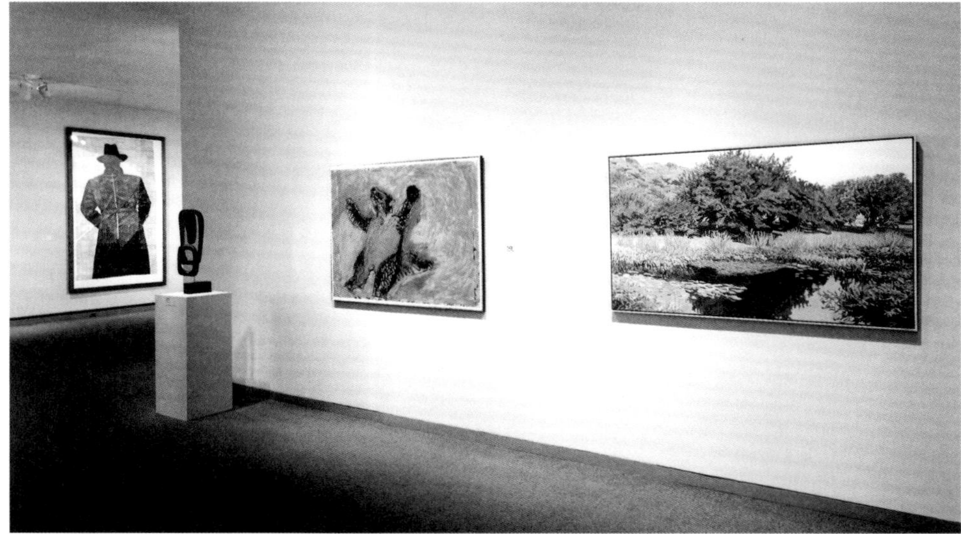

41

41. Installation view, *Massachusetts Masters: Afro-American Artists*, Museum of Fine Arts, Boston, 1988

AAMARP AT 590 HUNTINGTON AVENUE

1986

Michael Jones–AAMARP Artist Farewell Party
JUNE 27

FIGS. 42–43

1987

Art Pro Quo
SEPT 2–30

Bryan McFarlane: Fragments & Presence
OCT 25

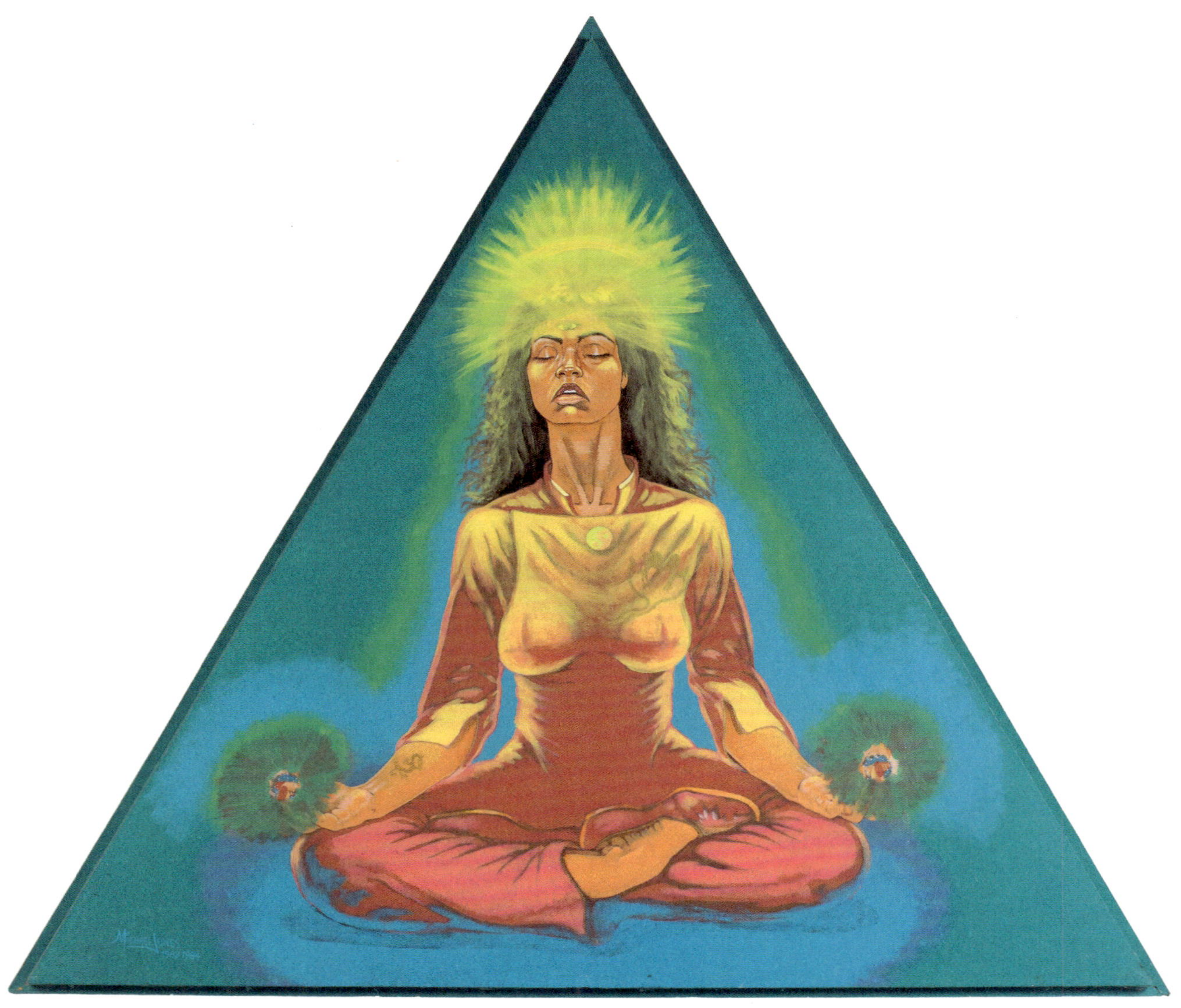

42

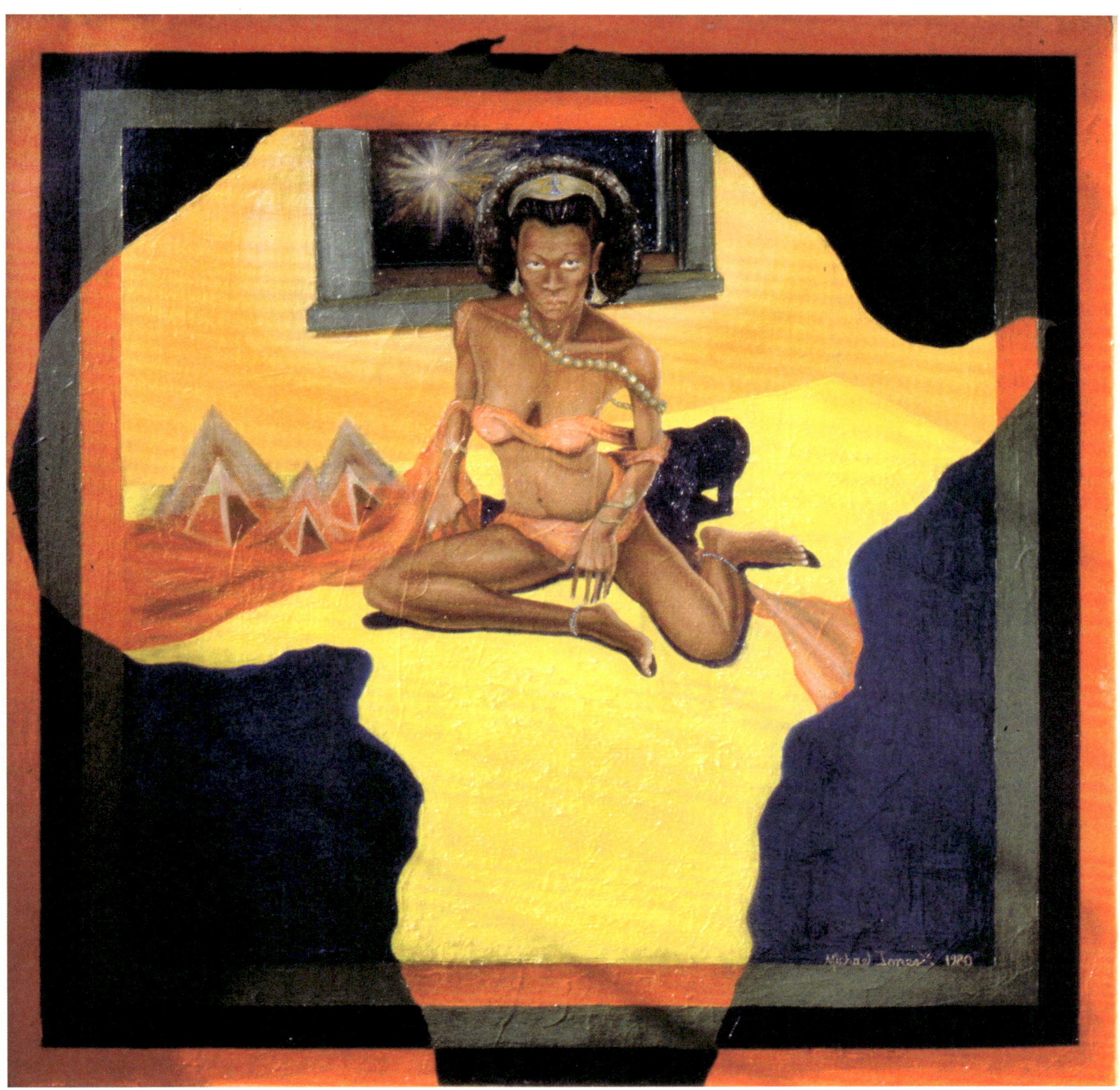

43

42. Michael Jones, *Meditation–
Inner Force–Lotus*, 1982–84.
Acrylic on shaped canvas and
artist frame. 76 × 66 inches
(193 × 167.6 cm)

43. Michael Jones, *Untitled*,
c. 1980. Acrylic on canvas.
Dimensions unknown

AAMARP DIVIDED BETWEEN 11 LEON STREET AND 590 HUNTINGTON AVENUE

1988

AAMARP '88: The Eleventh Year

FEB 7–MAR 4

Ellen Banks, John E. Barbour, Calvin Burnett, Dana C. Chandler Jr., Robin Chandler, Curtis Corbin, Allan Rohan Crite, Henry DeLeon, Milton Derr, Tyrone Geter, Paul Goodnight, Barbara Holt, Michael Jones, Napoleon Jones-Henderson, Jackie Jordan, Kofi Kayiga, Harriet Kennedy, John Keyes, Vusumuzi Maduna, Bryan McFarlane, Frank W. Morris, Robert Murrell, Roxanne Perinchief, Hakim Raquib, James Reuben Reed, Rudolph Robinson, Renée Stout, Edward Strickland, Susan Thompson, Bill Travis, Don West, Rene Westbrook, Diane Wignall, John Wilson, Richard Yarde

FIGS. 44–49

During February 1988–timed in celebration of African American History month and programmed alongside the exhibition *Massachusetts Masters: Afro-American Artists* organized by Edmund Barry Gaither at the Museum of Fine Arts, Boston (MFA)–*AAMARP '88: The Eleventh Year* assembled the work of thirty-five artists affiliated with the program in their annual showcase. The exhibition included longtime residents and affiliate artists, as well as many artists featured in *Massachusetts Masters*. At AAMARP and the MFA, Paul Goodnight, a figurative painter with an expressive sense of color presented work

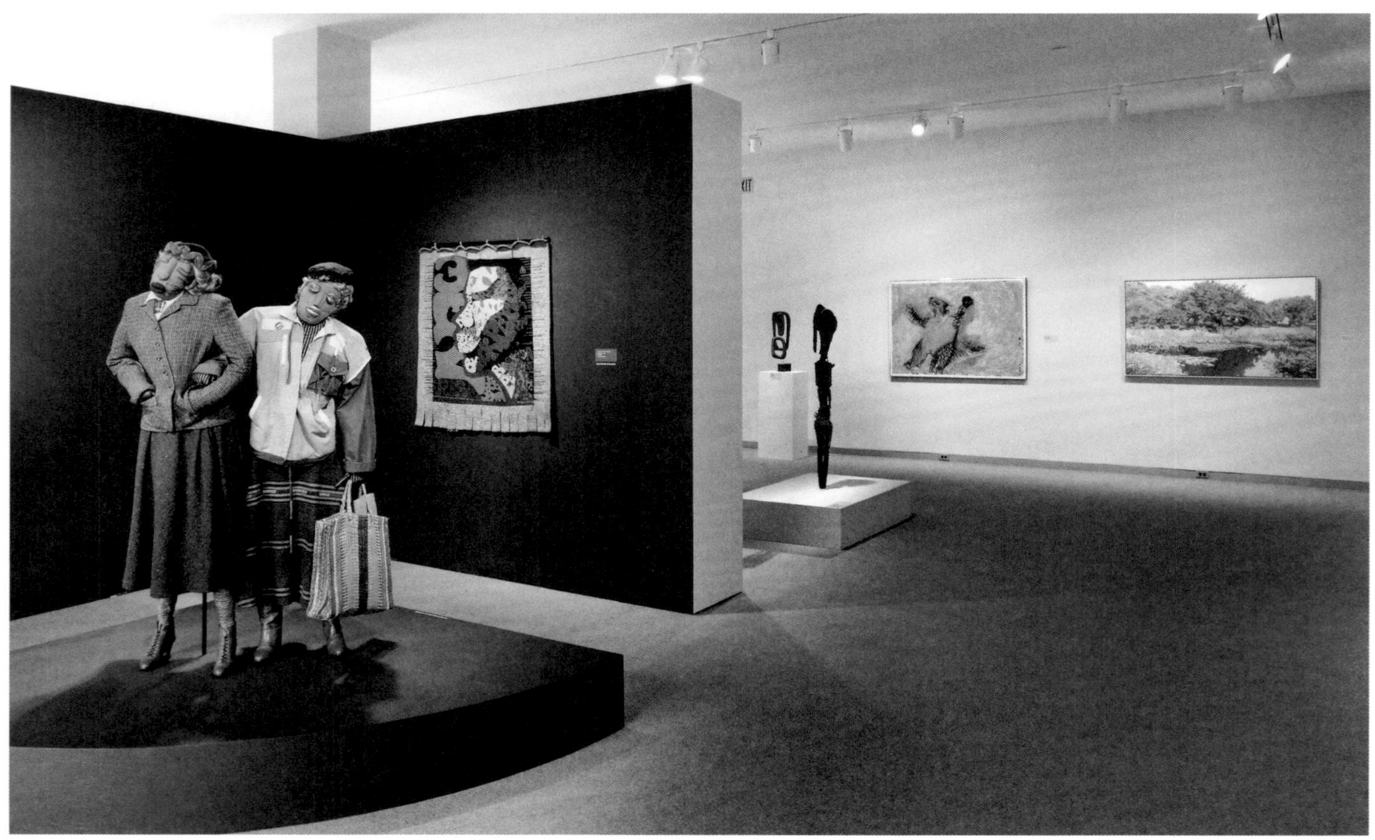

44

44. Installation view, *Massachusetts Masters: Afro-American Artists*, Museum of Fine Arts, Boston, 1988

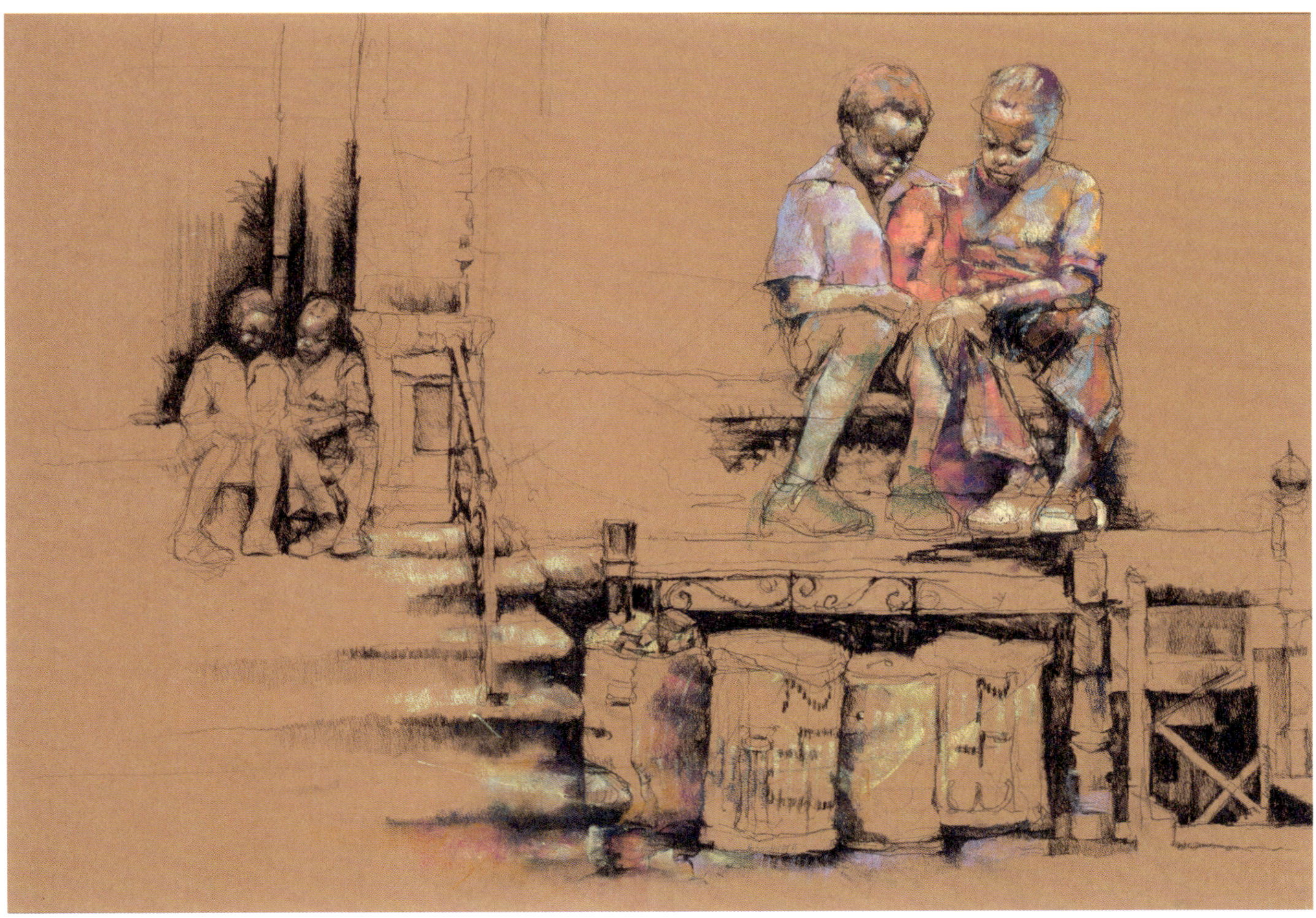

alongside magisterial woven textiles by AfriCOBRA member Napoleon Jones-Henderson. Both artists created images inspired by the lived experience and cultures of people of the African diaspora. Richard Yarde painted intricate, grid-like compositions in watercolor inspired by the segmented construction of the quilts his mother made. Yarde often painted at a grand scale, especially for watercolor, including a cycle of paintings about Harlem's famed Savoy Ballroom (1926–58), though scenes such as *Parlor* (1980) of a father and daughter in a domestic interior convey his unparalleled artistry through exuberant colors and patterns.

AAMARP '88 also struck a somber tone, as it was made in tribute to and in memory of Rudolph Robinson, a photographer and original AAMARP artist who had recently passed away. Robinson worked as photographer for the Museum of the National Center of Afro-American Artists for nearly twenty years, and as a freelance photographer for the Museum of Fine Arts, Boston. Robinson was energetic and prolific, photographing a wide range of subjects ranging from the nighttime scene *TRY BLACK* (1983), to his Invisible Man/Europe series documenting the growing communities of Black people living there. A highly skilled technician who believed in the transformational possibilities of the darkroom, Robinson was an influential member of AAMARP and a mentor to many, including Hakim Raquib. **JDB**

45. Paul Goodnight, *Endangered Species*, 1980. Pastel, charcoal, pencil, and pen and ink on paper mounted on paperboard. 21⅞ × 30½ inches (55.6 × 77.5 cm). Smithsonian American Art Museum, Washington DC; Gift of the artist

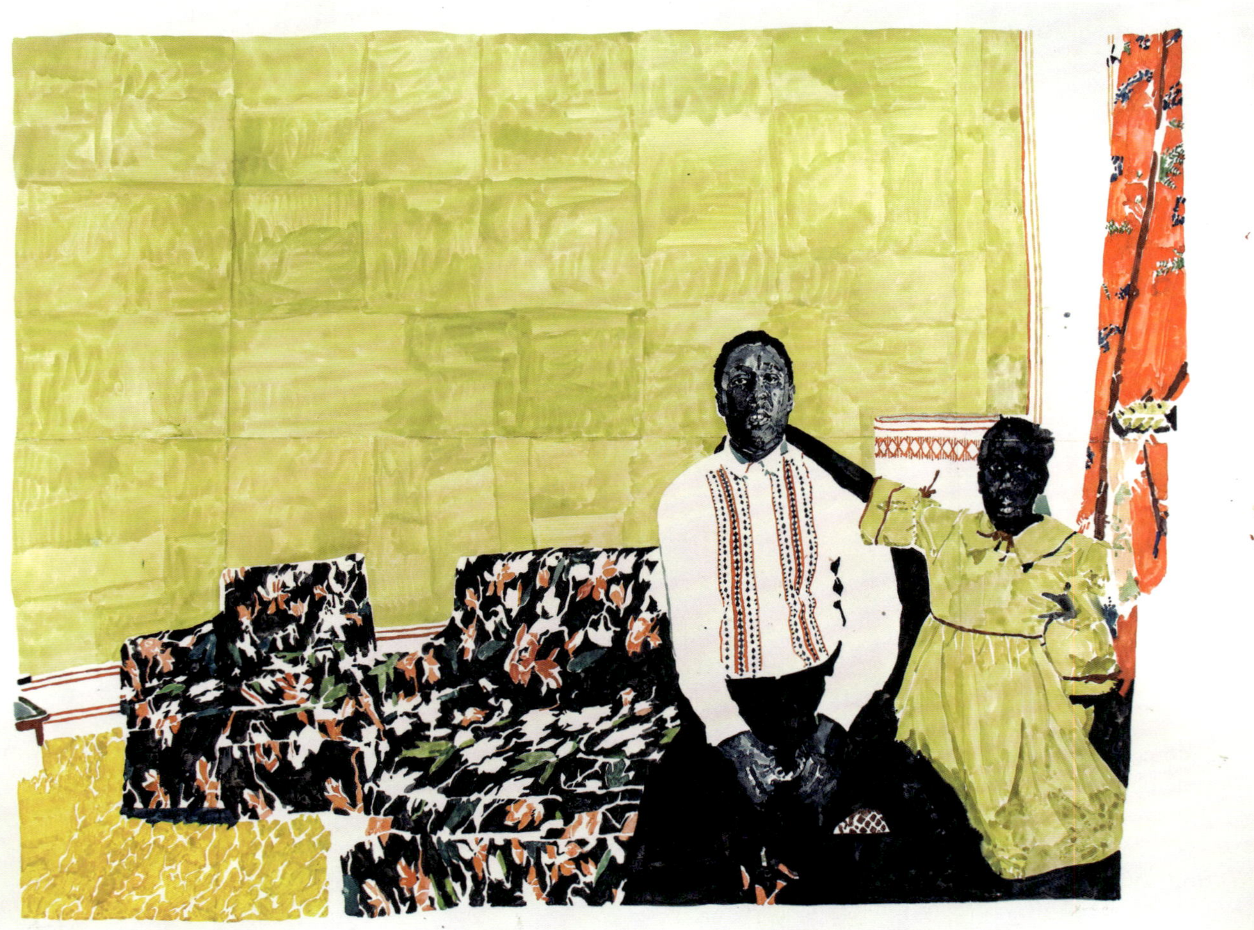

46

46. Richard Yarde, *The Parlor*,
1980. Opaque watercolor on
paper. 58⅞ × 78⅝ inches
(149.4 × 199.7 cm). Mount
Holyoke College Art Museum,
South Hadley, MA; Gift of the
American Academy of Arts
and Letters

47. Rudolph Robinson, *TRY
BLACK*, 1983. Gelatin silver
print. 15 × 16½ inches (38.1 ×
41.9 cm). Addison Gallery of
American Art, Phillips Academy,
Andover, MA; Museum purchase

48. Rudolph Robinson in
his studio, n.d.

49. Rudolph Robinson on
assignment for the Museum
of Fine Arts, Boston, c. 1987

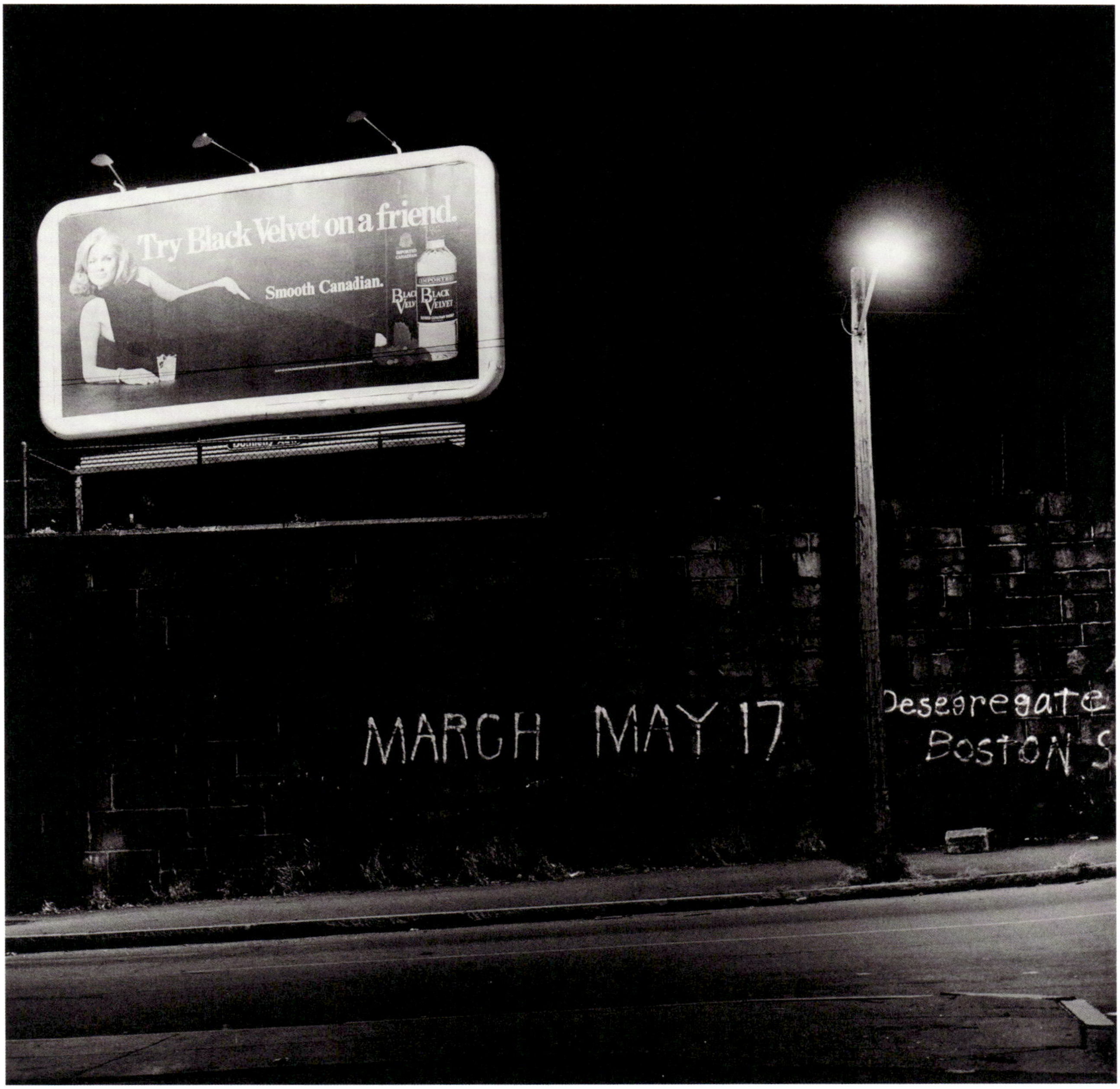

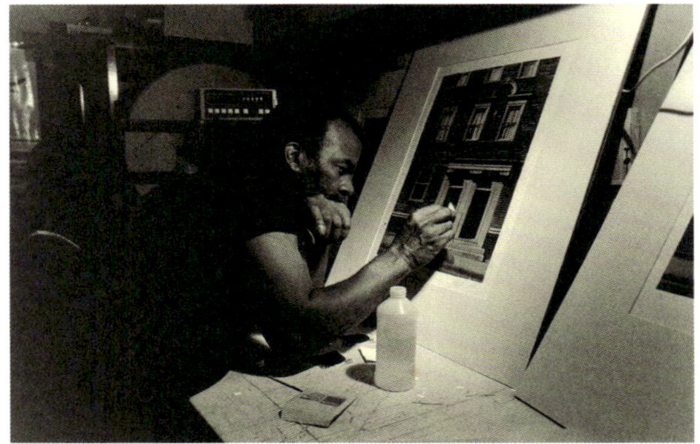
Try Black Velvet on a friend.
Smooth Canadian.
MARCH MAY 17
Desegregate
Boston S

47

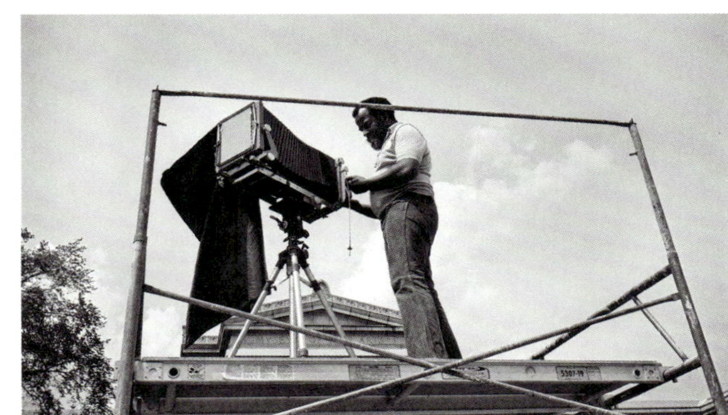

48

49

"AAMARP was my first studio experience, the first time I felt like a professional artist. Before then, I was painting in my bedroom at my parents' house in Pittsburgh. I met Dana Chandler when he was giving a talk in Richmond at the National Conference of Artists. He spoke about AAMARP, and it ended up that he invited my friend Jackie Jordan and me to share a studio there for six months. I was not a fan of Boston, but I was taken by the idea that we could be in a communal setting with other artists, hanging out and talking at any time. I had been making photorealist paintings like *Renée & Sam*, which I painted at AAMARP, until I first saw Joseph Cornell and Betye Saar's boxes just before arriving in Boston. Since I didn't feel safe in the city to take photographs to paint from, I stayed inside where I felt safe. I started creating boxes at AAMARP with found objects and constructions. Creating the boxes was a metaphor for putting myself in a box." Renée Stout

Judy Chicago: The Birth Project
MAR 11–APR 3

Vusumuzi Maduna: The African Spirit–Bicultural Synthesis, Part 2
MAY 1–30

Hakim Raquib: On Photography
JUNE 5

FIG. 51

At the end of the turbulent 1960s, when many were searching for meaning and direction, Hakim Raquib discovered photography. He ran into a friend who invited him to see the studio of the Roxbury Photographers Training Program (RPTP). The RPTP was a community-based initiative launched by the Massachusetts Institute of Technology's Creative Photography Laboratory. After training at the RPTP, Raquib took on extensive commercial assignments, including for the Polaroid Corporation, the *Boston Globe*, WGBH-TV, and more. He grew somewhat disillusioned with commercial work and soon returned to a mode of personal expression, especially while on an Oxfam America assignment in Zimbabwe in 1986 where he witnessed the ruins of Great Zimbabwe. According to artist and critic Edward Strickland, "the sky in Raquib's photographs of the ruins of Great Zimbabwe is often dark or in transition toward darkness. The ruins themselves are richly illuminated so that one's eyes are drawn to the textural detail of stone upon stone. It is as if the light in which we see stone walls bathed comes from their history and not from daylight."[21] This same skillful control of light is evident in *The Tent* (1992) from his Canvas Cathedral series. Raquib captures a nighttime Baptist tent revival congregation in Roxbury. While it is pitch black around the tent, light appears to emanate from underneath it, including in what might be described as a poetic flash of spiritual energy. **JDB**

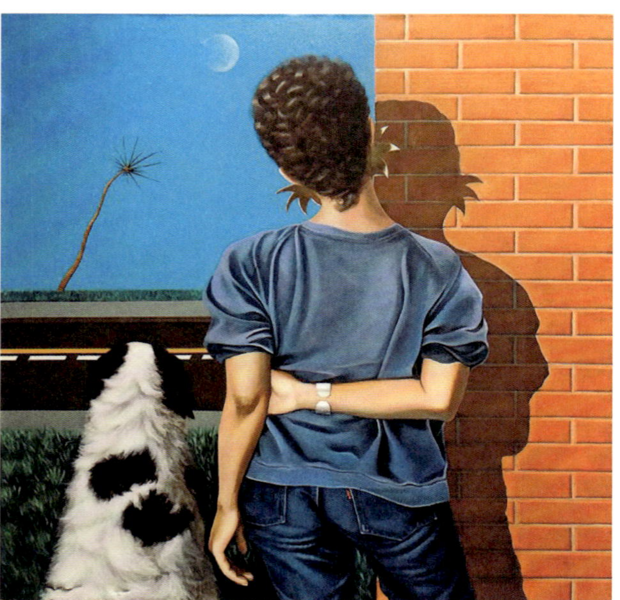

50. Renée Stout, *Renée & Sam* (detail), 1985. Acrylic on canvas. 36 × 36 inches (91.4 × 91.4 cm). Collection of Lauren Thomasson

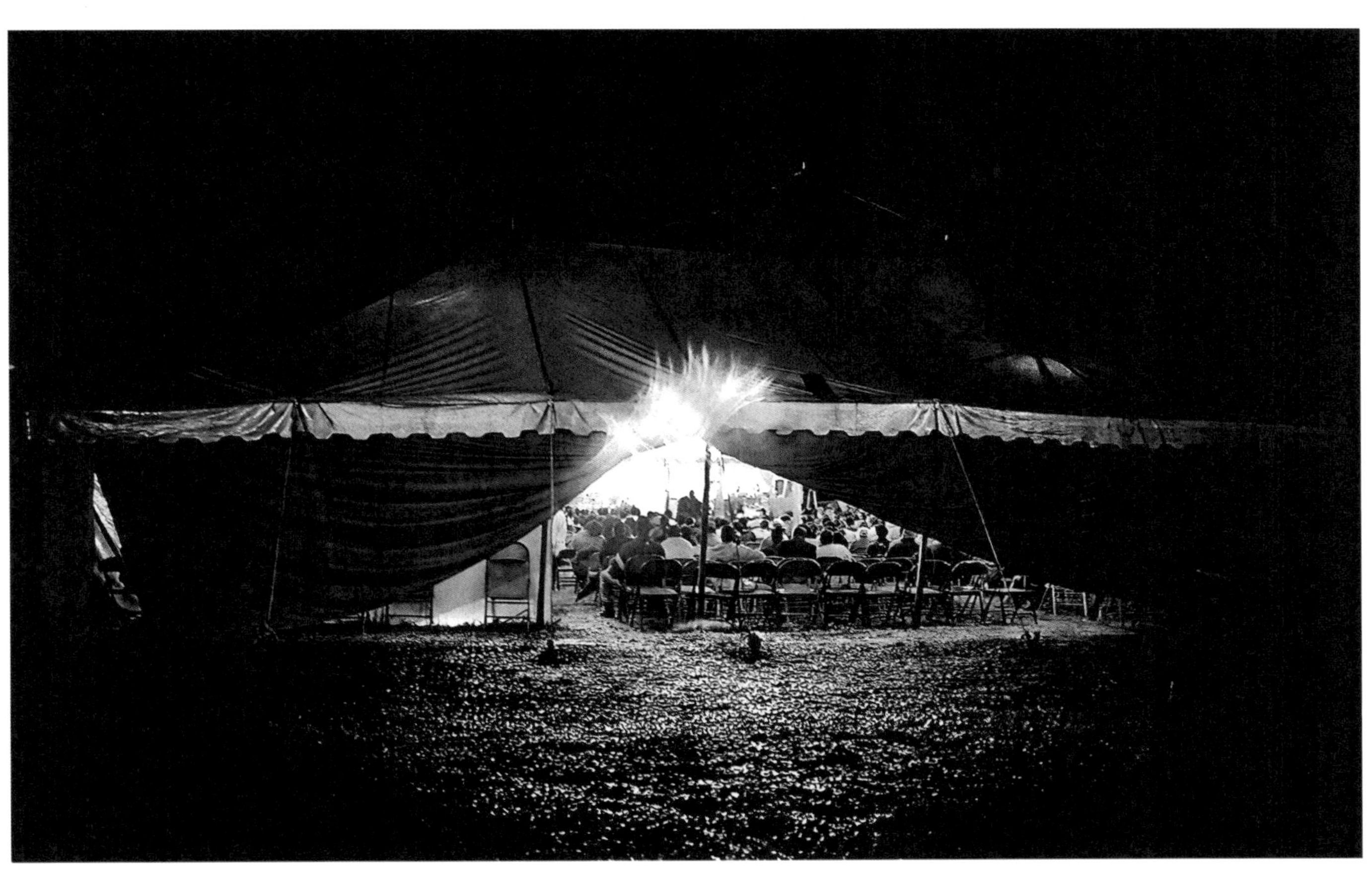

51

51. Hakim Raquib, *The Tent*,
1992. From the series Canvas
Cathedral. Gelatin silver print.
28 × 18 inches (71.1 × 45.7 cm)

"I owe an immense debt of gratitude to the African American Master Artists-in-Residence Program. It served as the springboard that propelled my career as a visual artist. In the early stages of my photographic journey, opportunities for artists of color to pursue a professional path in the arts—especially in Boston—were scarce. AAMARP changed that.

Under the visionary leadership of its founder, Professor Dana Chandler—an activist and artist committed to racial justice and equality—AAMARP offered a platform where Afrocentric expression could flourish freely, without the pressure to conform. Dana's guidance helped shape my artistic direction in profound ways.

One of the most transformative gifts AAMARP gave me was a studio space with twenty-four hour access. That space became my sanctuary—a place to experiment, refine my craft, and grow. Being surrounded by other like-minded artists created a vibrant, inspiring atmosphere that fueled my creativity.

The program also opened doors for me to exhibit my work locally, nationally, and internationally—an essential cornerstone for recognition. Beyond my own development, AAMARP allowed me to give back. I mentored youth through workshops held at the center, and I'm proud to say that several of those young artists went on to study at Northeastern University and Massachusetts College of Art and Design.

AAMARP's open-door policy welcomed community organizations and families, forging lasting relationships that led to future collaborations. During my residency, I had the privilege of engaging with renowned national and international artists who exhibited at AAMARP, and I participated in countless cultural events and seminars. I truly cannot think of another residency program in Boston that offered such a rich and inclusive experience." Hakim Raquib

Diane Wignall: Contemporary Glass Works

SEPT 11–OCT 7

The Fantastic Image

OCT 9–NOV 4

Myryn-Ellen Barret, Arne Bass, Kerry Burke, Calvin Burnett, Kate Caish, Dana C. Chandler Jr., Allan Rohan Crite, Milton Derr, Robert Dodge, Polly Doyle, Mateo Galvano, Paul Goodnight, Kofi Kayiga, Claudia Keel, Mary Ellen Latas, Marcia Lloyd, C. J. Lori, Vusumuzi Maduna, Carlyn Marcus, Patricia McNabb, J. Morrix, Daniel Ouelette, Carole Pryharski, James Reuben Reed, Robert Rutman, Julia Seltz, Shan Shan Sheng, Edward Strickland, Arnold Stuck, Arnold Trachtman, Bill Travis, Wen-ti Tsen, Rene Westbrook, and John Wilson

1989

Rene Westbrook: War and Prophecy

JAN 8–31

FIG. 52

"When I was finishing my BFA at MassArt, I wanted to continue learning from artists who were on the front lines of creative excellence and social activism. AAMARP was the perfect environment for those seeking mastery of their craft.

Dana Chandler created a Mecca at AAMARP for artists whose work was bold and experimental. The range and caliber of the various talents there made it a place to commune and learn from those already in the pipeline for success.

I was thrilled and humbled when Dana accepted me into the program. It was also when my work began to expand from my classical training in sculpture to more cutting edge experimental work. While at AAMARP I was highly productive. The camaraderie among the crew was dynamic and guaranteed the exchange of ideas and techniques. During those heady days, I understood their drive to master one's self as part of the pursuit of an audacious authenticity.

I am certain that my association with AAMARP helped to anchor my art career in ways I could not have expected. AAMARP must be allowed to flourish and continue its great work for the next generation of visionaries and creative leaders in the city. The blueprint laid down by the early members of this esteemed community deserves to be part of an ongoing, living legacy that AAMARP promised at the outset of its mission." Rene Westbrook

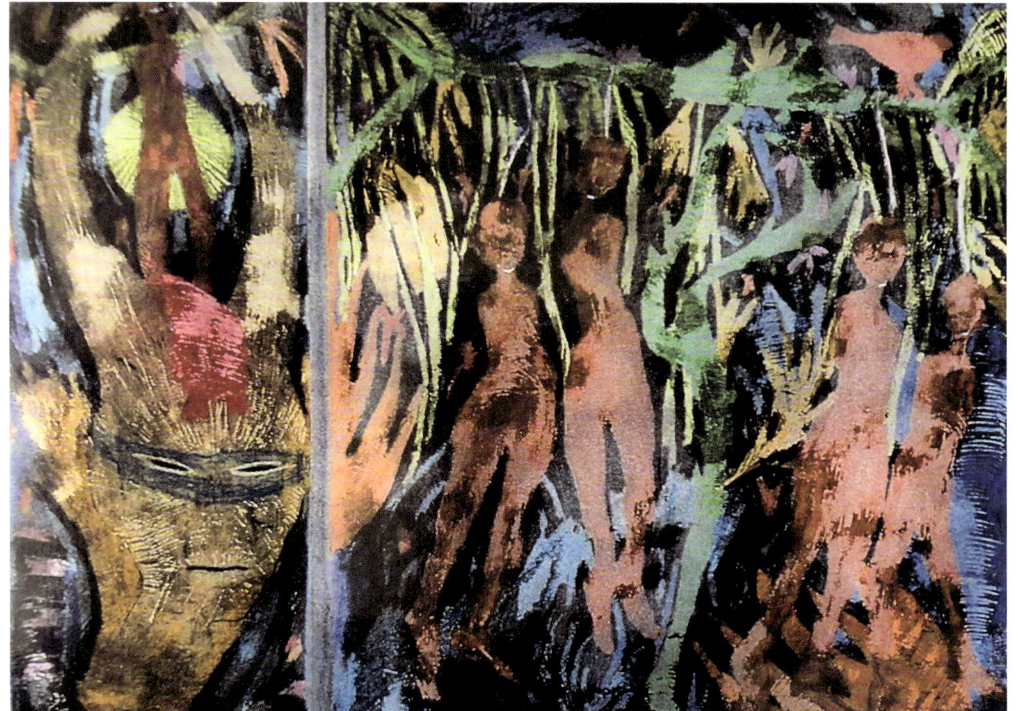

52

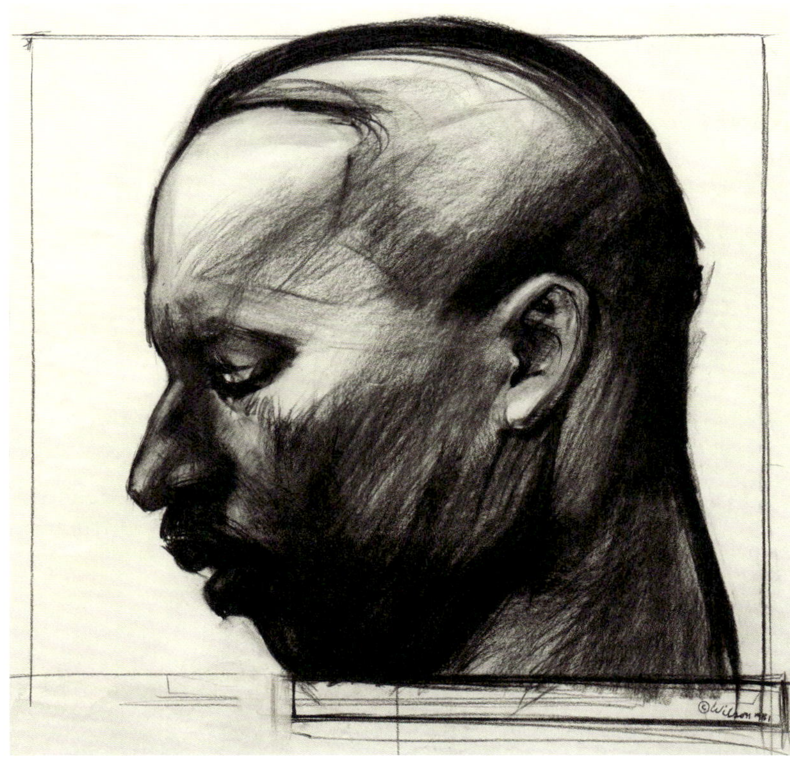

53

52. Rene Westbrook, *Strange Fruit*, 1986. Oil pastel, graphite, and turpentine wash on paper. 20 × 30 inches (50.8 × 76.2 cm). Musuem of the National Center of Afro-American Artists, Boston, MA; Museum purchase

53. John Wilson, *Study for "Martin Luther King, Jr." (Buffalo)*, 1981. Charcoal on paper. 28½ × 28 inches (72.4 × 71.1 cm)

AAMARP AT 76 ATHERTON STREET IN JAMAICA PLAIN

1990

Baker's Dozen: A Tribute to Martin Luther King

BOSTON CITY HALL

JAN 9–FEB 28

Ellen Banks, John Barbour, Gloretta Baynes, Calvin Burnett, Dana C. Chandler Jr., Robin Chandler, Allan Rohan Crite, Milton Derr, Gordon Gaul, Paul Goodnight, Napoleon Jones-Henderson, Barbara Holt, Reginald L. Jackson, Kofi Kayiga, Harriet Kennedy, John Keys, Marcia Lloyd, Vusumuzi Maduna, Bryan McFarlane, Frank Morris, Robert Murrell, Roxanne Perinchief, Hakim Raquib, James Reuben Reed, Edward Strickland, Susan Thompson, Bill Travis, Don West, Ken Whyte, John Wilson, Betty Winston, Richard Yarde

FIG. 53

1991

Dana Chandler: Upon My Fiftieth Year: Visions From an Elder

APR 14–JUNE 15

Edward Strickland: A Human Presence

SEPT 15–OCT 15

FIG. 54

Don West: Mozambique

OCT 20–NOV 31

Kofi Kayiga: Recent Images

DEC 1–JAN 17, 1992

FIG. 55

Kofi Kayiga moved to Boston in 1981 after nearly ten years as head of the painting department at the Jamaica School of Art, where AAMARP artist Bryan McFarlane was his student. In Boston, McFarlane introduced Kayiga to Dana Chandler, who welcomed the elder Jamaican artist into the fold. During a prolonged stay in Uganda, Kayiga became deeply interested in traditional African religious rites, which he began to see differently when he returned to Jamaica with a heightened consciousness of the island's African retentions. Inspired by this vivid cultural hybridity—as well as childlike mark-making, whose "unconscious base" the artist cites as his greatest influence—Kayiga arrived at an intuitive way of working.[22] He sees himself as a conduit for the repeating forms and motifs he registers directly on canvas and paper with an unrestrained immediacy. At AAMARP, the scale of Kayiga's work grew dramatically, as it did for many artists, though curator Edmund Barry Gaither maintains that his smaller works are the primary source for all others, the "interior landscapes," such as *Moonlight* (1987), that are the most "directly felt works" in his oeuvre.[23] **JDB**

1992

AAMARP Artists Celebrate African American History Month

FEB–APR 19

Gloretta Baynes, Calvin Burnett, Dana C. Chandler Jr., Paul Goodnight, Reginald L. Jackson, Kofi Kayiga, Frank Morris, Hakim Raquib, Edward Strickland, Susan Thompson, Keith Morris Washington, Don West, etc.

1993

Dana C. Chandler Jr.: The Last Picture Show

MAY 9–JUNE 30

"Recent Images by America's Most Controversial Africancentric Artist" Open House

JUNE 27

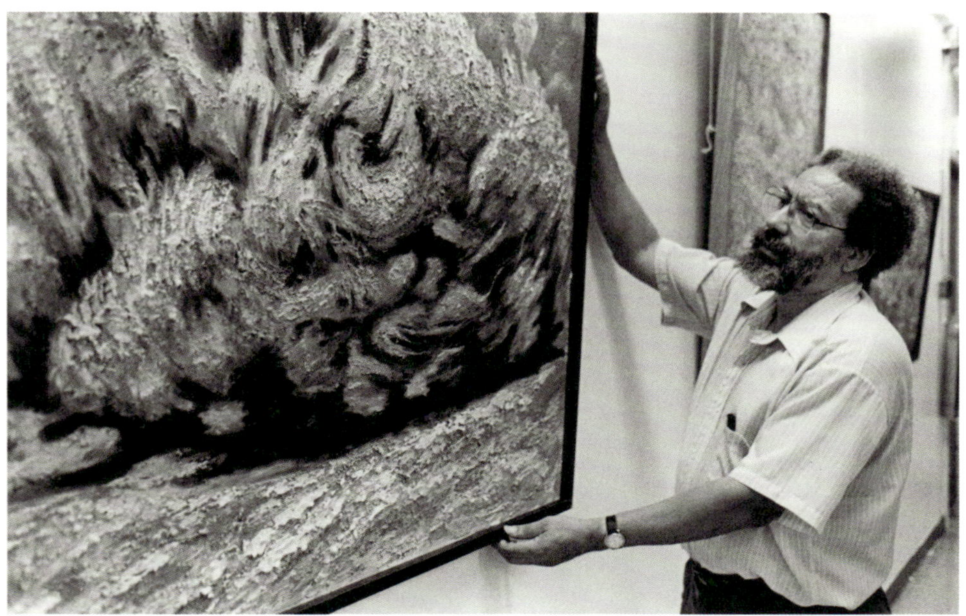

54

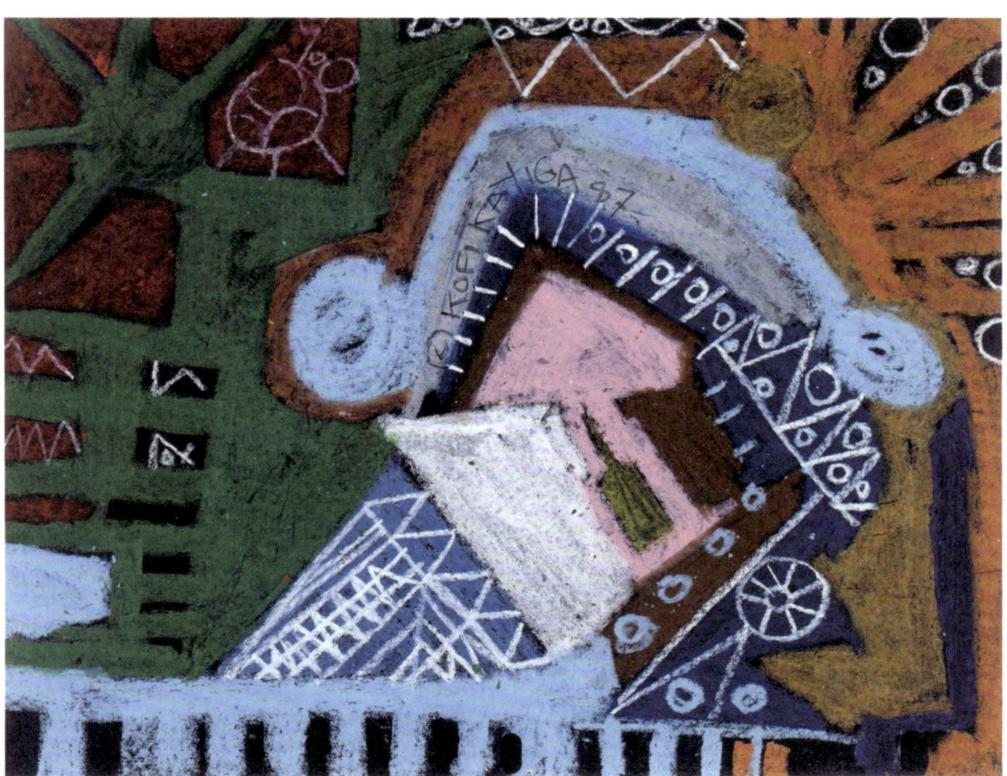

55

54. Edward Strickland hanging his painting *Meadow Sweet*, July 16, 1992

55. Kofi Kayiga, *Moonlight*, 1987. Pastel on paper. 8¼ × 10½ inches (21 × 26.7 cm)

(SEE ATTACHED)

Dana C. Chandler Jr.'s *Urban Newsletter Art Piece* and the Fight for AAMARP

FAYE R. GLEISSER

On the surface, *Urban Newsletter Art Piece* is a twenty-five page, double-sided packet of densely collaged, annotated, and photocopied documents, cumulatively testifying to the immense social, artistic, political, and material contributions of Dana C. Chandler Jr. individually, and the African American Master Artists-in-Residence Program (AAMARP) collectively, from 1979 to 1993. Looking closer, however, the document serves myriad purposes and offers variable lessons for conceptualizing and navigating how the history of *making evidence* of Black life, achievement, and ingenuity under conditions of anti-Blackness and white supremacy debt economies is always already an aesthetic, material, legal, and political endeavor.

First and foremost, Chandler created the document as an immediate and direct rebuttal to the changes then immanently threatening the existence of AAMARP and his role within it: in May 1993, Northeastern University provost Michael Baer announced a devastating, 75 percent cut to the residency program's already diminished budget and the termination of Chandler as its director. Although Northeastern's presidents, first Kenneth Ryder, and then his successor John Curry, had supported and advocated for the program over the years, the residency had essentially been "put in storage" around 1989 (as the newsletter attests), due to the university's negligence to properly renovate and make usable the studio spaces promised to AAMARP in the 76 Atherton Street building. In the meantime, the administrators had rerouted parts of the residency's budget to the renovation of studio space for other artists in the building, all while creating mock-ups for its new, multimillion dollar renovation of the Dodge Library and renovations of the Transportation Department's facilities on the building's second floor. Provost Baer justified his decisions for defunding AAMARP and dismissing Chandler with unfounded claims and criticisms that as director Chandler had not effectively worked to integrate the residency's artists with campus initiatives, stating moreover that, "departments like AAMARP do not provide the university with documentable evidence of adding new students to the university community." Baer asserted that he wanted new leadership that would help to "rejuvenate the program to make it interactive with the other programs on campus" in order to "refocus" AAMARP because "that program wasn't focused at all."[1]

Chandler's document vociferously refutes these claims and reveals their political stakes. Each page is filled with news clippings capturing contradictions in the administrator's narrative. Significantly, the excerpts from published interviews not only catch Baer in the act

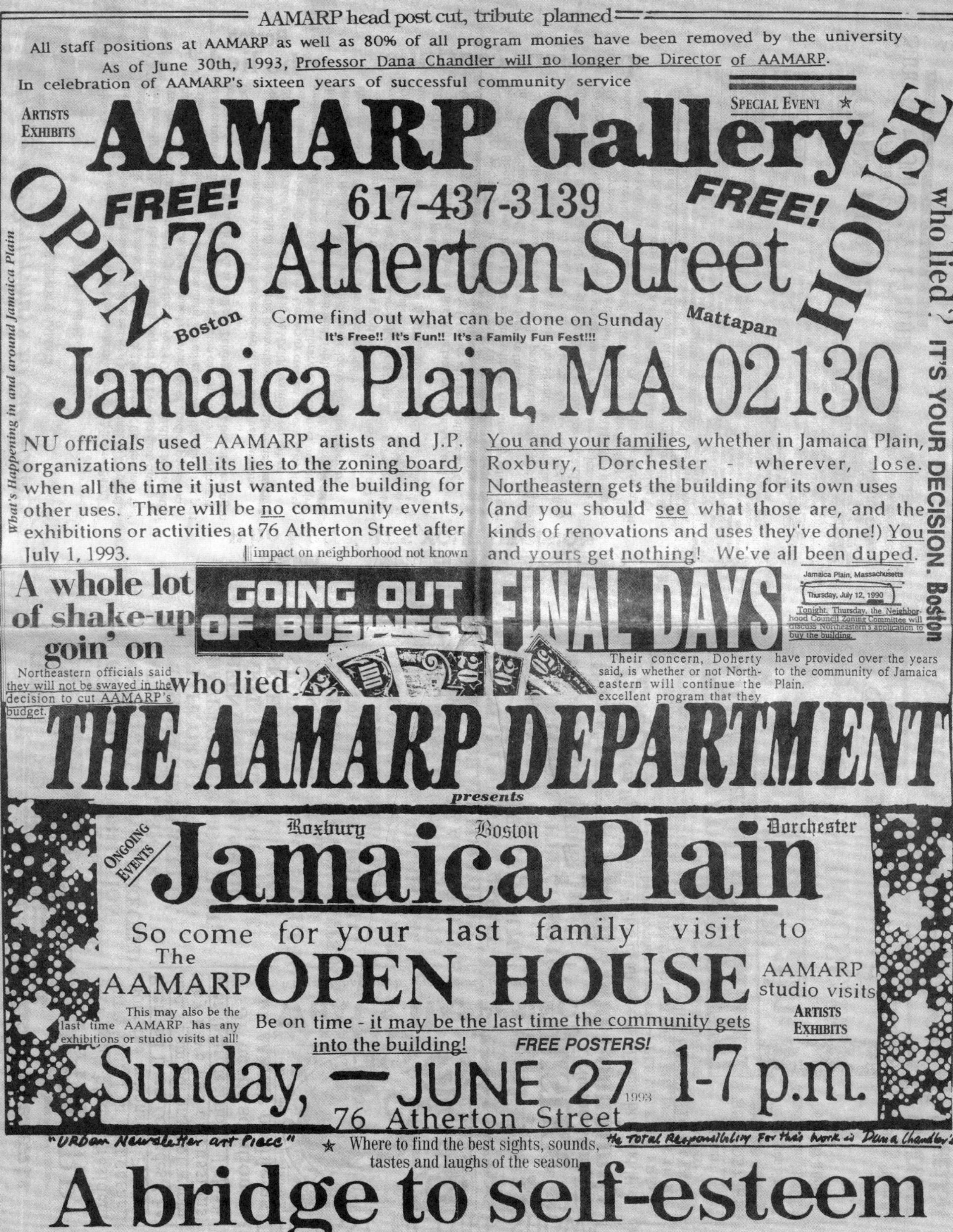

AAMARP head post cut, tribute planned
All staff positions at AAMARP as well as 80% of all program monies have been removed by the university
As of June 30th, 1993, Professor Dana Chandler will no longer be Director of AAMARP.
In celebration of AAMARP's sixteen years of successful community service
SPECIAL EVENT
ARTISTS EXHIBITS
AAMARP Gallery
OPEN
FREE!
617-437-3139
76 Atherton Street
FREE!
HOUSE
who lied?
IT'S YOUR DECISION. Boston
What's Happening in and around Jamaica Plain
Boston
Come find out what can be done on Sunday
Mattapan
It's Free!! It's Fun!! It's a Family Fun Fest!!!
Jamaica Plain, MA 02130
NU officials used AAMARP artists and J.P. organizations to tell its lies to the zoning board, when all the time it just wanted the building for other uses. There will be no community events, exhibitions or activities at 76 Atherton Street after July 1, 1993.
impact on neighborhood not known
You and your families, whether in Jamaica Plain, Roxbury, Dorchester - wherever, lose. Northeastern gets the building for its own uses (and you should see what those are, and the kinds of renovations and uses they've done!) You and yours get nothing! We've all been duped.
A whole lot of shake-up goin' on
Northeastern officials said they will not be swayed in the decision to cut AAMARP's budget.
GOING OUT OF BUSINESS
FINAL DAYS
who lied?
Jamaica Plain, Massachusetts
Thursday, July 12, 1990
Tonight, Thursday, the Neighborhood Council Zoning Committee will discuss Northeastern's application to buy the building.
Their concern, Doherty said, is whether or not Northeastern will continue the excellent program that they
have provided over the years to the community of Jamaica Plain.
THE AAMARP DEPARTMENT
presents
ONGOING EVENTS
Roxbury
Boston
Dorchester
Jamaica Plain
So come for your last family visit to
The AAMARP
OPEN HOUSE
AAMARP studio visits
ARTISTS EXHIBITS
This may also be the last time AAMARP has any exhibitions or studio visits at all!
Be on time - it may be the last time the community gets into the building!
FREE POSTERS!
Sunday, — JUNE 27 1993 1-7 p.m.
76 Atherton Street
"Urban Newsletter art piece"
Where to find the best sights, sounds, tastes and laughs of the season.
the Total Responsibility for this work is Dana Chandler's
A bridge to self-esteem

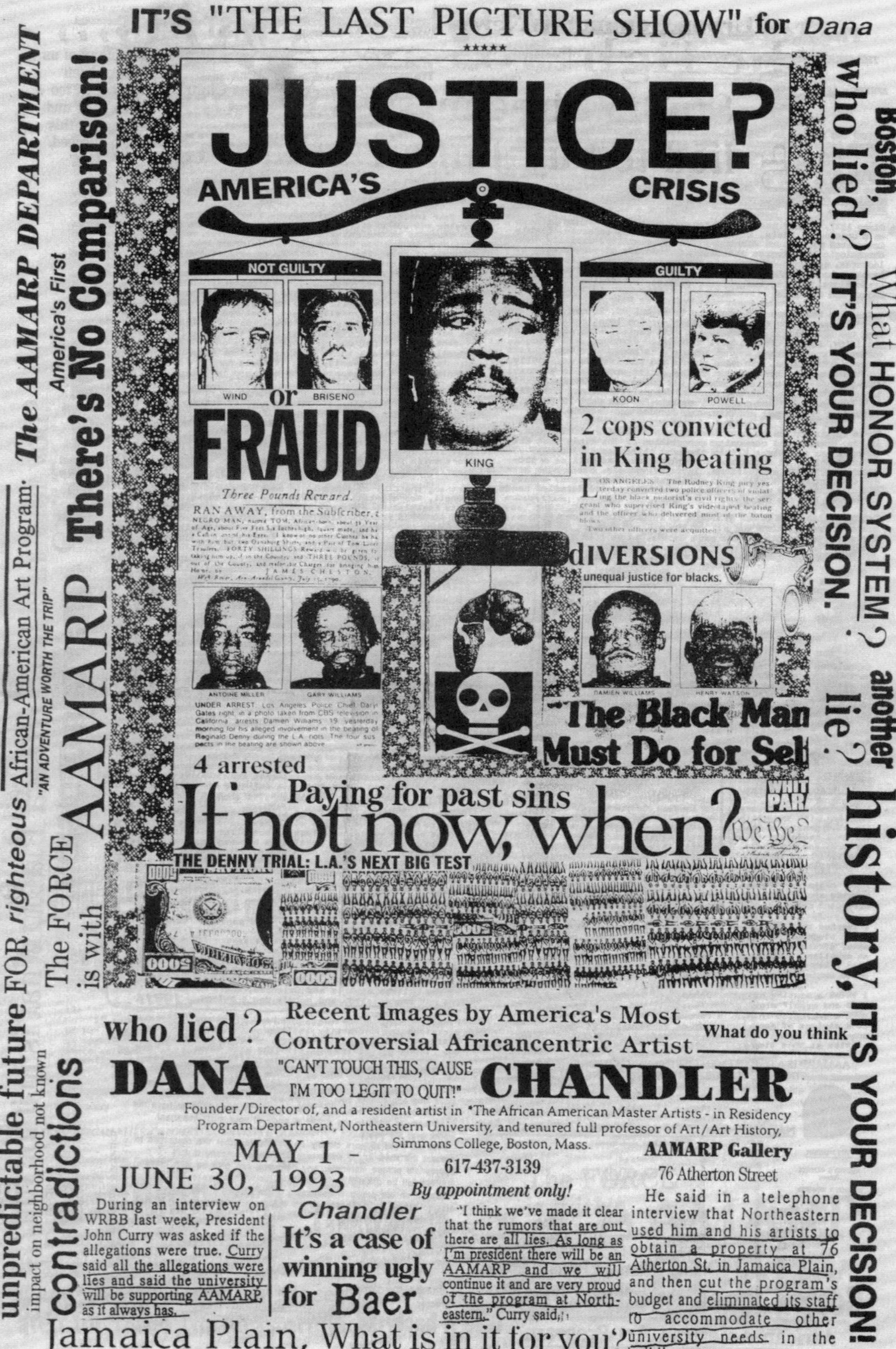
IT'S "THE LAST PICTURE SHOW" for Dana

JUSTICE?
AMERICA'S   CRISIS
NOT GUILTY   GUILTY
WIND   BRISENO   KOON   POWELL
or FRAUD
KING
2 cops convicted in King beating
Three Pounds Reward.
RAN AWAY, from the Subscriber
dIVERSIONS
unequal justice for blacks.
ANTOINE MILLER   GARY WILLIAMS
DAMIEN WILLIAMS   HENRY WATSON
"The Black Man Must Do for Self
4 arrested
Paying for past sins
If not now, when?
THE DENNY TRIAL: L.A.'S NEXT BIG TEST
The AAMARP DEPARTMENT
America's First
There's No Comparison!
"AN ADVENTURE WORTH THE TRIP"
AAMARP
The FORCE is with
FOR righteous African-American Art Program.
unpredictable future
impact on neighborhood not known
contradictions
Boston who lied?
What HONOR SYSTEM? another lie?
IT'S YOUR DECISION.
history, IT'S YOUR DECISION!
who lied?
Recent Images by America's Most
Controversial Africancentric Artist
What do you think
DANA   "CAN'T TOUCH THIS, CAUSE I'M TOO LEGIT TO QUIT!"   CHANDLER
Founder/Director of, and a resident artist in *The African American Master Artists - in Residency
Program Department, Northeastern University, and tenured full professor of Art/Art History,
Simmons College, Boston, Mass.
MAY 1 - JUNE 30, 1993
617-437-3139
By appointment only!
AAMARP Gallery
76 Atherton Street
Chandler
It's a case of winning ugly for Baer
During an interview on WRBB last week, President John Curry was asked if the allegations were true. Curry said all the allegations were lies and said the university will be supporting AAMARP as it always has.
"I think we've made it clear that the rumors that are out there are all lies. As long as I'm president there will be an AAMARP and we will continue it and are very proud of the program at Northeastern." Curry said.
He said in a telephone interview that Northeastern used him and his artists to obtain a property at 76 Atherton St. in Jamaica Plain, and then cut the program's budget and eliminated its staff to accommodate other university needs in the building.
Jamaica Plain, What is in it for you?

of lying but additionally, when juxtaposed with Chandler's correspondence and records over the years, reveal that the provost was taking credit for ideas that Chandler had proposed years prior. For example, in a typeset proposal dated 1990 and reprinted in the newsletter, Chandler outlines a plan for 76 Atherton to become a "Community–University Multi-Cultural Facility"—precisely the idea for interaction and collaboration that Baer would wrongly claim Chandler had failed to envision or enact. These lies are further offset by pages upon pages of the residency's robust calendar, listing hundreds of programs, exhibitions, and school groups it had hosted since 1979, showing how, despite the university's previous cuts and destaffings, AAMARP nevertheless persisted and served a wide range of communities. All this, too, appearing alongside reprinted correspondence from prestigious organizations, such as the National Archives of American Art praising Chandler's work with AAMARP, as well as quotes from interviews with established Boston City Council members speaking to the program's critical impact citywide—animated further by Chandler's handwritten annotations that model and solicit the work of reading between the lines. Indeed, throughout the wealth of documented contributions, the reappearing phrase "(see attached)," directs readers of the newsletter to become activated participants in, and witnesses for, a people's court of opinion. The phrase, *(see attached)*, also effectively offers a choreographic instruction: Look here, and here, and here. Thus directing readers to become personally accountable and involved (and thereby *attached*), via the sustained practice and skill of counteracting the institution's unfounded claims of inaction through the very act of coming to learn the lived reality of AAMARP's abundance, ambition, and impact.

In so doing, *Urban Newsletter Art Piece* solicits what art historian and Black studies scholar Sampada Aranke has theorized as "politicized looking": a mode of coming-to-know that makes meaning of the absence of visual evidence of state- or institution-sanctioned anti-Black violence—be it in the physical form of murder or the interconnected, slower violence of character assassination, defunding, and disenfranchisement—while also confronting the "evidentiary limits" of state, court, and legal apparatuses. By developing a visual and material language of documentation to counter them, "these modes of looking," as Aranke puts it, "encouraged an activation of context, a refusal to accept state narratives, and an active engagement with Black visual histories that

cite and sight a long history of the Black freedom struggle."[2] Here, Aranke is speaking specifically of the state-sanctioned murders of the Black Panther Party for Self-Defense leaders, Fred Hampton and Bobby Hutton in the late 1960s and the group's collaged works that substantiate evidence of murder while rejecting dehumanizing anti-Black frameworks of witnessing that sensationalize and reproduce violence. Importantly, these histories and the murders of Hampton and Hutton are not outside of the scope of what Chandler addresses when fighting for AAMARP and his own integrity as its director. While confronting and refuting the misinformation, distortions, and disavowal of Baer, he situates this seemingly mundane budgetary "refocusing" as part of longer, evidenced histories of anti-Black violence, dehumanization, and racial capitalism—what he visualizes when he posits justice not as a given but as a question, and a crisis, central to American history.

Page 5 of the newsletter exemplifies this history lesson: Chandler brings together news stories and headlines pinpointing the skewing of the courts, extractive processes of property relations, and the lies surrounding the residency's management through damning visual and material juxtapositions that disrupt linear chronologies of liberalism and social progress. He compresses timelines and histories, making clearer the transhistorical stakes of AAMARP and its defunding. For example, beneath the text, "Justice? America's Crisis," images of Officer Laurence Powell and Sergeant Stacey Koon, two white officers convicted for their role in beating Rodney King in 1991, appear paired with a news story featuring the Black men who came to be known as the "LA four," Antoine Miller, Henry Watson, Damian Williams, and Gary Williams, who were arrested for beating Reginald Denny, a white man, during the 1992 Los Angeles uprising. A snippet of text reading "unequal justice for blacks," hovers not far from the embedded detail of an infamous print made by white enslavers to show their "economical" use of space on slave ships during the transatlantic slave trade. Encircling these visual and material histories, questions swirl: near the bottom of the page, "If not now, when?" and "Jamaica Plain, What is in it for you?" This strategy of collaging historical flashpoints in Black life and resistance to white supremacist structures of power resonates with Chandler's contemporaneous photocollage prints from the early 1990s, as exemplified by *For the Children We Strive* (1991), wherein the faces of Marcus Garvey, Martin Luther King Jr., Medgar Evans, Malcolm X, and Nelson

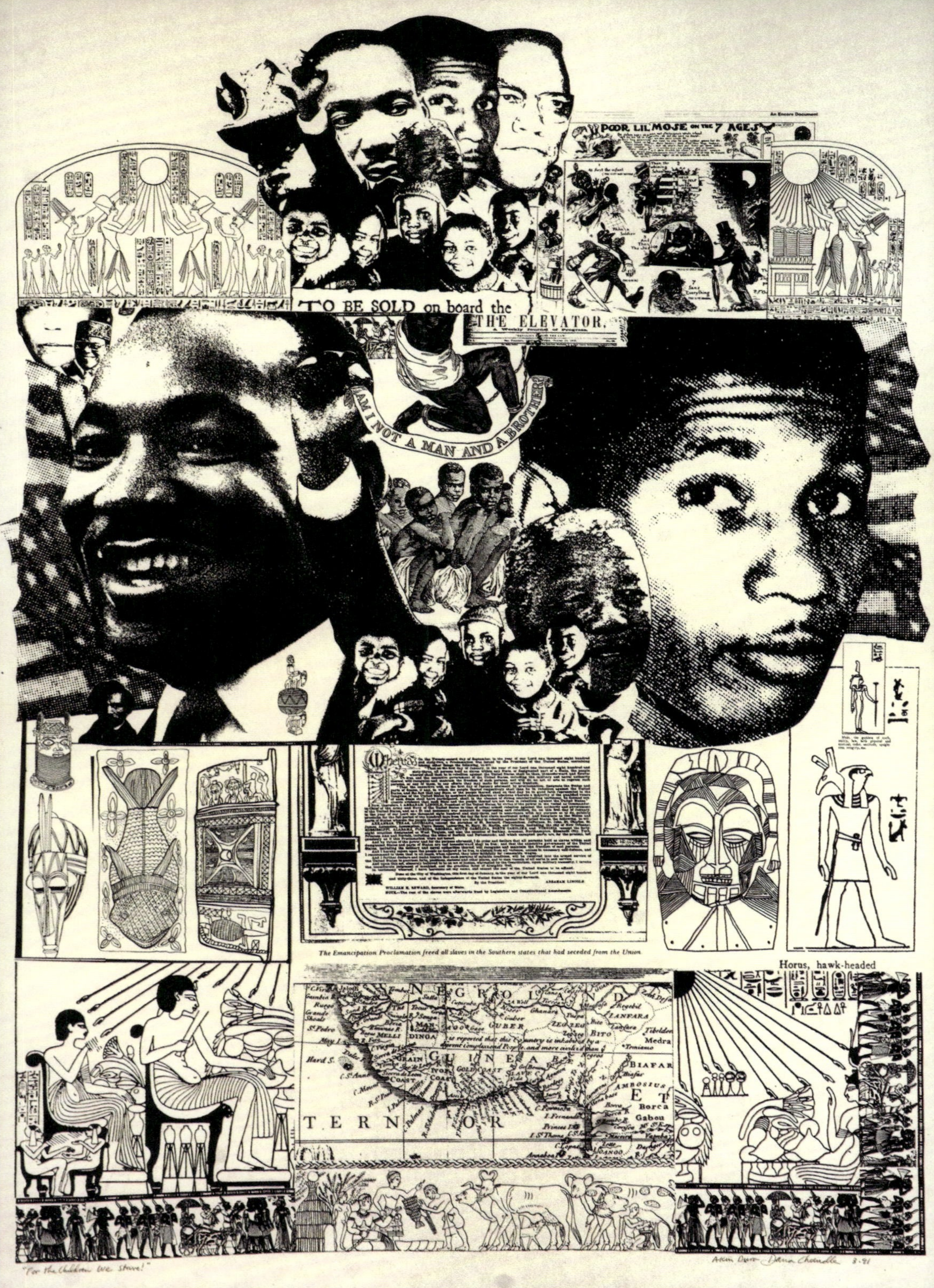

Akin Duro — Dana Chandler 3-91

Mandela, are juxtaposed with fugitive slave ads, abolitionist imagery, and the hieroglyphic imaginaries of ancient Egyptian culture.

Slyly, the newsletter—like the collages—demonstrates how Black Americans in the United States must *constantly* and *persistently* do the resistive *work of refocusing* distortive and exploitative narrations of injustice on a daily basis, in all spheres of society, across centuries. This practice of refocusing as a kind of evidence-making carries high stakes. For Chandler, as the director of AAMARP, this meant combating distortive narrations that conceal what political geographer Ruth Wilson Gilmore has called "organized abandonment," wherein institutions and administrators enact slow violence under the aegis of renovation, rejuvenation, and risk management procedures.[3]

Looking again to page 5, in the lower left-hand corner, Chandler indicts Northeastern of this organized abandonment, and offers annotations that make clearer the entanglements of land possession, property relations, and the dispossession of Black labor and arts. In a newspaper clipping, Chandler "said in a telephone interview that Northeastern used him and his artists to obtain a property at 76 Atherton St. in Jamaica Plain, and then cut the program's budget and eliminated its staff to accommodate other university needs in the building." Elsewhere in the newsletter, Chandler points to the types of strategies he developed in order to sustain the building renovations that the university promised but neglected to make good on. In 1990, for example, Chandler worked with the Home Builders Institute (part of the National Home Builders Association), to trade building renovations for educational experience when the budget had been cut and Chandler fought to make the studios readily available to the artists: "It was a trade-off—renovations for AAMARP, training for urban construction workers." The effort to sustain the residency was not only undertaken by Chandler. Rather, it was a cross-generational endeavor for its myriad members, as evidenced by Dana's brother Jeff Chandler (an artist still active in the collective), lending his skills in construction and carpentry, and later, artist Keith Morris Washington framing out parts of the studio space.[4]

In addition to modeling strategic navigation and collaborations, *Urban Newsletter* is an artwork. Art historically, it resonates within and shares a range of practices and contexts, connecting Chandler's aesthetic gestures on the pages of the document to earlier, Dada-esque critiques of propaganda from the early twentieth century, as well as with the anti- or para-institutional zines and conceptual mail art newsletters of activist art groups such as Asco, PESTS, Guerrilla Girls, Godzilla, and Videofreex, active at different points between the 1970s and '90s. These ephemeral, paper-printed, and circulated texts harbor and present resonant critiques of the racist, classist, and gendered gatekeeping of the media, of authorities, and cultural institutions. The artists, though responding to distinctive and incommensurate barriers and violences, mobilized a shared reformulation of information to reveal the institutionalized distortions that conceal anti-Black, anti-immigrant, sexist, and neocolonial violence; their efforts name and materialize the impact of displacement of marginalized people and communities while also developing a unique visual and aesthetic language rooted in soliciting and sustaining solidarity work.

Not coincidentally, these newsletter art practices are poised to tell a significant and as of yet inadequately studied story of the intertwined support networks of Black, brown, Asian American, and Indigenous art institutions, residencies, and exhibition histories that emerged defiantly and collaboratively to sustain art communities thriving beyond, and often in opposition to, the normalized conditions of care fostered by white-dominated arts and academic institutions. See, for example, a page from PESTS' 1987 newsletter, a publication that similarly utilized collage, graphic art elements, and annotated commentary to document a buzzing cross-racial, cross-ethnic, nonwhite art scene while raising awareness of what the group called the "artworld apartheid" of New York City.[5] On page 4 of their newsletter *Peststrip*, the members of PESTS (an anonymous group of women of color artists and curators active in the mid to late 1980s), offer listings of relevant exhibitions, including, for example, a show of Oliver Jackson's work at Liz Harris Gallery in Boston. This gallery was a contemporary of AAMARP, one of the first active spaces for Black American artists to show their work in the city at that time. As such, it is highly likely that the various artists who exhibited there would have passed through AAMARP's studios, and vice versa, that AAMARP artists would have attended the gallery's events. All to say, Chandler's *Urban Newsletter Art Piece* not only documents the local and citywide contributions of AAMARP; it also tells a story of the residency's role within a larger national and international ecosystem of cross-generational Black,

Brilliantly, in keeping with this expanding ethos of guerrilla journalistic and conceptual artworks, Chandler printed 5,000 copies of the newsletter using Northeastern's own resources. As Chandler recalls: "I did it all by hand. The secretary typed up a list of all the events we had; anything I could possibly think of. I took it to the printer, printed by the university, which had its own printing press. I distributed it all across the university and throughout the community; did this on a regular basis, hand carrying flyers to barber shops, beauty parlors, bars, churches all across Roxbury and Jamaica Plain. Hand carried to Channel 4, Channel 7, all television stations and radio stations; made it a point to meet people at those places, so that they knew me on a first name basis; made it difficult for the university to come down on me."[6]

Thinking of the longer history of news production and the role of Black criticism of the white-dominated press, Chandler's circulation of the newsletter accrues additional meaning when situated within precedents of W. E. B. Du Bois in *The Crisis* and Ida B. Wells's pathmaking 1892 pamphlet on lynching, *Southern Horrors*.[7] As critical communication scholar Jordana Cox argues, the news itself is the "cultural production of the present," wherein the idea of newsworthiness is a technology of rendering who is, and who isn't, present in these narratives, and how and to what ends.[8]

In this moment, as contemporary witnesses of this document, we must be careful not to receive it in a vacuum of a white cube gallery or glossy exhibition catalogue. Chandler's work in the newsletter is about much more than keeping score or holding Northeastern administrators accountable to their promises. The force of its politicized looking can still be felt in the documents gathered, shared, and shared again through the immersiveness of the attachments. Cumulatively, the pages offer a multifold argument: the residency is active (still!); Black artistic practice works across the thresholds of aesthetics and evidence-making; and the legacy of AAMARP exceeds institutional imaginaries of value, while simultaneously revealing how such imaginaries rely on and often perpetuate infrastructural, legal, and affective attachments.

Perhaps it is the "when" of the newsletter that remains the most haunting and critical part of its form:

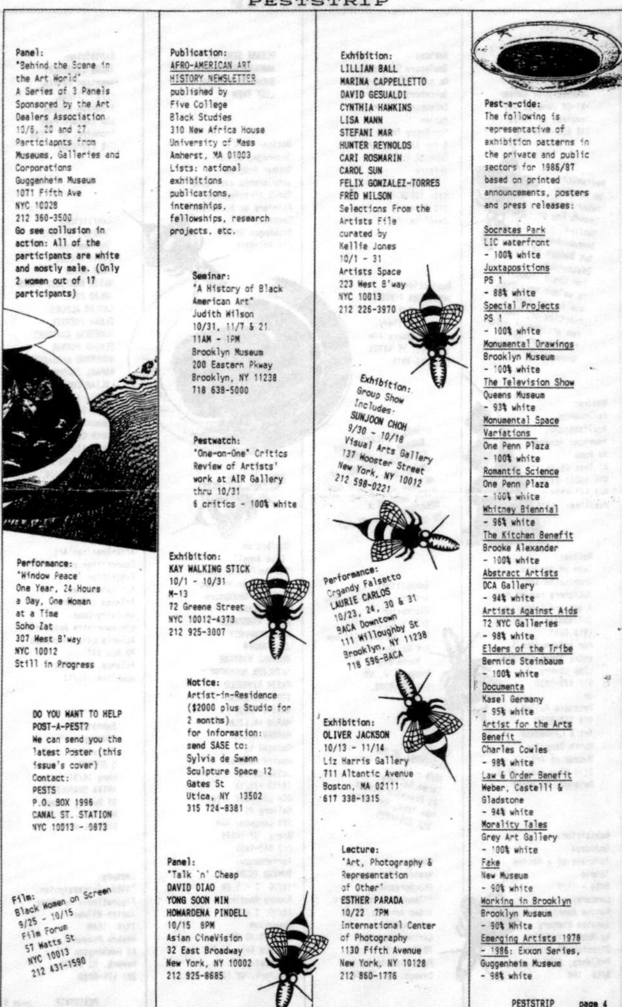

Panel:
"Behind the Scene in the Art World"
A Series of 3 Panels
Sponsored by the Art Dealers Association
10/6, 20 and 27
Participants from Museums, Galleries and Corporations
Guggenheim Museum
1071 Fifth Ave
NYC 10028
212 360-3500
Go see collusion in action: All of the participants are white and mostly male. (Only 2 women out of 17 participants)

Performance:
"Window Peace"
One Year, 24 Hours a Day, One Woman at a Time
Soho Zat
307 West B'way
NYC 10012
Still in Progress

DO YOU WANT TO HELP POST-A-PEST?
We can send you the latest Poster (this issue's cover)
Contact:
PESTS
P.O. BOX 1996
CANAL ST. STATION
NYC 10013 - 9873

Film:
Black Women on Screen
9/25 - 10/15
Film Forum
57 Watts St
NYC 10013
212 431-1590

Publication:
AFRO-AMERICAN ART HISTORY NEWSLETTER
published by Five College Black Studies
310 New Africa House
University of Mass
Amherst, MA 01003
Lists: national exhibitions publications, internships, fellowships, research projects, etc.

Seminar:
"A History of Black American Art"
Judith Wilson
10/31, 11/7 & 21
11AM - 1PM
Brooklyn Museum
200 Eastern Pkway
Brooklyn, NY 11238
718 638-5000

Pestwatch:
"One-on-One" Critics Review of Artists' work at AIR Gallery
thru 10/31
6 critics - 100% white

Exhibition:
KAY WALKING STICK
10/1 - 10/31
M-13
72 Greene Street
NYC 10012-4373
212 925-3007

Notice:
Artist-in-Residence
($2000 plus Studio for 2 months)
for information:
send SASE to:
Sylvia de Swann
Sculpture Space 12 Gates St
Utica, NY 13502
315 724-8381

Panel:
"Talk 'n' Cheap
DAVID DIAO
YONG SOON MIN
HOWARDENA PINDELL
10/15 8PM
Asian CineVision
32 East Broadway
New York, NY 10002
212 925-8685

Exhibition:
LILLIAN BALL
MARINA CAPPELLETTO
DAVID GESUALDI
CYNTHIA HAWKINS
LISA MANN
STEFANI MAR
HUNTER REYNOLDS
CARI ROSMARIN
CAROL SUN
FELIX GONZALEZ-TORRES
FRED WILSON
Selections From the Artists File
curated by Kellie Jones
10/1 - 31
Artists Space
223 West 8'way
NYC 10013
212 226-3970

Exhibition:
Group Show Includes:
SUNJOON CHOH
9/30 - 10/18
Visual Arts Gallery
137 Mooster Street
New York, NY 10012
212 598-0221

Performance:
Organdy Falsetto
LAURIE CARLOS
10/23, 24, 30 & 31
BACA Downtown
111 Willoughby St
Brooklyn, NY 11238
718 596-BACA

Exhibition:
OLIVER JACKSON
10/13 - 11/14
Liz Harris Gallery
711 Altantic Avenue
Boston, MA 02111
617 338-1315

Lecture:
"Art, Photography & Representation of Other"
ESTHER PARADA
10/22 7PM
International Center of Photography
1130 Fifth Avenue
New York, NY 10128
212 860-1776

Pest-a-cide:
The following is representative of exhibition patterns in the private and public sectors for 1986/87 based on printed announcements, posters and press releases:

Socrates Park
LIC waterfront
- 100% white
Juxtapositions
PS 1
- 88% white
Special Projects
PS 1
- 100% white
Monumental Drawings
Brooklyn Museum
- 100% white
The Television Show
Queens Museum
- 93% white
Monumental Space Variations
One Penn Plaza
- 100% white
Romantic Science
One Penn Plaza
- 100% white
Whitney Biennial
- 96% white
The Kitchen Benefit
Brooke Alexander
- 100% white
Abstract Artists
DCA Gallery
- 94% white
Artists Against Aids
72 NYC Galleries
- 98% white
Elders of the Tribe
Bernice Steinbaum
- 100% white
Documenta
Kasel Germany
- 95% white
Artist for the Arts Benefit
Charles Cowles
- 98% white
Law & Order Benefit
Weber, Castelli & Gladstone
- 94% white
Morality Tales
Grey Art Gallery
- 100% white
Fake
New Museum
- 90% white
Working in Brooklyn
Brooklyn Museum
- 90% White
Emerging Artists 1978
- 1986: Exxon Series, Guggenheim Museum
- 98% white

59

restructuring knowledge production that offer a critical view of histories of white supremacist violence and extractive power relations in the name of "refocusing" DEI initiatives or critical race studies coincides with largely silent left-leaning, self-proclaimed liberal art museums and universities enacting anticipatory over-compliance. Chandler's incisive cross-historical insights, aesthetic language, and archiving of collectivized, collaborative strategies, feel as salient as ever

Harassment hurts
A climate of corruption

Lowndes and Baer said lies.

AAMARP head hieghtens accusations

By David R. Exum
News Staff

The director of the African American Masters Artists Residency program at Northeastern heightened allegations this week that university officials manipulated, then fired him.

But Northeastern administrators continued to call the allegations "lies," saying the director, Dana Chandler, is a disgruntled employee making false claims to get his job back.

During an interview on WRBB last week, President John Curry was asked if the allegations were true. Curry said all the allegations were lies and said the university will be supporting AAMARP as it always has.

"I think we've made it clear that the rumors that are out there are all lies. As long as I'm president there will be an AAMARP and we will continue it and are very proud of the program at Northeastern." Curry said.

Chandler said his position is being eliminated because he

could not be controlled or manip-ulated by Dean of Arts and Sciences Robert Lowndes and Provost Michael Baer.

Chandler previously claimed that Northeastern granted money to AAMARP to purchase the program's facility in Jamaica Plain and gained approval in the community by saying the building would be used for a minority artist program open to the public.

Chandler then claimed Northeastern cut funding for the program and eliminated him and the one other staff member effective at the end of June.

"I'm too strong for them. I cannot be controlled," Chandler said this week. "I don't understand why an intelligent human being has to be controlled. I won't take a position that makes me subservient, they want someone who will take orders," Chandler said.

Chandler said he was not blaming Curry specifically for his removal from the position. Instead, Chandler pointed to Lowndes and Baer as banning together on the decision.

"I don't blame President

Curry but I'm concerned about the actions of Provost Baer and Dean Lowndes," he said. "I am not privy of whom they have had discussions over their decisions. I think they only think I'm a lowly project director and I'm better than that."

An art review of an AAMARP exhibit by *The Boston Globe* in February is what Chandler said Baer and Lowndes used to make their decision. The review said that AAMARP exhibit was unbalanced, off course and bothersome because "the AAMARP shows don't even have a thread of unity. They're a hodgepodge," the review said.

"They read the article and believe the author. I met him (Baer) once in 1991 and never since to my knowledge have I ever seen him at Atherton Street," Chandler said.

According to Lowndes, the accusations made by Chandler are incorrect. The decision made by Lowndes and Baer was in January — before the review ran in *The Globe*.

"No decision was made on the basis of that article," Lowndes said. "These decisions were planned and discussed before that article came out. The article was based on a critic's opinion of arts and exhibits and we don't make our decisions on it. Baer may have referred to it, but it is simply not true," Lowndes

Baer also said the accusations from Chandler were not true. Baer said he did not know about any secret meetings and requested that Chandler let him know where and when they took place.

"There was a review that was not complimentary but it was not part of our decision. We want to make that program more meaningful to students," Baer said.

The Jamaica Plain Neighborhood Council, which supported North-eastern's facility at 76 Atherton St. because it could directly provide programs for the city's young residents, recently questioned the universities decision.

"How can they cut costs from 75 percent and still provide a great program?" said Bernie Doherty, a council member. "My question is going to be 'How can you assure us that this organization will not be seen as a cost to young urban blacks who want to get a leg up in life?' (Northeastern) has a commitment to this urban community; There is a real need for this program in this neighborhood," Doherty said.

According to Doherty, the council is not involved in the decision by the university over the fate of Chandler, which is not their concern.

Their concern, Doherty said, is whether or not Northeastern will continue the excellent program that they have provided over the years to the community of Jamaica Plain.

Northeastern officials said they will not be swayed in the decision to cut AAMARP's budget. Chandler has said he may seek legal action if the decision is not overturned.

The director of the African American Masters Artists Residency program at Northeastern heightened allegations this week that university officials manipulated, then fired him.

Events to end

Studio director says NU officials lied to buy Jamaica Plain facility

University denies any wrong-doing in program cuts

By David R. Exum
News Staff

Officials at the African American Masters Artists in Residency Program at Northeastern said this week the university misled them into purchasing new Northeastern

property in Jamaica Plain, with promises of funding and support, weeks before their budget was cut by nearly 75 percent.

Northeastern officials have denied that they have misled the program's director, Professor Dana Chandler,

saying the university's budget could no longer fully support the minority artists program.

Northeastern granted money for AAMARP to purchase the program and received approval from the Jamaica Plain neighborhood by saying that the building will be used for a minority artist facility which will be open to the public.

Now that the building has been approved by the community, Chandler said, Northeastern is cutting AAMARP out of its budget and using the facility for other uses. Chandler claims that the building is now closed to the public.

According to Mary Breslauer, a spokesperson for the university, the administration plans to focus AAMARP in a direction that is geared towards interaction with academic programs at the university. Breslauer also said that the program now does not relate to any academic program at Northeastern.

(Continued on page 4)

Chandler then claimed Northeastern cut funding for the program and eliminated him and the one other staff member effective at the end of June.

Northeastern officials said they will not be swayed in the decision to cut AAMARP's budget.

• "How can they cut costs from 75 percent and still provide a great program?" said Bernie Doherty, a council member. "My question is going to be 'How can you assure us that this organization will not be seen as a cost to young urban blacks who want to get a leg up in life?' (Northeastern) has a commitment to this urban community; There is a real need for this program in this neighborhood," Doherty said.

who lied? IT'S YOUR DECISION.

• AAMARP director calls a foul on NU officials

AAMARP 1993–NOW

Compiled by
MEGHAN CLARE CONSIDINE MCC
and JEFFREY DE BLOIS JDB

Artist reflections by
**KHALID KODI, GLORETTA BAYNES, L'MERCHIE
FRAZIER, KEITH MORRIS WASHINGTON,
DON WEST, JEFF CHANDLER, SHEA JUSTICE,
RICARDO GOMEZ, and MARLON FORRESTER**

After the fallout from the events of 1993, many AAMARP artists resolved to go underground. While Chandler declared, "There will be no community events, exhibitions or activities at 76 Atherton Street after July 1, 1993," in his *Urban Newsletter Art Piece* (1993), that did not prove to be true. This included for Chandler himself, who showed his work at AAMARP a year later in a two person show with Ronald W. Bailey—chair of the African American Studies Department of Northeastern at the time, and coauthor of *Lower Roxbury: A Community of Treasures in the City of Boston* (1993)—and again in 1998 in a solo exhibition only a few years before he retired to New Mexico. Northeastern appointed well-respected artist and art critic Edward Strickland as Chandler's

replacement as director, and Strickland attempted to rehabilitate AAMARP's image with the university, even as Chandler continued working in his studio at 76 Atherton Street. There were far fewer exhibitions and programs, and when there were, they were funded by the artists themselves, without institutional support from the university. While not nearly as many people attended AAMARP events and openings—primarily due to the distance from Northeastern's campus to the building in Jamaica Plain—the remaining collective members concentrated on community partnerships in Boston, and an expansive idea of community rooted in their many international connections. Much less is known about the program's activities after 1993, and no archive offers

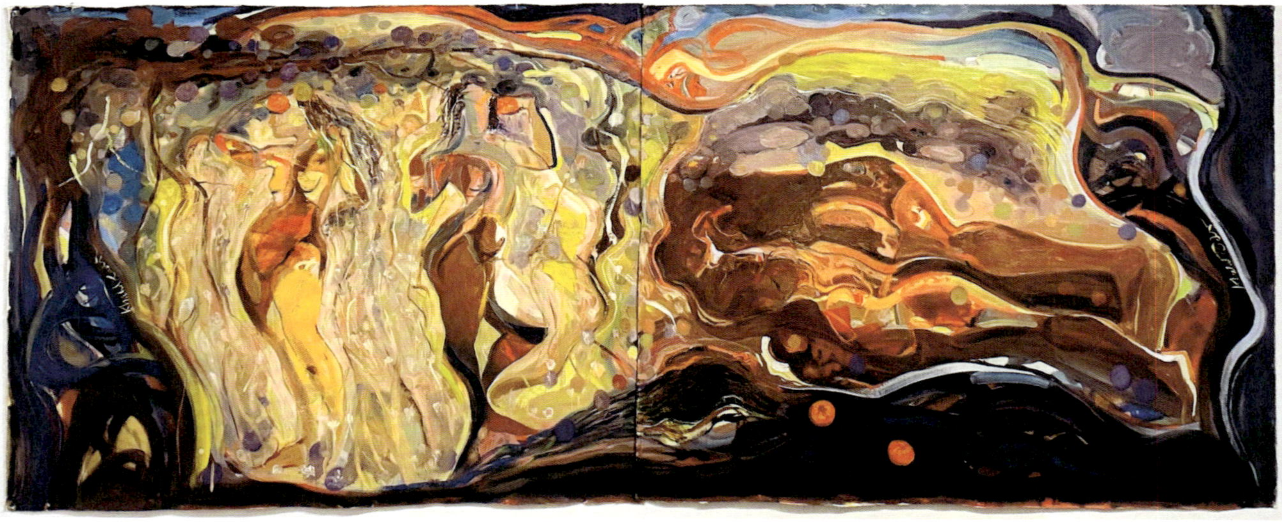

74 AAMARP 1993–NOW

61. Khalid Kodi, *Excessive Narrative: Echoes of Eden*, 2025. Oil on canvas. 68 × 170 inches (172.7 × 431.8 cm)

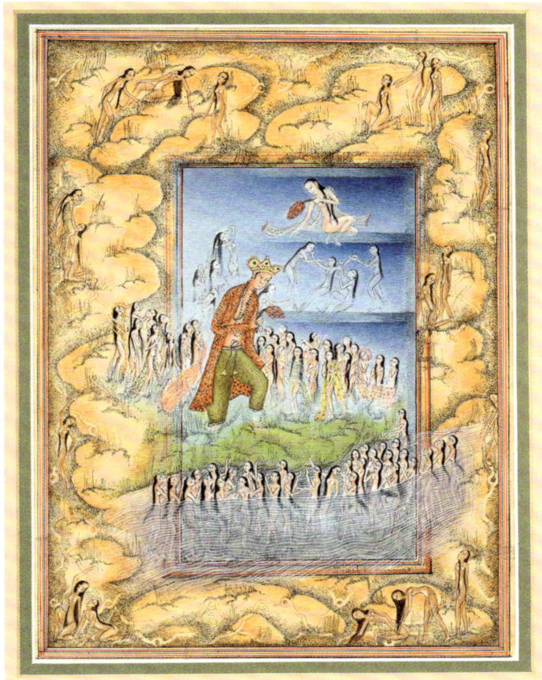

62

comprehensive evidence of what unfolded at the program in the years since. However, what *is* certain is that the artists continued to make work following the groundbreaking example set in AAMARP's earliest years.

1995

Khalid Kodi and *Out of Pakistan*

FIGS. 61–62

Khalid Kodi joined AAMARP in the early 1990s, when he immigrated to Boston from Sudan to attend MassArt. Since then, he has made works in a range of media, from sculpture and participatory installations, to small- and large-scale paintings invested in what he describes as "excessive narrative." Kodi's conception of excessive narrative is embodied in artworks that do not simply illustrate, but interrogate where narrative, memory, and visual excess meet. This sense of excess is informed by Kodi's upbringing in Sudan, his European-style art education, and ongoing engagement with African American art and artists, as well as the frictions and intersections between Islam, Christianity, and the

Indigenous spiritual practices giving shape to post-colonial African futures. In this sense, Kodi's artworks, such as *Excessive Narrative: Echoes of Eden* (2025), "encapsulate the complexity of cultural and political entanglements that shape identity, history, and artistic expression within African and African diasporic contexts."[1] Kodi remains deeply connected to Sudan, mentoring young Sudanese artists and activists, bringing rival groups together to attempt to resolve conflicts, and even hosting workshops in war zones. Because of his upbringing and deep connections to the African continent, his presence at AAMARP augments the historically Pan-Africanist bent of the collective. With artist Walter Crump, Kodi organized *Out of Pakistan* in AAMARP's galleries in 1995, featuring a group of Pakistani artists working and studying at Boston-area colleges, including Ambreen Butt, Rashid Rana, and Shahzia Sikander, reinvigorating the program's rich history of exhibiting groundbreaking artists from outside of the collective. **JDB**

"My journey to AAMARP was less a geographical migration than an existential one. Coming from a European-style education in Africa—where art history was rich in European classicism but silent on African visual traditions—I made a deliberate choice to pursue graduate study in the United States. What drew me here was not a fascination with dominant American culture, but a profound admiration for artists like Richard Diebenkorn and David Park, and a curiosity about the Harlem Renaissance as an intellectual and aesthetic insurgency.

Joining AAMARP marked a pivotal moment in my life as an artist, educator, and critic. It was more than a collective—it was a space of unlearning and reimagining. Here, African and African American aesthetic values were not marginalized but centered, interrogated, and celebrated. Through dialogue and practice with fellow artists, I encountered an epistemology rooted in resistance and beauty, in cultural memory and radical imagination.

AAMARP became a methodology, a way of thinking through the visual, of challenging inherited binaries between "African authenticity" and "Western modernity." It allowed me to develop a hybrid visual language, one that resists commodification and reclaims Blackness as a site of power and possibility.

In my continued engagement with African educational institutions and global audiences, I strive to offer alternative narratives. Such narratives reflect the depth of African American art beyond stereotypes, and the

62. Ambreen Butt, *Feudal prince and his disciple puppets*, 1993. Watercolor and white gouache on handmade Wasli paper. 8 × 11 inches (20.3 × 27.9 cm)

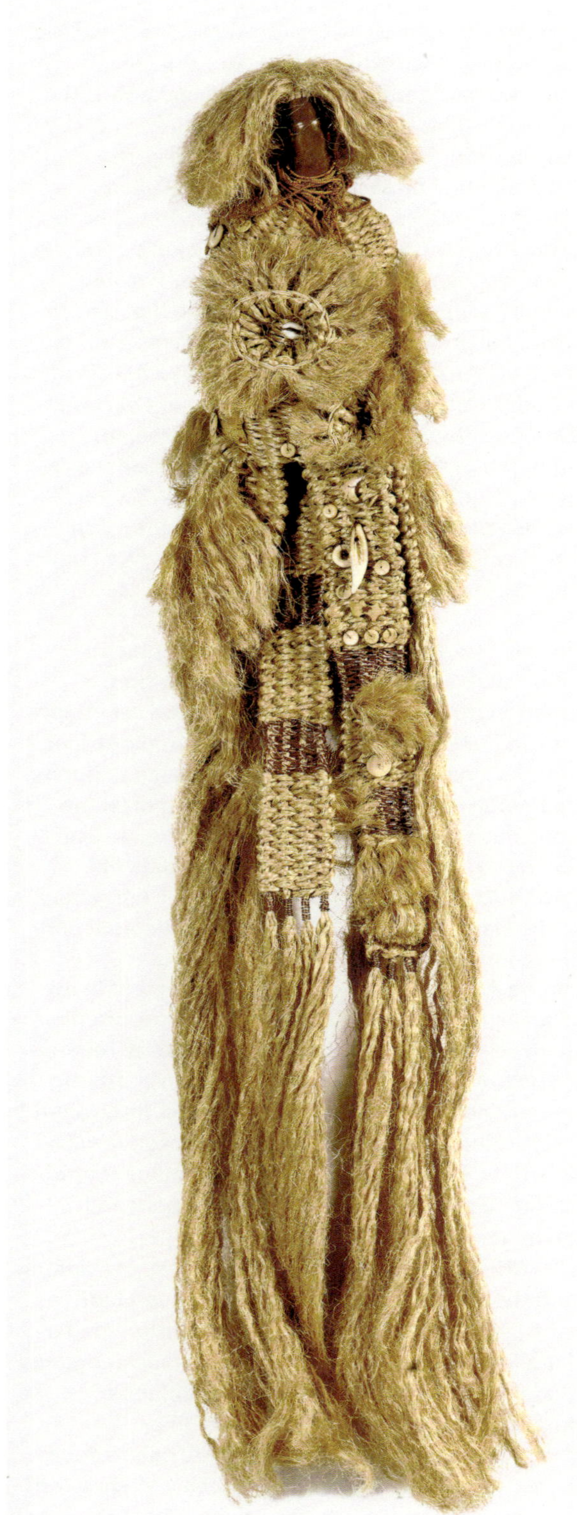

1998

AAMARP Women's Show

Gloretta Baynes, L'Merchie Frazier, and Susan Thompson
FIGS. 63–70

In 1998, the *AAMARP Women's Show* featured the work of Gloretta Baynes, L'Merchie Frazier, and Susan Thompson, three important multimedia artists and pillars of the program. All three were included in *Eyes On Africa* (1995), an exhibition "inspired by African origins, African settings, and African forms," which also featured Theresa-India Young, an important touchstone for all three artists. Thompson joined AAMARP in 1985, one month before the move from 11 Leon Street to 590 Huntington Avenue. Prior to working at AAMARP, Thompson had a small studio in the attic of Allan Rohan Crite's House Museum at 410 Columbus Avenue in Boston's South End. After meeting Crite, Thompson showed the elder artist wall hangings and costumes she had made for her child's grade school play, and he decided then and there she was an artist and began introducing her to others in the Boston art community. With Crite as her mentor, Thompson went on to master a range of artistic techniques, especially transforming various fabrics, sometimes found, often dyed or painted by the artist, into narrative quilts, such as *Freedom, Justice, Equality* (1989–2012). *Freedom, Justice, Equality*, a collaborative work with Crite based on one of his drawings, depicts protesters marching in a street scene like those in Crite's paintings. Others, like the indigo-dyed, pieced quilts *Call of the Ancestors 1 and 2* (both 2017), are more abstract and meditative, with shadowy, featureless figures against a patchwork landscape.

A member since 1988, Gloretta Baynes had several stints leading the program in the late 1990s following the death of Edward Strickland, and later throughout the early 2000s. Baynes has extensive experience working as a curator and arts administrator in addition to her leadership position at AAMARP, including as assistant director at the Museum of the National Center of Afro-American Artists in Roxbury. Baynes is an expert draftsperson who works extensively with airbrush techniques, fabric, and digital media. *African Trio* (c. 1992) is indicative of

63. Theresa-India Young, *Native Dancer*, 2000. Sisal rope, shells, copper, and beads. 54 × 12 inches (137.2 × 30.5 cm)

Baynes's aesthetic, featuring three women delicately rendered with fine lines, their mostly nude bodies covered with intricately detailed jewelry. Other paintings are Afrofuturist in style, featuring more-than-human figures set against other worldly landscapes. Baynes's travel to such places as Cuba and Ghana often informs whole bodies of work, or are the subject themselves, such as *Ghana* (c. 1992). Following in AAMARP's rich tradition of Pan-Africanist work, the multimedia wall piece *Ghana* takes the shape of a woman's body, with a black, yellow, and green fan as a head and a raffia skirt. The figure's torso features an array of airbrushed symbols, such as a head in profile emerging from the African continent, with the flags of Ghana and the Pan-African flag on top and bottom respectively. Among airbrushed patterns is a photograph of Kwame Nkrumah, the first president of Ghana and a founding member of the Organization of African Unity, fashioning *Ghana* into a meaningful symbol of embodied solidarity between African nations and people of the African diaspora.

Like Baynes, L'Merchie Frazier has had a variety of roles in the Boston arts ecosystem, most prominently through designing educational programs at the Museum of the National Center of Afro-American Artists in Roxbury for seven years and serving as the director of Education and Interpretation for the Museum of African American History, Boston/Nantucket. Frazier conceives of herself as a visual activist and a public historian, and her artwork as a form of reparative justice. She has been a member of AAMARP since 1999, making works in a variety of media, from quilts dedicated to Black American history to shrine-like devotional sculptures related to her extended stays in Brazil. These works, such as *Ogun: God of War to Love* (1995/2015), are based on *terreiros*, or houses of worship in Candomblé, an African diasporic religion practiced in Brazil. Dedicated

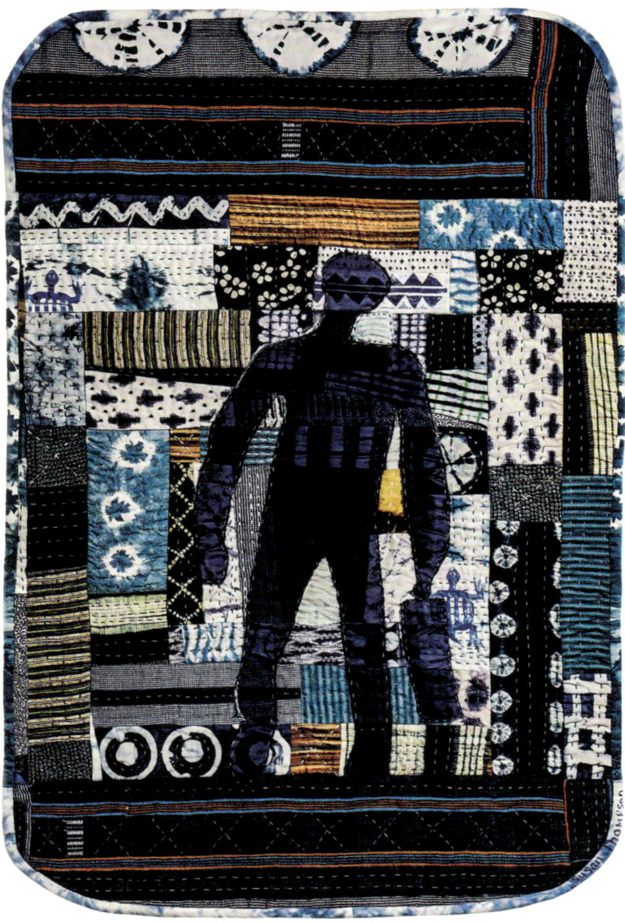

64

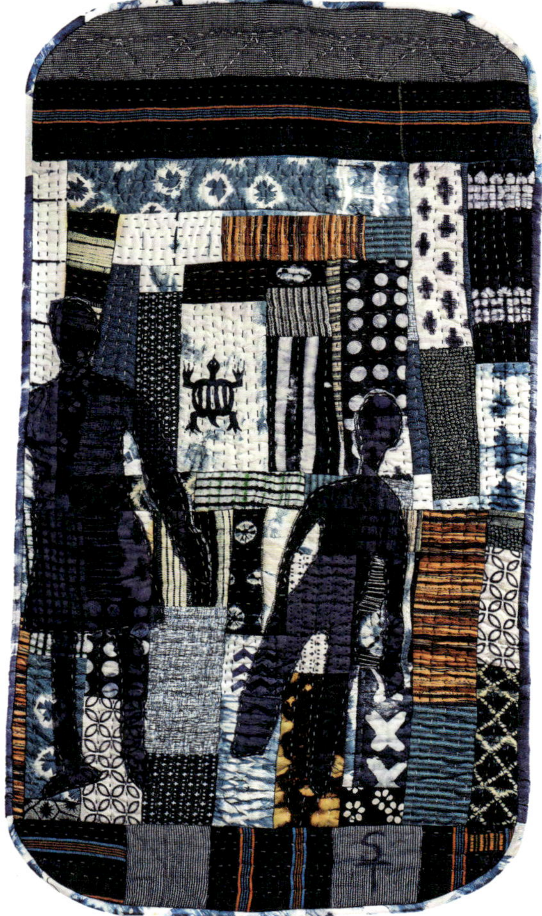

65

64. Susan Thompson, *Call of the Ancestors 1*, 2017. Pieced quilt with applique. 54 × 35 inches (137.2 × 88.9 cm)

65. Susan Thompson, *Call of the Ancestors 2*, 2017. Pieced quilt with applique. 56 × 31 inches (142.2 x 78.7 cm)

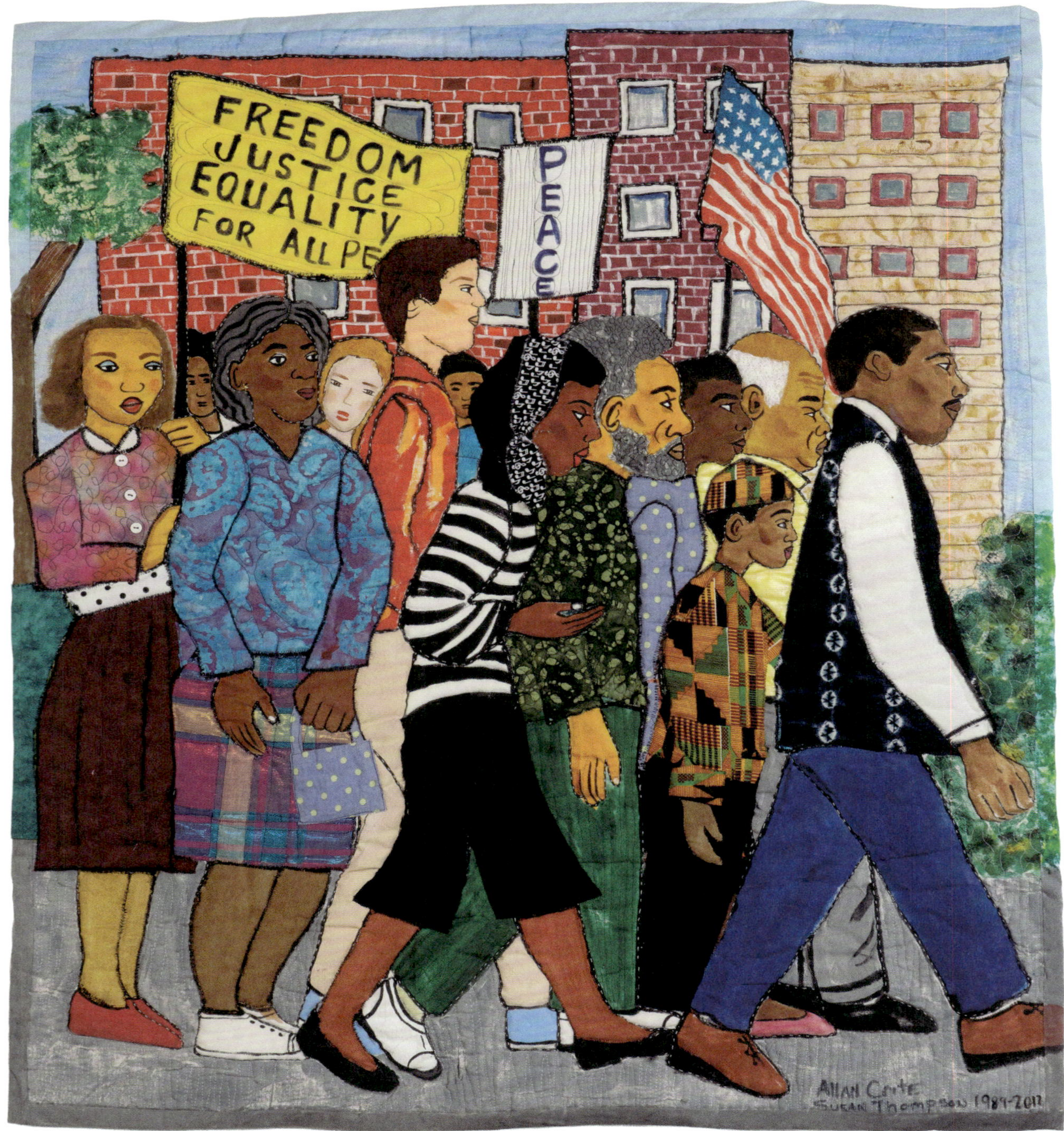

66

66. Allan Rohan Crite and Susan Thompson, *Freedom, Justice, Equality*, 1989–2012. Fabric collage, applique, and painted quilt. 45 × 40 inches (114.3 × 101.6 cm)

to Ogun—a central figure in Yoruba religion who is the patron saint of metallurgy—this shrine features beaded metallic effigies, image transfers, a dedicatory poem written by the artist, and a framed quote from Mel King, an influential community organizer and lifelong resident Boston's South End. Another work, *Ericka Huggins: Liberation Groceries* (2019), is a tribute to the activist and leading member of the Black Panther Party. Representative of Frazier's approach to underrecognized figures in American History, *Ericka Huggins* features the titular figure set against a black background holding a bag of groceries emblazoned with the Black Panther Party logo designed by Dorothy Zellner. This image of Huggins alludes to her involvement in the People's Free Food Program, a community service program focused on providing free breakfast for children before school, and by extension, to the role of Black women in enacting revolutionary change more broadly. Steadfastly interested in holography, the palimpsestic, gauzy qualities of the translucent fabrics Frazier uses testifies to the diversity of material innovations taking place at AAMARP. Frazier's advocacy within the Women of Color Quilter's Network exemplifies the ongoing national and international connections forged through AAMARP. **JDB**

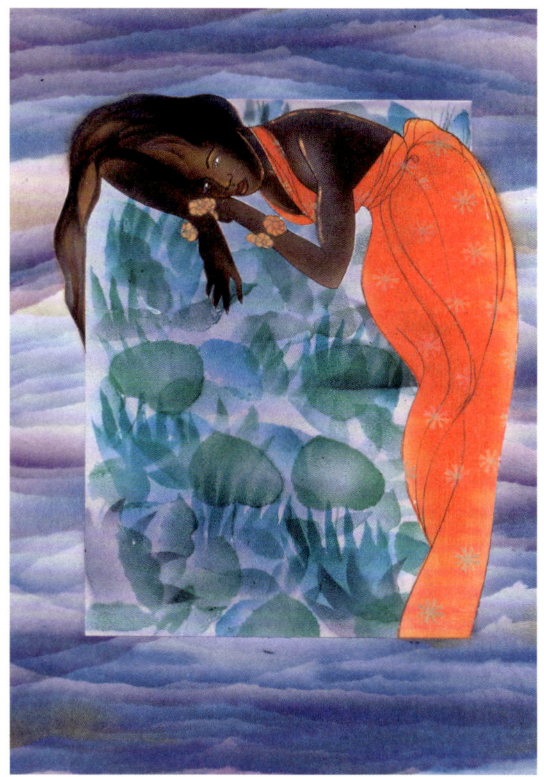

67

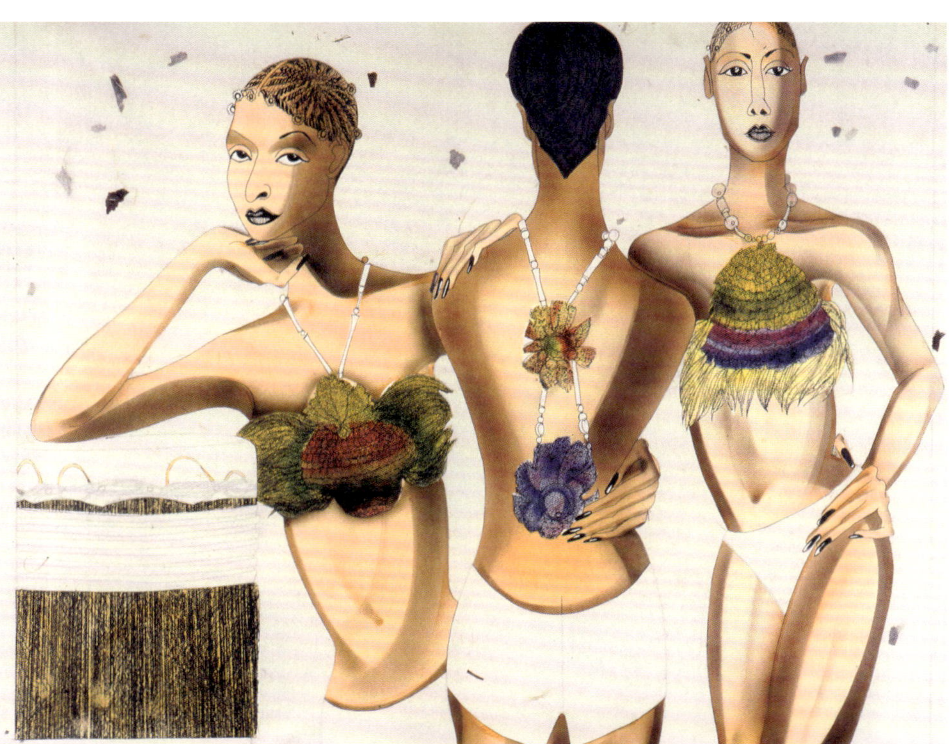

68

67. Gloretta Baynes, *Dreamer 2*, 1993. Airbrush. 20 × 15 inches (50.8 × 38.1 cm)

68. Gloretta Baynes, *African Trio*, c. 1992. Airbrush. 20 × 30 inches (50.8 × 76.2 cm)

"In high school at Cambridge Rindge and Latin School, I discovered my passion for art and activism as a member of the Black Student Union. At age sixteen, I applied for a scholarship to MassArt, where my portfolio was reviewed by Professor Calvin Burnett, an AAMARP affiliated master artist. I was accepted and awarded the scholarship, around the same time that my desire to connect with fellow Black artists grew. This search led me to the Black Artist's Union (BAU) at MassArt, where I found inspiration in the murals and works of Dana Chandler and Gary Rickson, as well as the exhibitions at the Museum of the National Center of Afro-American Artists. In 1980, Dana invited me, along with other BAU members, to participate in the AAMARP exhibition *Young Black Artists Under 36*. Some years later, Dana asked me to be a resident AAMARP artist, and he often had me design promotional flyers for the exhibitions at that time. Dana Chandler's letter "A Proposal to Eradicate Institutional Racism at the Boston Museum of Fine Arts" (1970) was a pivotal document that advocated for inclusion and equity, resulting in the monumental and historical 1970 exhibition *Afro-American Artists: New York and Boston* at the Museum of Fine Arts, as a joint endeavor with the Museum of the National Center of Afro-American Artists. The letter also contributed to my decision to become a museum professional, curator, and arts administrator. Those skills and insights were invaluable in my administration of AAMARP as a former Director, and Chair Emeritus. The AAMARP collective embodies a praxis of revolutionary change, synthesizing a new visual language directed toward social justice. The didactic themes of the Black Arts movement are integral to the fabric of AAMARP, where we continue to lift up the voices of the African diaspora." Gloretta Baynes

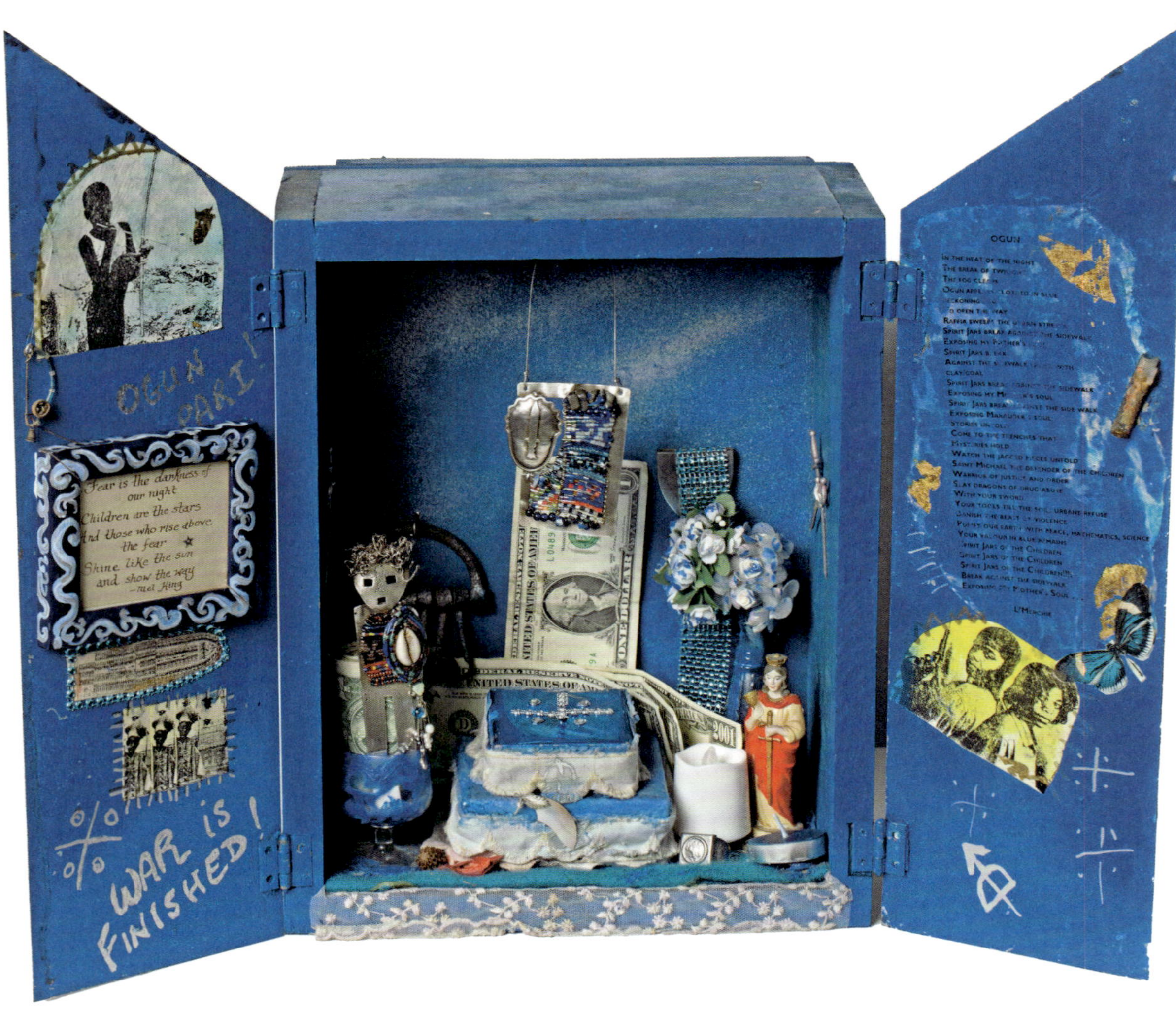

69

69. L'Merchie Frazier, *Ogun: God of War to Love*, 1995/2015. Mixed media assemblage. 18 × 12 × 6 inches (45.7 × 30.5 × 15.2 cm)

70. L'Merchie Frazier, *Ericka Huggins: Liberation Groceries*, 2019. Nylon, synthetic tape, and Thinsulate fabrics. 47 × 37 inches (119.4 × 94 cm)

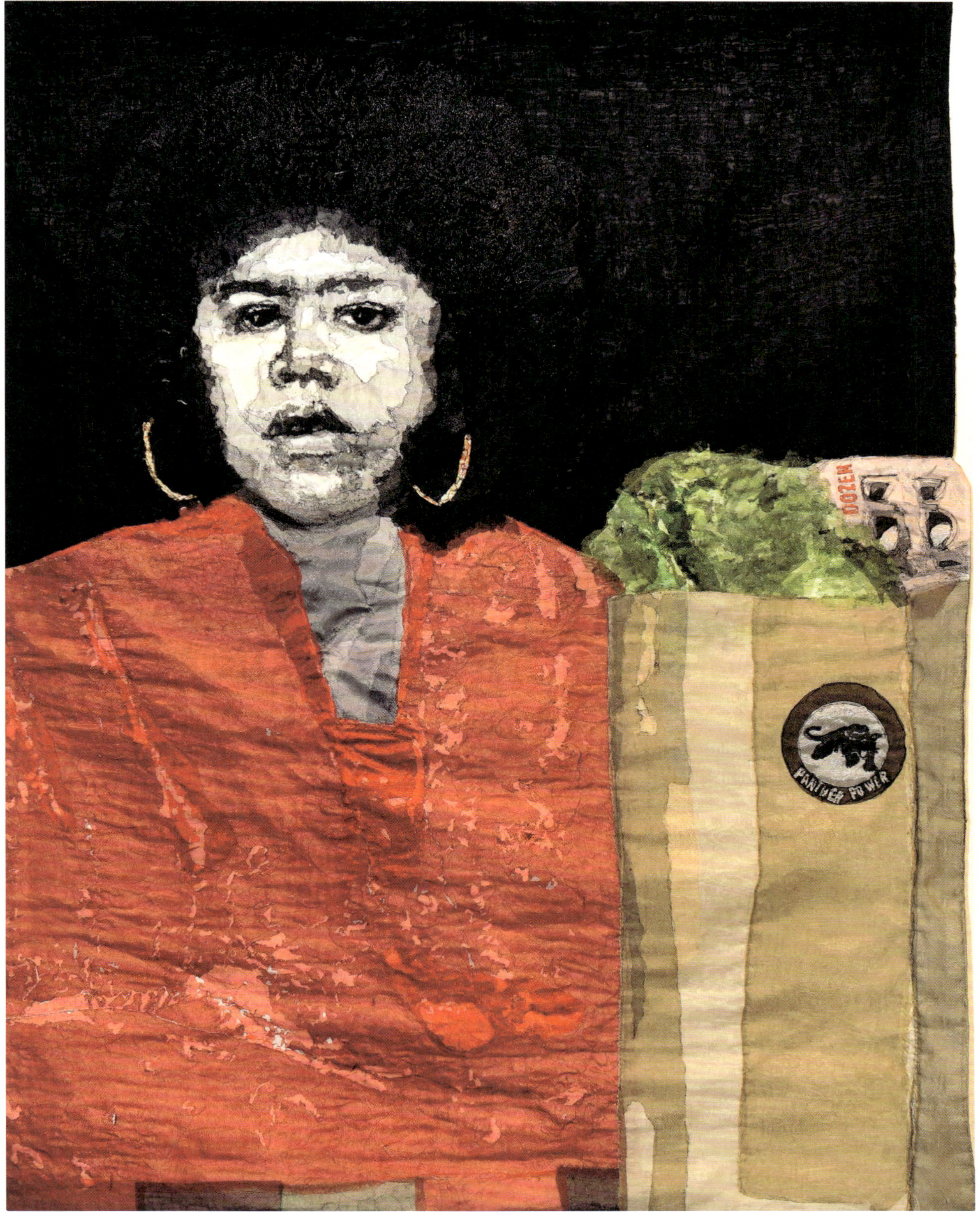
PANTHER POWER
DOZEN

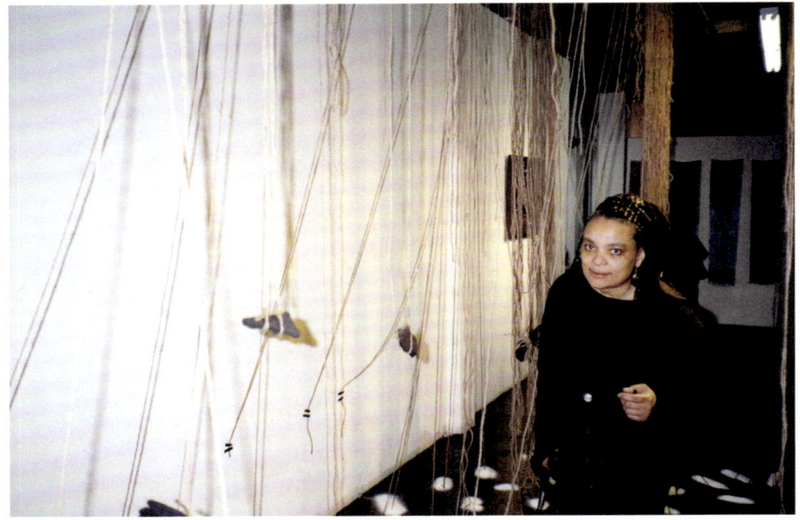

71. Sharon Dunn installing *Hemp Environment* at AAMARP, 1999

72. Sharon Dunn painting a mural in Jamaica Plain, 1981

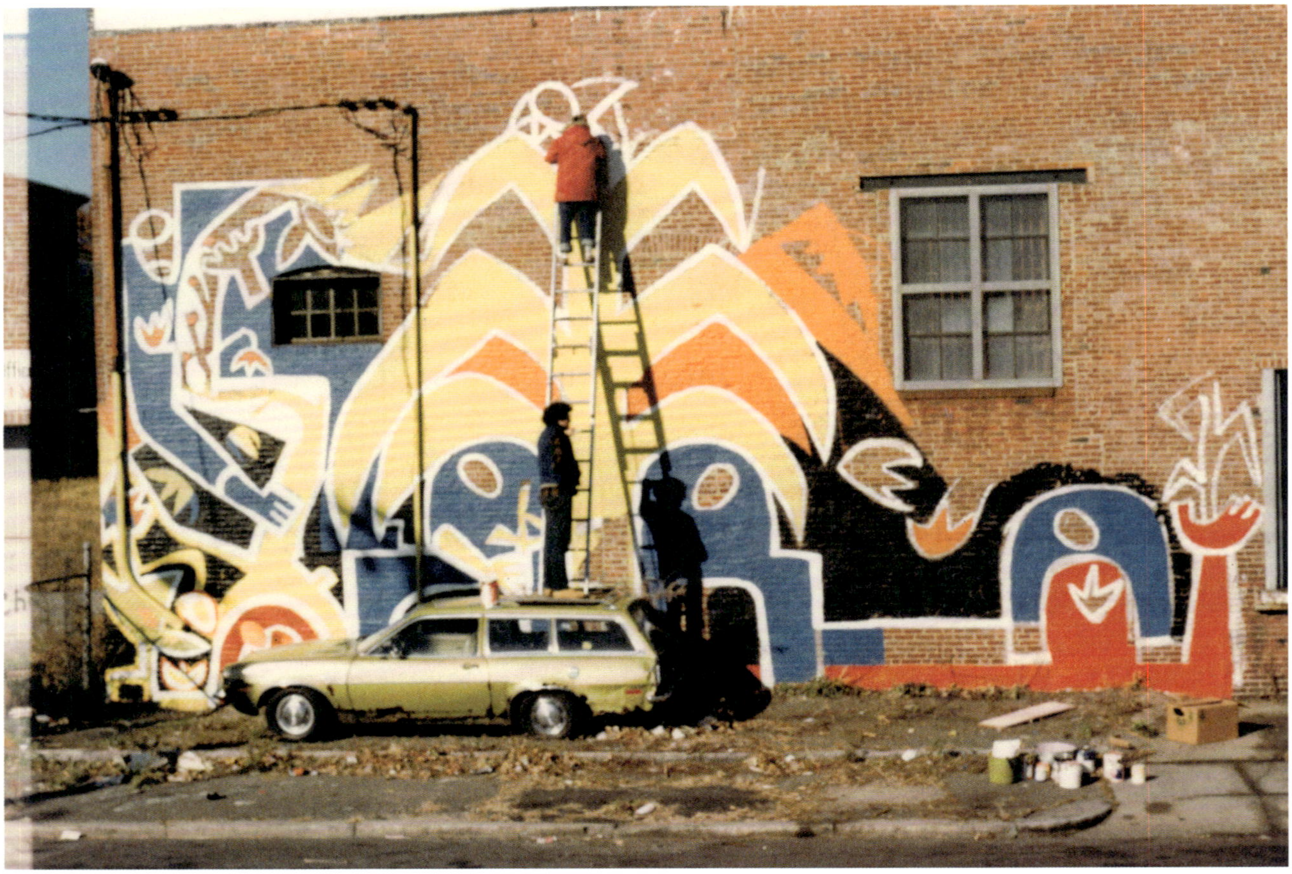

71

72

"The African American Master Artists-in-Residence Program represents a powerful collective movement. AAMARP proudly continues the legacy of earlier Black artistic guilds from the eighteenth, nineteenth, and twentieth centuries, including the Harlem Renaissance, Spiral, Weusi, Obassi, and AfriCOBRA, to intentionally utilize aesthetics and creative expression to advance Black liberation across all periods of time and geographic locations. These organizations confronted the impact of slavery, colonialism, and imperialism by waging resistance against systemic, racist exclusion from the Western art canon. These self-identified, self-acknowledged networked organizations created an artistic archive to deliberately present and record Black material and cultural production, thereby achieving a liberation model.

My ongoing series of works, The Quilted Chronicles, joyfully documents this rhythm of self-identification. Spanning over five hundred years of Black and Indigenous experience, these artworks provide connective tissue to elevate stories of hidden people, places, and events. They boldly reclaim, restore, and reimagine an expanded historical narrative, moving from invisible to visible. Through a rich textural visual language, my aim is to unapologetically engage in reparative dialogue and conversations.

American media often sensationalized the Black Panther Party, typically portraying them as a symbol of armed violence. However, in stark contrast to this narrative, the Panthers waged a triumphant protest that exposed substandard neighborhood grocery stores. Reimagining this protest, the Quilted Chronicle *Ericka Huggins: Liberation Groceries* (2019) captures a pivotal 1972 media moment. It depicts the Black Panther Party's distribution of 10,000 bags of groceries to communities in Oakland, California, demonstrating a deliberate strategy of loudly announcing ourselves as our own best resource for freedom." L'Merchie Frazier

1999

Sharon Dunn

FIGS. 71–72

When multidisciplinary artist Sharon Dunn was invited to take residence at AAMARP in the mid-1990s, she was already a well-known figure within the community. Not only was she the daughter of Robert Haggins, personal photographer to Malcolm X from 1959 to 1965, but she was also the painter of *Black Woman* (1979), a beloved icon of Boston's mural movement, located at 4 Yarmouth Street in the South End. *Black Woman* anticipates themes and approaches that would become core to Dunn's practice, namely an appreciation for site-specificity and environment coupled with considerations of ancestral legacy and cultural memory. Her later, ephemeral installations, such as *Floor Piece* (1994/2026) were influenced by African and diasporic altars and floor rituals, including the Haitian *vèvè* floor drawings central to Vodou cosmologies. *Floor Piece* features small balls of organic materials with supposed healing properties (beeswax and turmeric, for example), and Dunn has described the work as an intuitive attempt to "call up sacred geometry summoned as if from a dream."[2] *Hemp Environment* (1999) was exhibited at AAMARP the year it was completed, and also explored the spiritual valences of geometry and organic material, with long, loose strands of hemp anchored to the floor in small mounds of salt, a substance she would continue to experiment with for many years as a symbol of and conduit toward ancestral memory. Like many AAMARP artists, Dunn has traveled and researched widely, including to Cuba, Nicaragua, the United Kingdom, Nigeria, and Ghana. These travels form fertile ground for ongoing investigations of syncretism, ritual, and the sacred. **MCC**

"As I quietly reflect on my AAMARP residency, I close my eyes in peace, with a deep inner contentment and with a healing breath . . .

The experience gave me an opportunity to quietly embark on a new creative, mindful, and self-reflective process . . . and to begin a lifelong journey towards a meditative, contemplative new body of personal expressive/mixed-media and abstract intuitive photographic work.

At the time, I did not know I was about to begin the slow, subtle inner journey . . . towards a new ancestral opening, with new sensory door awareness . . . and new emergent creative insights. The experience gave me a quiet, safe, intellectual, physical, and spiritual space that allowed me to try, to explore and to thrive . . . it gave me the peace of mind to listen to an inner self I had not fully met . . .

I carry deep respect, fond memories of creative-insightful conversations and studio exchanges . . . and I carry lifelong loving and heartfelt warmth for AAMARP studio neighbors and colleagues . . . who inspired and informed my journey . . . and opened ancestral passages." Sharon Dunn

1999

Keith Morris Washington

FIG. 73

In the late 1990s, thanks to his generous studio space at AAMARP, Keith Morris Washington began an ongoing series of large-scale paintings he called Within Our Gates: Site and Memory in the American Landscape. Each work takes as its subject the site of an American lynching; as the artist says, he is "mediating spaces, investigating a past still present, interrogating tradition, questioning discrepancies extolled in Hudson River / Luminist Painting." The presentation of *George Armwood: Front Lawn of Judge R. Duer's Home; Princess Anne, Maryland* (1999) is always accompanied by the following text written by the artist. **JDB**

PRINCESS ANNE, Md., Oct. 18 — In the wildest lynching orgy the state has ever witnessed, a frenzied mob of 3,000 men, women and children, sneering at guns and tear gas, overpowered 50 state troopers, tore from a prison cell a Negro accused of attacking an aged white woman, and lynched him in front of the home of a judge who had tried to placate the mob.

Then the mob cut down the body, dragged it through the main thoroughfare for more than half a mile and tossed it on a burning pyre.

Fifty State policemen were beaten to the ground and the others were swept aside by the fury of the townsmen and farmers, who used a heavy wooden battering ram to smash three doors and reach the cell of the terrified prisoner, George Armwood, twenty-four years old.

Armwood was dragged by the neck through the streets, to the home of Judge Robert F. Duer, who, earlier in the day had called the Somerset County grand jury in special session next Monday to hear testimony against the Negro.

While the prisoner pleaded desperately for his life and members of the mob shouted, "lynch him!" a rope was placed about his neck. The other end was swung over the limb of a tree directly in front of the judge's dwelling.

To accompanying shouts of "let him swing," the struggling Negro was hoisted into the air. Five minutes later he was cut down, dead.

Under the oak tree, despite the presence of women and children, all the victim's clothes were torn from his body and he hung there for several minutes nude.

Then members of the mob, shouting, seized the loose end of the rope and dragged the body half a mile on Main

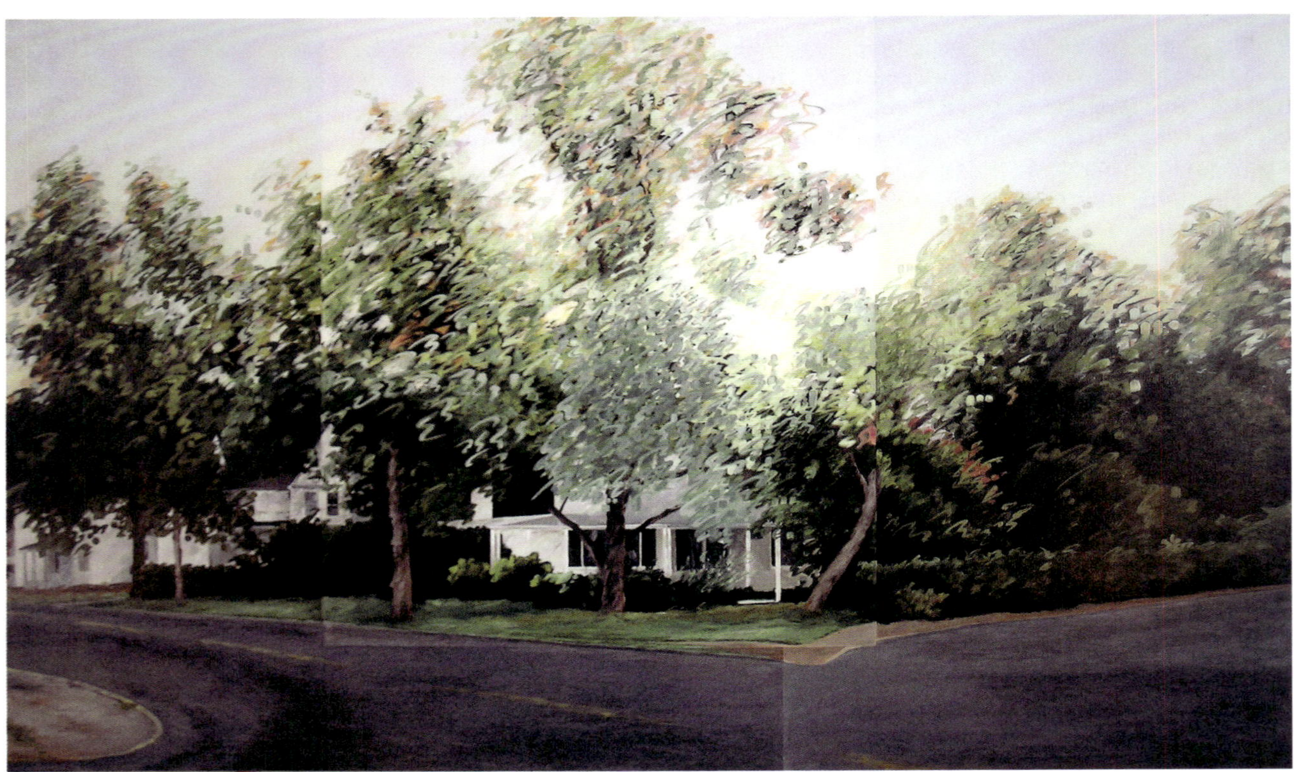

73. Keith Morris Washington, *George Armwood: Front Lawn of Judge R. Duer's Home; Princess Anne, Maryland*, 1999. Oil and acrylic on linen. 72 × 119 inches (182.9 × 302.3 cm). Fitchburg Art Museum, Fitchburg, MA; Museum Purchase, Sinon Collection Fund, Marjorie Doyle Rockwell Fund, General Collection Fund, in honor of Susan Roetzer's service as president of the Fitchburg Art Museum Board of Trustees, 2016–2021

Street to a blazing pile in the center of the thoroughfare. The dead man was lifted high by half a dozen men and flung to the flames.

Hundreds of persons, packed so thickly about the fire that police could not fight their way through, watched the body burn.   Keith Morris Washington

"I moved to Boston in 1976 and two years later began attending the MassArt. While a student at MassArt I joined the Black Artists Union, a student-run organiza-tion founded by members of AAMARP. AAMARP already had a distinguished international reputation at that time, and I was honored to show my work there while still a student.

In the early 1990s I got a studio space there and was there until 2010. I was less tuned into the community, per se, and was more drawn to having twenty-four-hour access to the space. I was in dialogue with many AAMARP artists who I knew before joining as a mem-ber. In the late '90s we still had shows but kept a relatively low profile as it related to Northeastern's administration. For a few years I served as co-chair with Susan Thompson. I am deeply grateful for that space. Without it, I wouldn't have been able to make the large landscapes and portraits that are still the primary focus of my practice today."   Keith Morris Washington

2000 TO NOW

Don West

FIGS. 74–75

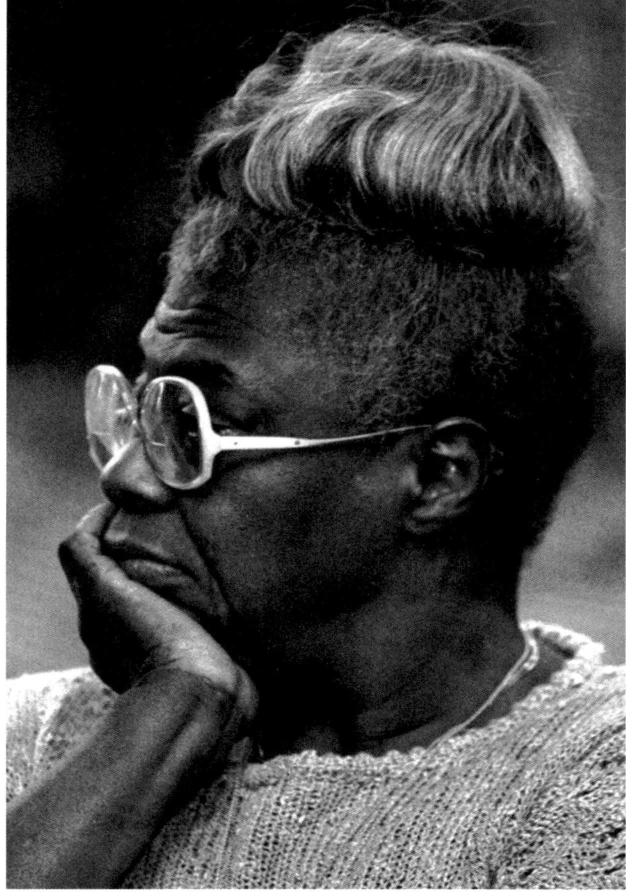

74

Growing up slightly isolated as one of few Black children in posh Brookline, Massachusetts, Don West first approached cameras with a shy curiosity, seeing them as a "passport to get close while keeping a distance."[3] After stints at Morgan State College (now University; an HBCU in Baltimore, Maryland), touring the country as a musician, and teaching meditation practices to incar-cerated individuals in the Bay Area, West returned to Boston in 1980. By this point, his longtime fascination with photography as a hobby had evolved into something deeper. Proximity to the civil rights and Black Power movements lent a certain edge to the artist's philosophy of image-making, and he came to see photography as a political project, counteracting the racism and bias present in mainstream media. West worked as a freelance photographer for United Press International, as well as for the *Bay State Banner*, Boston's weekly Black newspa-per. Through this work, he came to know Boston's Black community and grew close with AAMARP-affiliated photographers, including Rudolph Robinson and Hakim Raquib. He was eventually recruited to the collective by Dana Chandler and still maintains a studio at AAMARP today. Through West's work with the *Banner*, he had the opportunity to serve as an official photographer for politicians visiting Boston, such as Nelson Mandela and Barack Obama, as well as protests, exhibitions, athletic events, and local political chronicles, such as the rise of Mel King's historic 1983 mayoral campaign and his Rainbow Coalition. These formative experiences in photojournalism, and specifically portraiture, provided the basis for what would become West's most ambitious project, the Portraits of Purpose series. Today the decades-long series features well over a hundred photo-graphs of Black civic and artistic leaders, as well as their allies. An early iteration of this body of work was featured in the 1993 ICA/Boston exhibition *On the*

74. Don West, *Elma Lewis*, c. 1985. From the series Portraits of Purpose. Gelatin silver print. Printed dimensions variable

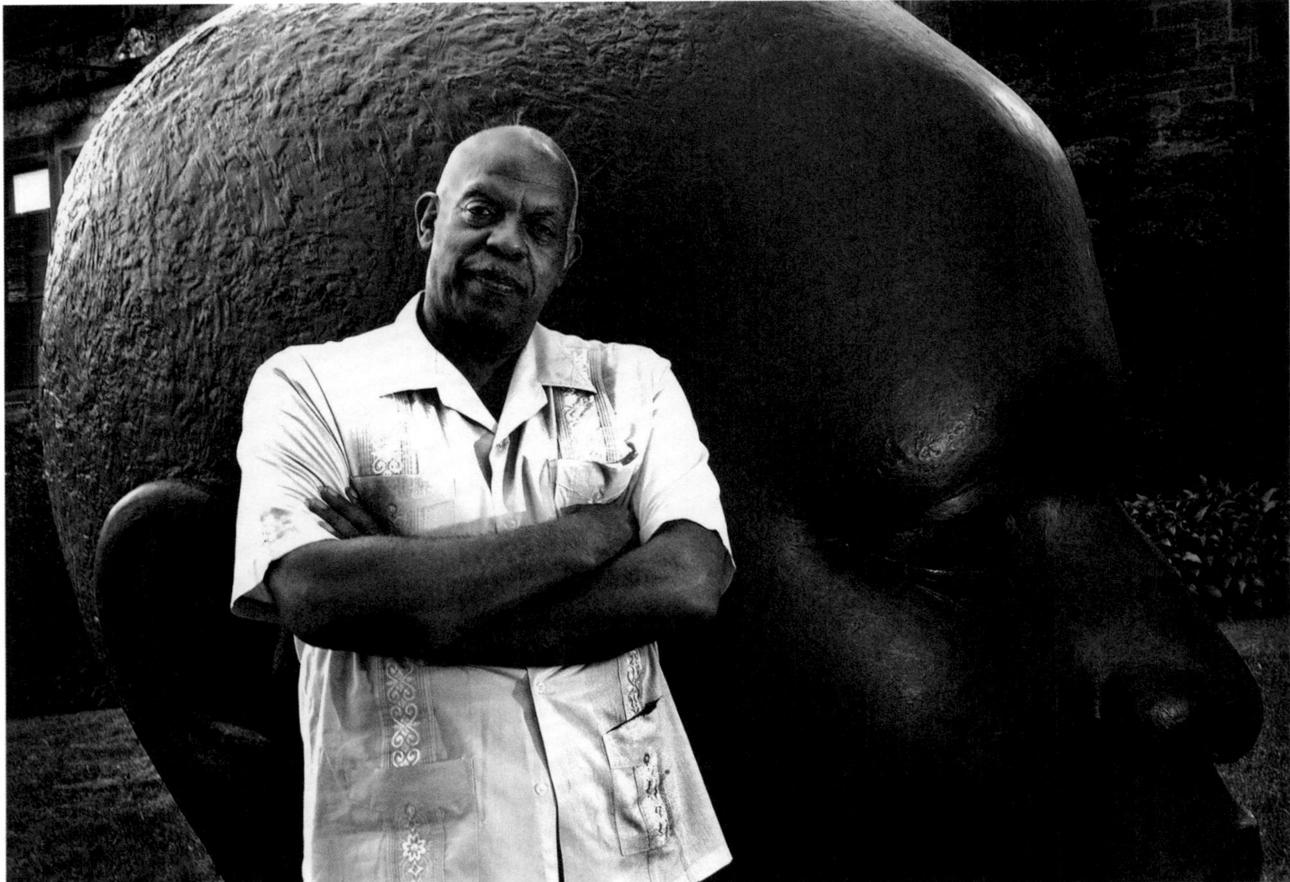

Subject: Voices from Massachusetts, which provided a local context for the accompanying touring exhibition *Malcolm X: Man, Ideal, Icon* organized by Kellie Jones. Particularly notable are West's sensitive portraits of Elma Lewis, the legendary Boston arts educator and institution-builder, in deep and focused observation, and of her mentee, Edmund Barry Gaither, founding director and curator of the Museum of the National Center of Afro-American Artists, standing proudly alongside John Wilson's outdoor sculpture *Eternal Presence* (1985). Together these images, among many others, testify to a robust arts ecosystem that was inextricably tied to the political project of self-determination in Boston. **MCC**

"Dana Chandler was responsible for me meeting my wife, Libbie Shufro. To be exact, he offered her the opportunity to showcase her organization El Pueblo Nuevo (a Latina artist group) in his large studio at Northeastern and I covered the event as a news photographer for a publication.

This occasion was just one of many Dana offered the community to have space to share their work with a wider audience. This opportunity was extended to local Black artists and evolved into an organization named the African American Master Artists-in-Residence Program.

This artist group evolved into a local, national, and international resource for students, scholars, and the general public to gain insight into an expanding culture within a culture.

Dana, himself a prolific artist involved with issues of the day concerning Black people, was always on the lookout to bring more artists of varied backgrounds into the fold and called on me to join. This was an honor and a unique opportunity to expand my knowledge and understanding of the history of art in it's many incarnations.

After over forty years, AAMARP is still serving the community, and continues to grow with new artists and contemporary ideas." Don West

75. Don West, *Barry Gaither*, c. 1985. From the series Portraits of Purpose. Gelatin silver print. Printed dimensions variable

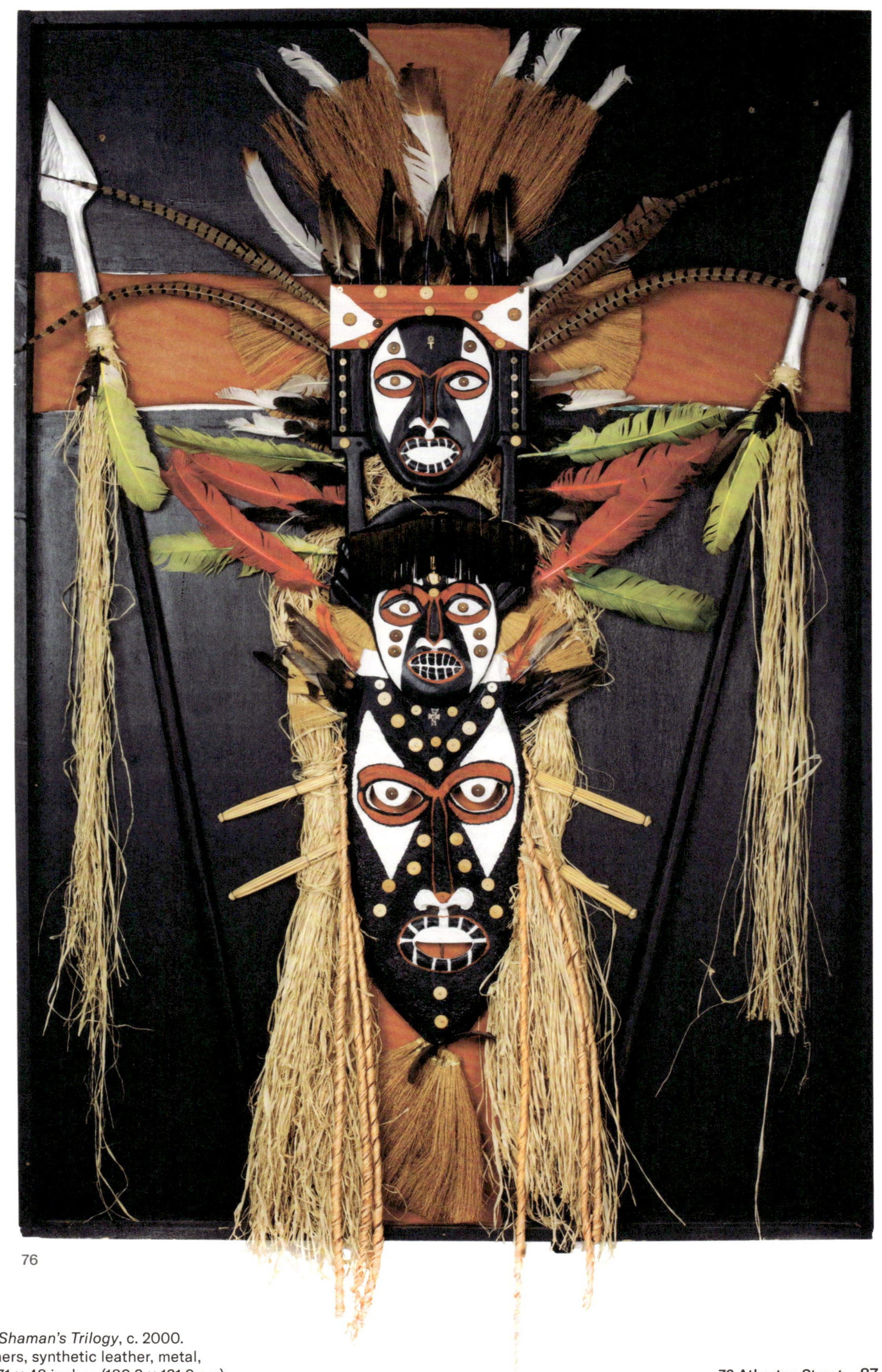

76

76. Jeff Chandler, *Shaman's Trilogy*, c. 2000.
Wood, raffia, feathers, synthetic leather, metal,
and acrylic paint. 71 × 48 inches (180.3 × 121.9 cm)

2000

Jeff Chandler

FIG. 76

Self-taught sculptor, woodworker, and percussionist Jeff Chandler–Dana Chandler's younger brother by sixteen years–got his start at AAMARP thanks to his experience working in construction. His woodworking skills were indispensable in renovating AAMARP's industrial studios at 76 Atherton Street and he frequently helped install the exhibitions on view in the galleries. Since the beginning, Chandler has worked with materials close at hand. His earliest works were made from reclaimed kitchen cabinets, bedroom sets, and other cast-off wood found at construction sites. As his work progressed and became more expansive in scale, he took on his own studio at AAMARP. In such works as *Shaman's Trinity* (c. 2000), Chandler incorporates cross-cultural forms and motifs linked to spiritual traditions, like African shamanic traditions related to spirit possession, ancestor reverence, and healing rituals. Chandler's work often demonstrates meaningful forms of mentorship and exchange among collective members. In some works, he has made figurative carvings using fellow member Don West's street photographs as a model, while others were carved using *bubinga* (African rosewood), brought back from the continent for him by Hakim Raquib. Chandler also solicits unique coins from AAMARP members when they travel internationally and embeds them into hand-carved walking sticks to evoke movement and travel. **JDB**

"AAMARP has afforded me the opportunity to travel the world without leaving my studio. I can learn from everyone who goes to different African nations, through the Caribbean, even those with connections to the American South. Just being in the building, I am affected by what everyone else does. I am so grateful to Dana that I was introduced to this organization in the way that I was because it offered me a model of how to be an artist. I could also see him in a new light, especially his effect on other people. The battle that Dana fought for the existence of AAMARP is being fought all over again. Dana left a template through his work and activism to fight for its survival. You can't sit around and deal with people who don't like you. You must learn how to fight." **Jeff Chandler**

Shea Justice, Ricardo "Deme5" Gomez, and Marlon Forrester

FIGS. 77–81

Growing up in Roxbury, Shea Justice was profoundly impacted at a young age by Dana Chandler's mural *Knowledge Is Power–Stay In School* (1972; p. 14), in Roxbury. Justice frequently cites Chandler as his biggest influence, and it was Chandler himself who eventually gave the younger artist a studio space at AAMARP as he was retiring to New Mexico and leaving the program. With the socially engaged, historically conscious work of Chandler as a model, Justice employs the medium of collage as a means of bringing the past into direct contact with the present to bear witness to American history. Shortly after the events of September 11, 2001, when the United States invaded Afghanistan as part of Operation Enduring Freedom–a decades-long war waged throughout the Middle East–Justice began a still-evolving project called *Scrolls of Justice*. For more than twenty years, Justice has continued adding dense admixtures of illustrations, paintings, handwritten text, and collage to miles of paper scrolls diaristic in form as part of an attempt to catalog the historical complexity of present day life in America. This sense of complexity and an exhaustive approach is encapsulated even in his smaller collages, such as *Constitution: Sojourner and Harriet* (2017), which captures the frenetic energy of Chandler's *Urban Newsletter Art Piece* (1993; p. 67) by combining newspaper clippings and sensitively rendered portraits of abolitionists Sojourner Truth and Harriet Tubman overtop of the United States Constitution, suggesting the racist underpinnings of the American project and its so-called founding fathers. Still other works, such as the beautifully rendered watercolor painting *Egleston Square Memorial* (2022; p. 6), marry the complexity of its subject to the dynamic possibilities of the medium to meditate on a temporary memorial for a lost child, a family's grief staged publicly.

Just as Shea Justice continues to advance a particular brand of socially engaged art-making at AAMARP, Ricardo Gomez, also known as Deme5, is a muralist working within the rich history of mural painting in Boston. Influenced by artists in Chicago, and in particular the *Wall of Respect*–a mural first painted collectively in 1967 that is a montage of portraits of key figures from African American history–the mural movement in Boston was built on notions of Black empowerment put forward by Dana Chandler, Sharon Dunn, and Gary Rickson, among others, in and around Boston's commu-

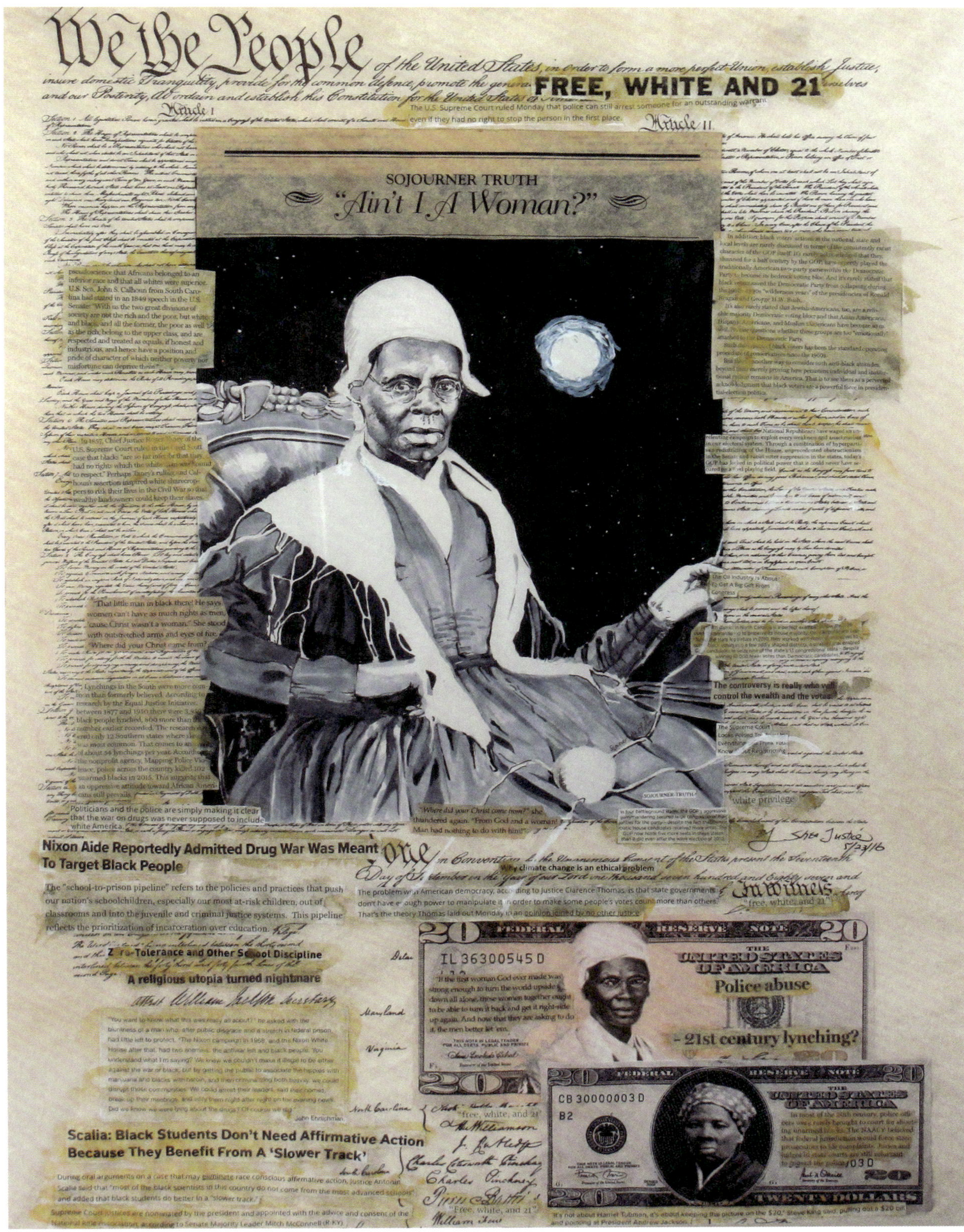

77. Shea Justice, *Constitution: Sojourner and Harriet*, 2017. Collage and ink on paper. 32 × 27 inches (81.3 × 68.6 cm)

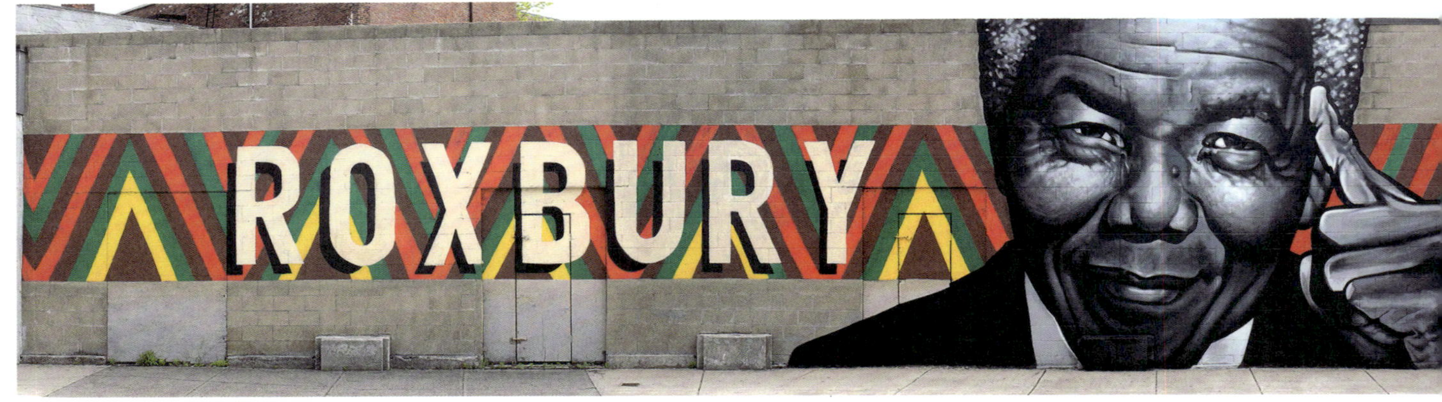

78

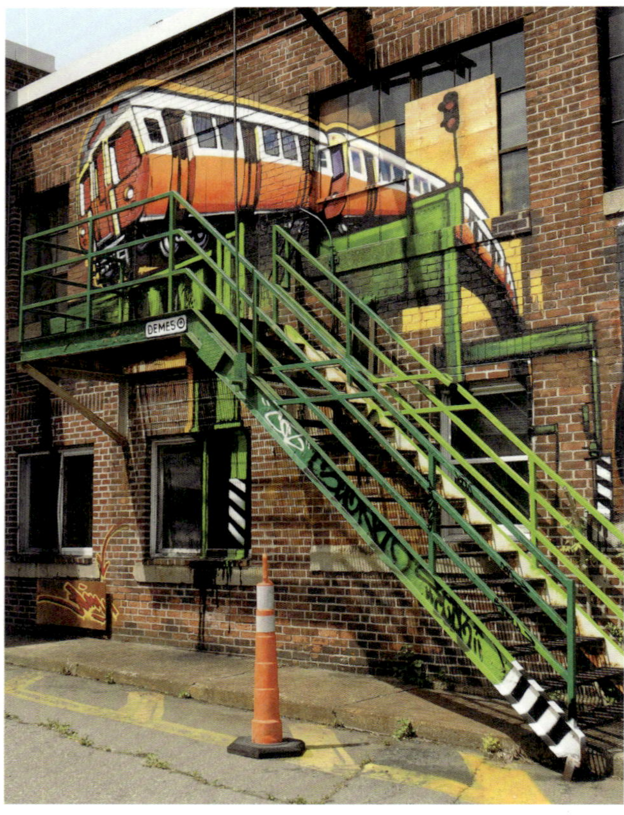

79

78. Ricardo "Deme5" Gomez and Thomas "Kwest" Burns, *Roxbury Love*, 2014. Warren Street, Roxbury, no longer extant

79. Ricardo "Deme5" Gomez, *Bartlett El*, 2013. Bartlett Yard, Roxbury, no longer extant

nities of color. According to artist and educator Stephen Hamilton, "younger generations of graffiti artists continued the legacy of this work, infusing it with visual innovations borne out of the hip-hop generation."[4] Included in this generation of artists is Deme5, one of the painters along with Zone, Thomas "Kwest" Burns, Marka27, and Rob "ProblaK" Gibbs (known collectively as the African Latino Alliance crew), who painted the mural *From the Pyramids to the Projects* (c. 2002) at Peters Park, an homage to poet Askia Touré, a prominent member of the Black Arts movement and Boston-based associate of AAMARP. In 2014, Gomez and Burns spray-painted a landmark, seventeen-by-one-hundred-foot mural called *Roxbury Love* featuring an iconic image of Nelson Mandela inspired by the South African activist and former president's visit to Boston in 1990, for which AAMARP artist Don West was official photographer. *Roxbury Love* was described as a "beacon of hope for the community, something folks could take pride in," and was widely loved and appreciated before it was unceremoniously demolished as part of plans to develop a two-building, ninety-nine-unit apartment complex.[5] The legacy of Gomez's visionary mural persists, even through smaller, temporary murals sited throughout the city, such as *Bartlett El* (2013), featuring an MBTA Orange Line train that appears to emerge from the wall of a brick building.

Marlon Forrester, the newest member of the collective, joined AAMARP in 2014 when he was approached by other members at an exhibition opening. Born in Guyana and raised in Boston, Forrester works in a range of media, from paintings and collages to performance and photography, that often take the representations and uses of the Black male body as a central concern. Forrester's work explores ideas of ritual and transforma-

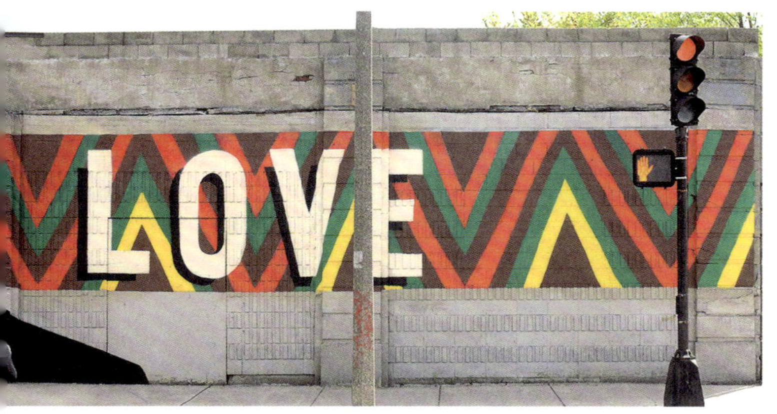

tion, often through themes and motifs drawn from basketball culture. Following an influential return visit to Guyana, Forrester increasingly examines the instability of identity and complex ideas of homeland for individuals of the Caribbean diaspora, situating him as part of a lineage at AAMARP that includes Kofi Kayiga and Bryan McFarlane. Forrester's earliest works, such as *Warrior Dance* (2012), depict crudely rendered figures performing traditional African ceremonies like the Zulu warrior dance to showcase strength, power, and unity. The beady eyed titular warrior at the center of the canvas, who holds a sword and sacrificial kill, is set against a geometrically dynamic and shifting background of vibrant colors and patterns inspired by Zulu attire. More recently, Forrester imagined an evolving body of work that begins with associations between ideas of flight, resistance, and freedom in the legend of flying Africans, popular folktales about enslaved Africans who rebel and liberate themselves by flying home. Forrester's approach in paintings from this series, such as *StTrayvonGeorge23* (2021), is framed conceptually by his notion of "psychic homeland," his multilayered sense of identity, belonging, and disequilibrium as a Guyanese American of the Caribbean diaspora. The complexity of experiences inscribed in each painting aims to counter historical exclusions and marginalization by centering the Black male body as a site of celebration, commemoration, and transformation. **JDB**

"I grew up in Grove Hall in Roxbury during the 1970s. Every day, whenever I went to school or took a bus to Downtown Boston, I saw at least one of Dana Chandler's murals. Initially I thought the images were of superheroes with bright colors and muscular figures. Being a comic book fan at the time they were definitely a sight to behold. I always heard the artist's name and wanted to meet him one day. I was lucky enough to meet Dana years later at art shows like the Copley Society's *Art In The Park* outdoor exhibition. We became good friends, and he became a mentor to me. As I developed as an artist, I found myself gravitating toward his style of art-making. Politically and historically minded and always speaking truth to power.

When he retired, he grandfathered me into AAMARP, and I've been a member ever since. It has been a great experience working and exhibiting with artists who share talent and vision that elevates the diaspora to new levels of creativity in telling our stories. Even now, a lot of the content of my work continues to deal with the many issues Dana has addressed. I give credit to Dana Chandler for helping me develop into the artist I am today, meeting other artists from the community, and inspiring me to have a focus that has not changed in all the years I have been drawing."
Shea Justice

"AAMARP has been a space where I can display my craft, continue to work, and be creative among a group of people I consider family. There is a sense of honor and humility that takes over whenever I step inside the building. An overwhelming feeling of belonging and a constant reminder not to take this opportunity for granted. AAMARP artists consist of a wide range of styles and mediums. As a member, I am grateful to bring yet another set of varied skills to the table. It's this solid community of artists that inspire me to continue my journey as a dedicated and passionate artist in the city of Boston." Ricardo "Deme5" Gomez

"AAMARP has afforded me the necessary space to contemplate and reflect on my process but also it has allowed me to be in a community of some of the baddest Black artists in Boston. To be in their presence and find fellowship with artists of their stature has changed my life and the trajectory of my artwork.

My residency has been a dream come true experience: exposing communities of young artists to a rich cultural history they never knew, incorporating new theoretical discourses in my practice, embracing the revolutionary call for social justice, working to transform both public and institutional spaces through the lens of painting and sculpture." Marlon Forrester

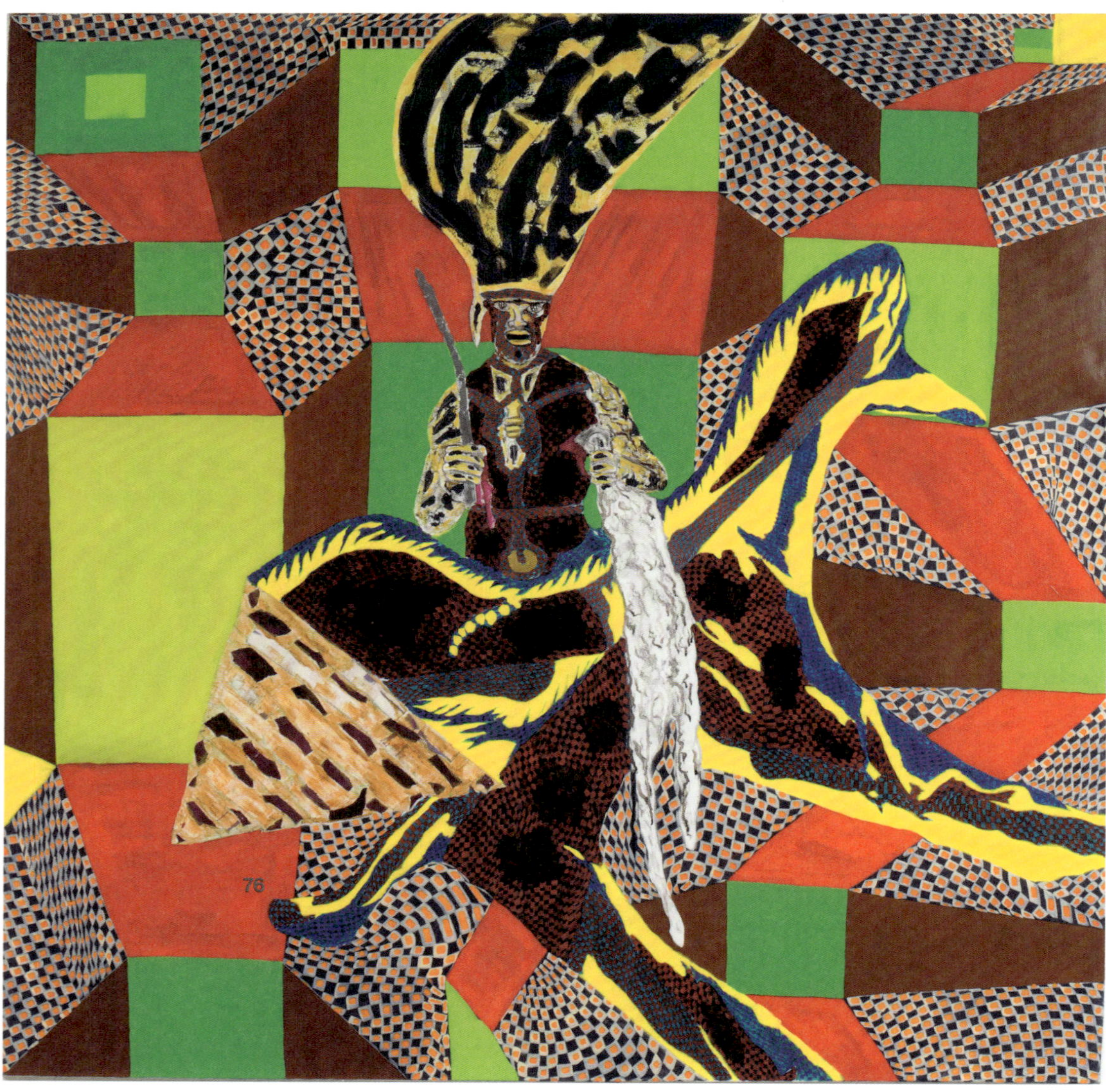

80

80. Marlon Forrester, *Warrior Dance*, 2012. Oil and mixed media on canvas. 64 × 64 inches (162.6 × 162.6 cm)

81. Marlon Forrester, *StTrayvonGeorge23*, 2021. From the series If Black Saints Could Fly 23: si volare posset nigra XXIII sanctorum. Oil, oil stick, acrylic, and gold leaf on linen. 86 × 52 inches (218.4 × 132.1 cm). Institute of Contemporary Art/Boston; Acquired through the generosity of James and Audrey Foster

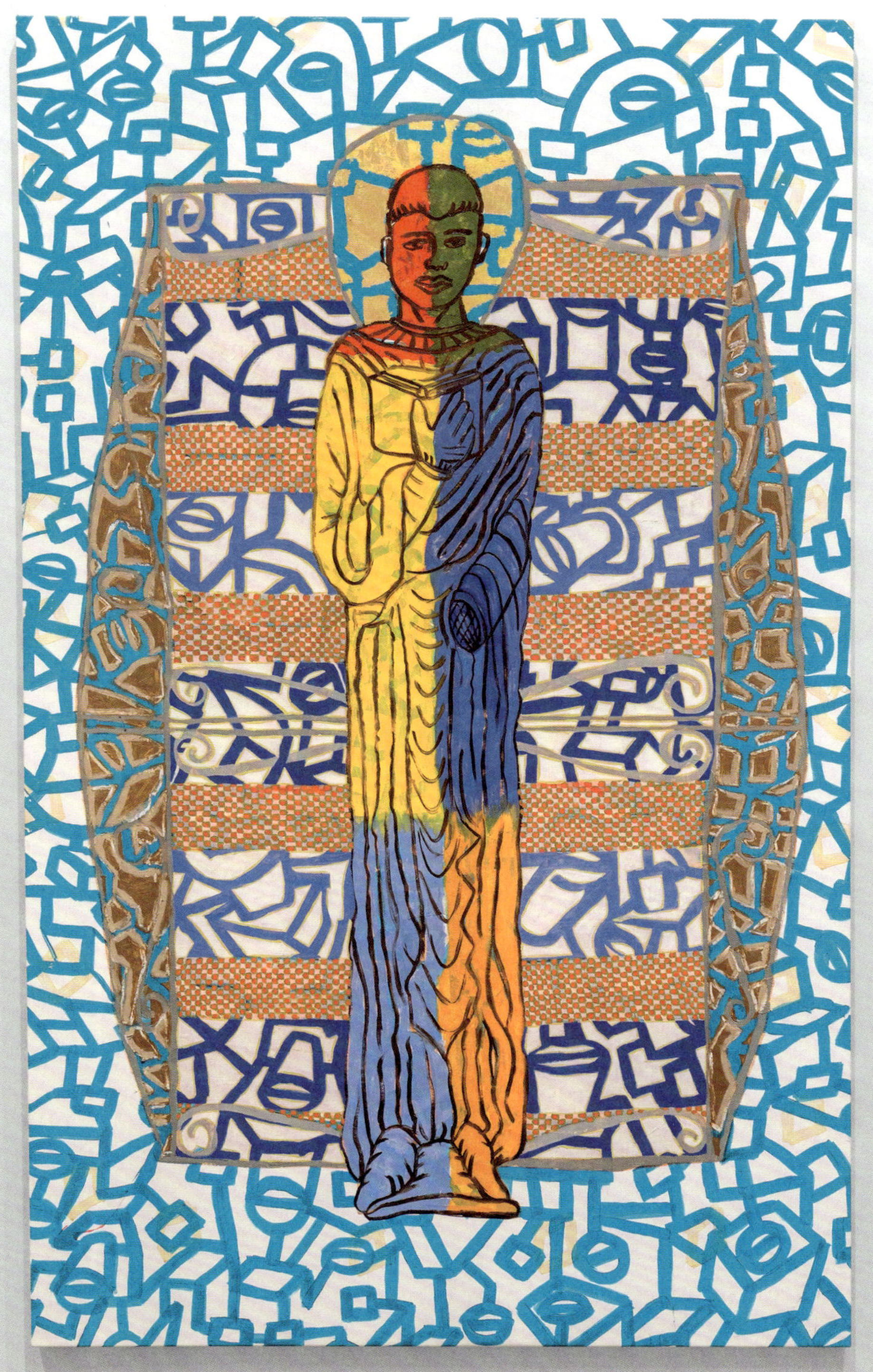

SUSTAINING COMMUNITIES

CONNIE H. CHOI

When the Studio Museum in Harlem opened in 1968, less than a decade before the African American Master Artists-in-Residence Program, it was with a recognition of the need to help sustain a vibrant Black Arts community and a deep commitment to championing new work being produced by artists. As Thelma Golden, Ford Foundation Director and Chief Curator of the Museum, notes:

> One of the gifts of the Studio Museum in Harlem's founders is that they wrote our mission in our name. In doing so they explicitly established a directive for our work, with Studio denoting the many ways our institution aligns itself with artist practices, evidenced most distinctly in our signature *Artist-in-Residence* program. We share this clarity in purpose with the African American Master Artists-in-Residence Program, a critical residency whose objective is made unmistakable in its naming, and which, since 1977, has profoundly shaped contemporary art through its unyielding support of Black artists.[1]

The Studio Museum's three founding initiatives—the *Artist-in-Residence* program, the Film Unit, and the Studio Program—were all grounded in this shared dedication to living artists, with a keen understanding of the institution's responsibility to provide support across multiple sectors, including advocacy, funding, and professional development. The goal was and always has been to offer space—for creativity, for conversation, for both rest and stimulation—with experiences rooted by a sense, and a knowing, of belonging. Today, the Studio Museum continues as an artist-centered institution with the same ethos outlined by its founders nearly sixty years ago: "it must be a living museum: a place not only to look, but a place to work and learn and create."[2]

This idea of a museum as an active space "to work and learn and create" proposes that museums are not just places for visitors to see art, but that they are also centers for nurturing the next generations of museum professionals, instilling in audiences of all ages an appreciation for the arts, and encouraging creativity and experimentation. In their proposal outlining the necessity for the Studio Museum, the institution's founders stated that "[w]e must learn to understand the great capacity of art to communicate across all manner of human boundaries, not just the lines that divide the past and the present but that separate one way of life and one spirit from another."[3] Museums, galleries, community centers, and other spaces committed to exhibiting the work of Black artists are as necessary now as they were fifty and sixty years ago precisely because they are so often dedicated to creating the conditions for this holistic experience. These spaces for and by people of African descent crucially attend to an ever-evolving constellation of Black voices, histories, and narratives, thereby serving as essential sites for engagement and meaning-making.

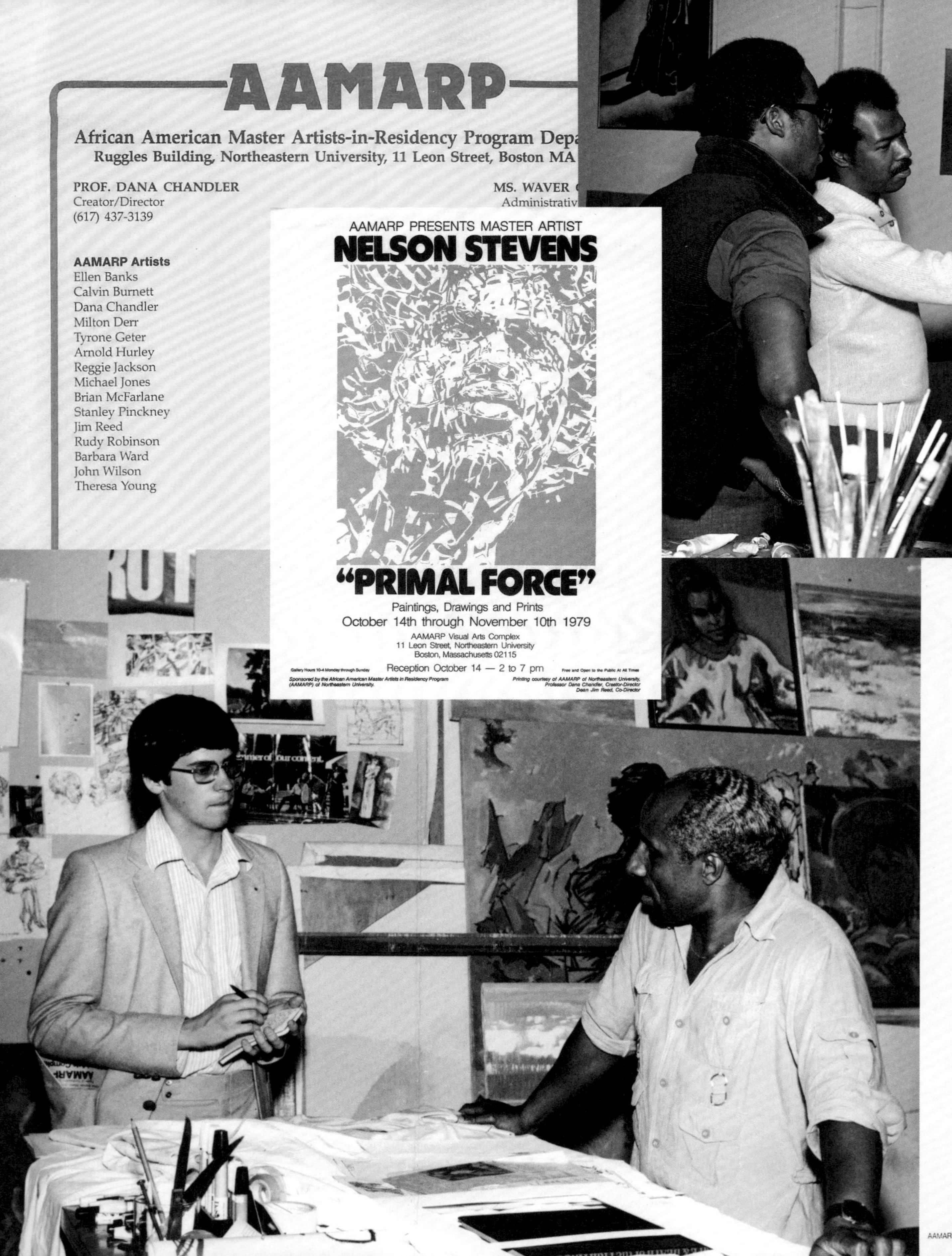
AAMARP
African American Master Artists-in-Residency Program Depa
Ruggles Building, Northeastern University, 11 Leon Street, Boston MA

PROF. DANA CHANDLER
Creator/Director
(617) 437-3139

MS. WAVER
Administrativ

AAMARP Artists
Ellen Banks
Calvin Burnett
Dana Chandler
Milton Derr
Tyrone Geter
Arnold Hurley
Reggie Jackson
Michael Jones
Brian McFarlane
Stanley Pinckney
Jim Reed
Rudy Robinson
Barbara Ward
John Wilson
Theresa Young

AAMARP PRESENTS MASTER ARTIST
NELSON STEVENS
"PRIMAL FORCE"
Paintings, Drawings and Prints
October 14th through November 10th 1979
AAMARP Visual Arts Complex
11 Leon Street, Northeastern University
Boston, Massachusetts 02115
Gallery Hours 10-4 Monday through Sunday
Reception October 14 — 2 to 7 pm
Free and Open to the Public At All Times
Sponsored by the African American Master Artists in Residency Program
(AAMARP) of Northeastern University.
Printing courtesy of AAMARP of Northeastern University,
Professor Dana Chandler, Creator-Director
Dean Jim Reed, Co-Director

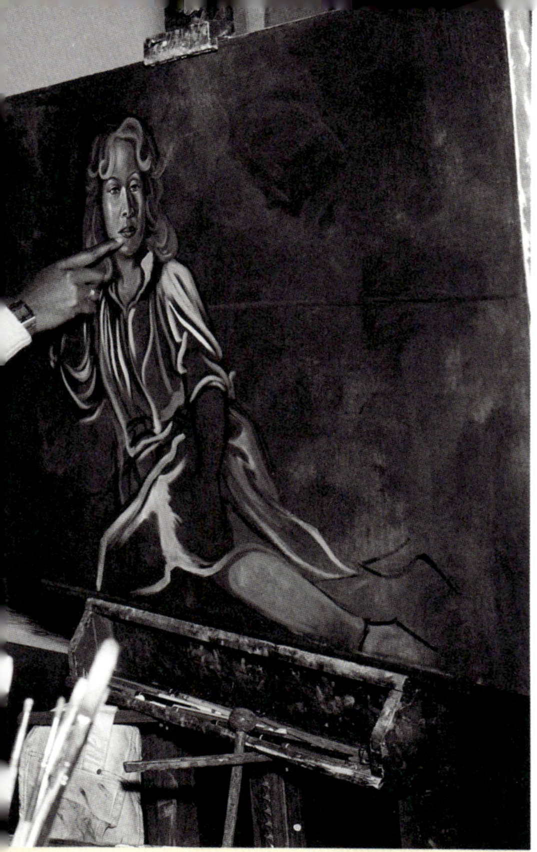

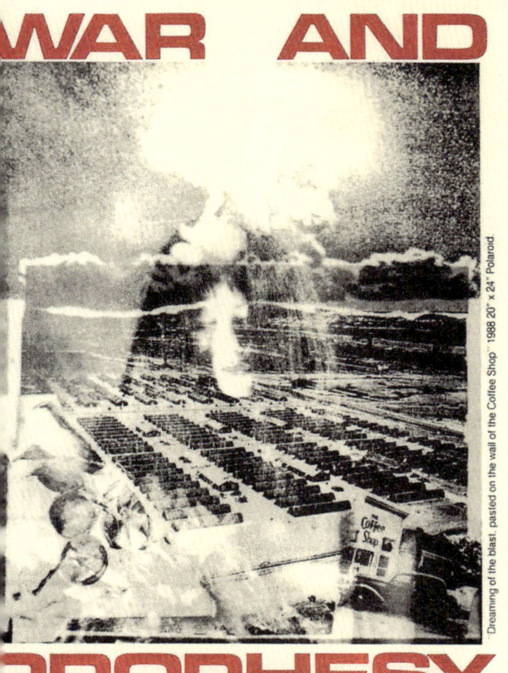

The African-American Master Artists-in-Residency Program is the first residency program of its kind in the country!

1. The purpose of the African-American Master Artists-in-Residency program is to bring to the Northeastern Community, African-Americans in and around Boston, and Americans of all ethnic groups everywhere, a group of highly competent and nationally famous African-American Artists whose collective credentials comprise many decades of African-American art history. The artists involved are indeed art history in the flesh, as their body of work has been shown internationally and individually. Work can be found in museum and private collections around the world.

2. To bring to the greater Boston and national community the collective skills of these artists by way of workshops, seminars, lectures, traveling exhibitions, demonstrations, and visiting lecture/discussions, and so on.

3. To instill pride and motivation in the minds of Black children and Black adults by sharing with them an image of collective competency and national prominence in the differing areas of the visual arts.

4. To foster knowledge and respect, of, and for, the field of visual arts by continuing a history of competency in visual arts which spans thirty-five+ years.

5. To provide students of all kinds from all areas with the opportunity to visit (on appointment or in a tour group) the studios of over thirteen artists and see them at work surrounded by their tools and finished/unfinished images in a creative art environment. We expect fruitful dialogue and possible apprenticeship will result from such interaction.

We hope as a group to clear up the mythologies and mysteries which surround our fields, and to display to many our diverse skills in the areas of painting, draughtsmanship, photography, printmaking, sculpture, illustration, film-making, tye-dying, jewelry making and other visual arts. We will be seeking funding for these endeavors and expect to get underway as soon as our studio facilities have been completed at Northeastern University.

Dana C. Chandler Jr. (Akin Duro), Director

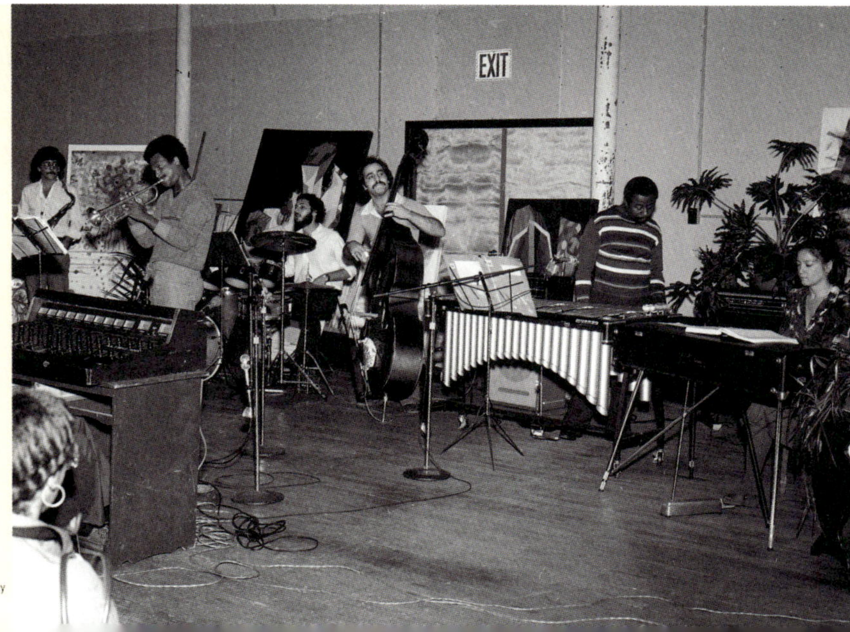

Acknowledgements

The first time I set foot in AAMARP's building at
76 Atherton Street in Jamaica Plain, Massachusetts, was
in 2021. I visited the studio of Marlon Forrester, who I
had invited to participate in the *2021 James and Audrey
Foster Prize*, an exhibition and prize key to the ICA/
Boston's efforts to nurture and recognize Boston-area
artists. Walking the halls together, I was immediately
struck by the power of the works lining the walls, which I
later learned were made by Gloretta Baynes, Reginald L.
"Reggie" Jackson, Khalid Kodi, and Bryan McFarlane,
among others. When I asked Marlon about the incredible
artworks I was seeing, he said: "This is just everything
that's been made at AAMARP. You need to catch up!"

Everything that followed was my attempt to do just
that, though what I quickly learned is that no exhibition
or catalogue can contain the staggering and multifarious
history of AAMARP. The stakes are high, the stakeholders are many, and the history is complicated, some of it
impossible to know. I am grateful to Marlon for inviting
me into that incredible space. I am honored that
AAMARP founder Dana C. Chandler Jr. trusted me to
take on the history of the program in the form of an
exhibition and publication. From our very first conversation, when I asked him about the possibility of doing an
exhibition about AAMARP, he immediately said: "Hurry
up and do it." His support instilled in me a sense of
urgency that subsequently drove every aspect of this
overdue project at a museum that, by and large, ignored
what was happening across town for so many years.
When he passed during the making of the exhibition and
catalogue, we rededicated ourselves to amplifying his
legacy as an artist and the program's visionary founder.
I am grateful to AAMARP's Executive Committee—
L'Merchie Frazier, Reggie Jackson, Hakim Raquib, and
Don West—for their great counsel, trust, and for guiding
many aspects of this project. The remaining collective
members—Gloretta Baynes, Jeff Chandler, Marlon
Forrester, Ricardo Gomez, Shea Justice, Kofi Kayiga
(and his wife Judith Smith, who also sadly passed before
the exhibition opened), Khalid Kodi, Bryan McFarlane,
and Susan Thompson—welcomed me into their studios
and worked with us to determine how to convey their

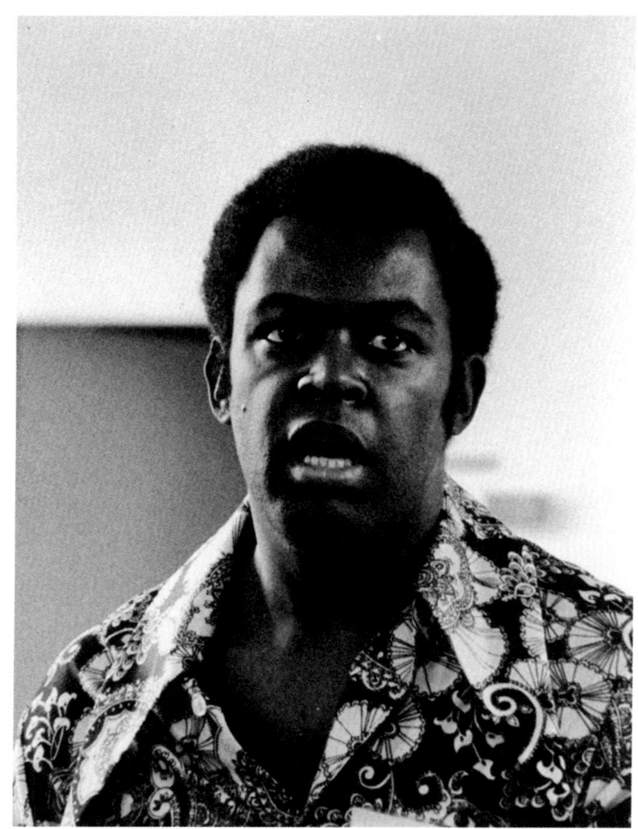

82

various contributions to the program. Conversations
with artists once affiliated with the program, or those
who exhibited there, lent further texture to my thinking.
These include Sharon Dunn, Tyrone Geter, Michael
Jones, Napoleon Jones-Henderson, Stanley Pinckney,
Renée Stout, Wen-ti Tsen, Keith Morris Washington,
and Rene Westbrook, many of whom expressed how
transformative the program was for them personally, and
for Boston's artistic community more generally. I am
indebted to Isis Kayiga, D. J. Chandler, Tracy Williams,
and other family members for their support. Every
aspect of this project belongs as much to Meghan Clare

82. Dana Chandler, n.d.

Considine, Curatorial Assistant, as it does to me. Meghan's fingerprints are to be found everywhere. Her enthusiasm matched my own, and her steadfast support and encouragement was invaluable.

Research for the exhibition followed two parallel paths: one through conversations with artists and key stakeholders, the other through archival research. Meghan and I are grateful to the generous staff at the archives of Northeastern University; Suffolk University; Emerson College; the University of Massachusetts, Boston; the Schomburg Center for Research in Black Culture; the Museum of Fine Arts, Boston; Simmons University; the Dallas Museum of Art; the Getty Research Institute; the Timothy Drescher Community Mural Slide Archive; and the Ellen Banks Archive in Spandau, Germany. Many conversations about shared research interests helped shape the project, including with Dzidzor Azaglo and Uta Poiger of Northeastern University's Reckonings project; Patricia Hills, professor emerita at Boston University; and filmmakers Abhi Indrekar and Michaela Henry.

At the ICA, support from Director Emerita Jill Medvedow gave the exhibition early life. Nora Burnett Abrams, Ellen Matilda Poss Director, joined the project midstream and helped bring it to fruition. The transformative support and steadfast belief of Ruth Erickson, Barbara Lee Chief Curator and Director of Curatorial Affairs, were instrumental in its realization. Early support from Assistant Curator Tessa Bachi Haas set the project on a solid course. At the ICA, I am grateful for the opportunity to work collaboratively across departments to realize complicated projects, especially with Liz Adrian, Director of Retail; Katrina Foster, Director of Development; Karin France, Director of Institutional Giving; Monica Garza, Charlotte Wagner Director of Education; Kelly Gifford, Deputy Director; Kay Moriarty O'Dwyer, Director of Individual Giving; Colette Randall, Chief Communication and Marketing Officer; and Mario Rossi, Chief Financial Officer.

All of the exhibition's lenders were incredibly supportive, including Childs Gallery (with thanks to Richard Baiano, Julie Edwards, and Maxima Baudissin, Arnold Trachtman's daughter); the Theresa-India Young Estate (with thanks to Jackie McRath); the Estate of John Wilson (with thanks to Martha Richardson of Martha Richardson Fine Art); the Benny Andrews Estate (with thanks to Kyle Williams, Director, and Moira Murdock, Archivist); Michael Rosenfeld Gallery (with thanks to halley k. harrisburg, Director); Mount Holyoke College Art Museum; Fitchburg Art Museum; Cambridge Public Library Archives and Special Collections (with thanks to Alyssa Pacy, Archivist); Addison Gallery of American Art; the Museum of the National Center of Afro-American Artists; Lauren Thomasson; and other private collections. I am deeply grateful to Nick Capasso, Director of Fitchburg Art Museum, who greatly informed my perspective thanks to his many years of supporting Black artists in Boston. I am grateful for the meaningful support for the exhibition from The Kristen and Kent Lucken Fund for Photography.

This catalogue would not have been possible without the transformative support of Wagner Foundation. The catalogue was ably coordinated by Considine, who made many vital contributions. Haas managed the many administrative details to keep the catalogue on track. Special thanks to Angela Torchio, the ICA's principal designer, for key support preparing images for this publication. I am proud and grateful that Edmund Barry Gaither—the standard-bearer of Black art in Boston for more than fifty years—contributed a preface to introduce the context from which this project arose. Faye R. Gleisser's incisive writing added much to this publication's scholarly remit. Connie H. Choi's reflection on the importance of Black-run spaces functions as a coda, lending a meaningful perspective rooted in the present. Matthew Christensen's editorial oversight ensured the overriding cohesiveness of the various materials gathered here. Miko McGinty, Rebecca Sylvers, Rita Jules, and Tina Henderson of Miko McGinty Inc. took these materials and enlivened them through their beautiful design. Mary DelMonico, as always, was an enthusiastic collaborator and copublisher. This catalogue follows the pathbreaking example of Kay Bourne, the former arts editor for Boston's *Bay State Banner* and tireless advocate for these artists, who herself was developing a book about AAMARP when she passed away in 2021.

It is my hope that the spirit of radical inclusivity modeled at AAMARP permeates every aspect of this project, as a way of staying true to the program's promise and to pass it on to future researchers. In a project with many complicated dimensions, I have aimed to approach every turn with the same "delicacy of heart" that French writer Jean Genet proposed in his 1970 "May Day Speech" on behalf of the Black Panthers at Yale University. I could not undertake work of such great complexity without the enduring support of my family. My love to Caty, Jan, and Alida who prop me up and give me purpose.

JEFFREY DE BLOIS
Mannion Family Curator

Notes

AAMARP IS FOR EVERYONE

1. Ever prolific, Chandler estimated that he lost 2,300 reproductions, 500 paintings, countless drawings, eight years' worth of personal records, as well as thousands of dollars' worth of cameras, hi-fi equipment, and art-making supplies. Dana C. Chandler Jr., *If the shoe fits, hear it!: Paintings and Drawings, 1967–1976* (Boston, MA: Northeastern University Art Gallery, 1976). Northeastern University Archives and Special Collections, African American Master Artists-in-Residence Program records, Box 1, Folder 4.
2. Following this event, in 1974 the Museum of the National Center of Afro-American Artists in Roxbury hosted an exhibition of Chandler's work entitled *The Way Back: Recent and Undestroyed Images*.
3. In *Time* magazine, Chandler appeared alongside his contemporaries including Melvin Edwards, Sam Gilliam, David Hammons, Joe Overstreet, and others whose work has been more widely received than Chandler's. "Art: Object: Diversity," *Time* 95, no. 14, April 6, 1970, https://time.com/archive/6877086/art-object-diversity/.
4. Jim Vrabel, "Mothers for Adequate Welfare," in *A People's History of the New Boston* (Amherst: University of Massachusetts Press, 2014): 81–91.
5. Edmund Barry Gaither, introduction to *Dana Chandler: Retrospective Exhibition 1967–1987* (Boston: Massachusetts College of Art, 1987), n.p.
6. Chandler, *If the shoe fits, hear it!*.
7. Dana C. Chandler Jr., Archives of American Art Oral History conducted by Robert Brown, March 11, 1993–May 5, 1993, transcript page 53.
8. Dana C. Chandler Jr., Archives of American Art Oral History, conducted by Robert Brown, March 11, 1993–May 5, 1993, transcript page 17.
9. As Chandler says himself, "I've had more people steal my work than buy my work." Dana C. Chandler, quoted in Greg Cook, "How Dana Chandler Brought Black Power to Boston Art, Murals and Museums," *Wonderland*, January 21, 2019, https://gregcookland.com/wonderland/2019/01/21/dana-chandler/.
10. Dana Chandler, quoted in *Black Art Notes*, ed. Tom Lloyd (1971; New York: Primary Information, 2020), backmatter.
11. Dana C. Chandler, in conversation with the author, May 2, 2025.
12. Larry Neal, "The Black Arts Movement," *The Drama Review: TDR* 12, no. 4, Black Theatre (summer 1968), 29, https://doi.org/10.2307/1144377, and https://www.jstor.org/stable/1144377. Similar sentiments were later voiced by artist Elizabeth Catlett in her well-known address, delivered by phone from exile in Mexico, to the Conference on the Functional Aspects of Black Art organized in 1971 at Northwestern University by AfriCOBRA founding member Jeff Donaldson, for which Chandler was in attendance.
13. Napoleon Jones-Henderson, in conversation with the author, April 23, 2025.
14. AAMARP description on Northeastern letterhead, undated, Northeastern University Archives and Special Collections, African American Master Artists-in-Residence Program records, Box 2, Folder 5.
15. AAMARP description on Northeastern letterhead, undated.
16. Dana C. Chandler Jr., Archives of American Art Oral History conducted by Robert Brown, March 11, 1993–May 5, 1993, transcript page 85.
17. AAMARP description on Northeastern letterhead, undated.
18. AAMARP description on Northeastern letterhead, undated.
19. Dana C. Chandler Jr., Archives of American Art Oral History conducted by Robert Brown, March 11, 1993–May 5, 1993, transcript page 81.
20. Elizabeth Catlett quoted in foreword to *A Black Revolutionary Artist and All That It Implies*, ed. Dalila Scruggs (Chicago, IL: Chicago University Press, 2024), 14.
21. Dana C. Chandler Jr., Archives of American Art Oral History conducted by Robert Brown, March 11, 1993–May 5, 1993, transcript page 81.
22. The range of activities at AAMARP is detailed in the chronology in this volume, beginning on page 24.
23. The phrase hospitable environment is borrowed here from Kenneth G. Ryder, quoted in Chandler, *If the shoe fits, hear it!*
24. Kenneth G. Ryder, quoted in Jo Campbell, Africa Feature, "Black Artists Link African Heritage with American Community," January 1979. Northeastern University Archives and Special Collections, African American Master Artists-in-Residence Program records, Box 1, Folder 1.
25. Dana C. Chandler, Jr., "To All AAMARP Resident Artists, re: Moving," August 12, 1985. Northeastern University Archives and Special Collections, African American Master Artists-in-Residence Program records, Box 2, Folder 6.
26. Chandler, "To All AAMARP Resident Artists."
27. Chandler, "To All AAMARP Resident Artists."
28. Dana C. Chandler Jr., in conversation with the author, May 7, 2025.
29. Dana C. Chandler Jr., Memorandum to Sergei Tschernisch, re: What's in a Name? Northeastern University Archives and Special Collections, African American Master Artists-in-Residence Program records, Box 2, Folder 6.
30. Chandler, Memorandum to Sergei Tschernisch.
31. Chandler, Memorandum to Sergei Tschernisch.
32. Gloretta Baynes, "AAMARP: A Historical Overview of the African American Master Artist-in-Residency Program at Northeastern University (Rough Draft #2)," unpublished. Kay Bourne Papers, Emerson College Archives and Special Collections, Art Box 10, AAMARP Folder.
33. Ryder, quoted in Campbell, "Black Artists Link African Heritage with American Community."
34. Gloretta Baynes, "AAMARP: A Historical Overview," unpublished.
35. See Faye R. Gleisser's response to Chandler's *Urban Art Newsletter Piece* in this volume, page 66.

36. L'Merchie Frazier, in conversation with the author, May 24, 2024.
37. Andrea Shea, "Northeastern University Tells African-American Artist Program to Vacate Space," WBUR, July 1, 2018, https://www.wbur.org/news/2018/06/29/northeastern-university-african-american-artist-program-to-vacate-space.
38. Maria Garcia, "City Intervenes in Black Arts Collective Eviction Case With Northeastern," WBUR, July 24, 2018, https://www.wbur.org/news/2018/07/24/city-intervenes-aamarp-northeastern.
39. Garcia, "City Intervenes in Black Arts Collective Eviction Case With Northeastern."
40. Hakim Raquib as quoted in Jon Seamans, "Artists Charge Northeastern with Lack of Support," *Jamaica Plain Citizen* news clipping included in Dana C. Chandler Jr., *Urban Newsletter Art Piece* (1993).
41. Dana C. Chandler Jr., in conversation with the author, May 29, 2025.
42. L'Merchie Frazier quoted in Shira Laucharoen, "When Artists Organize: The Fight Against Displacement in Greater Boston," *Boston Art Review*, no. 12 (2024), https://www.bostonartreview.com/read/isssue-12-art-stays-here-coalition-fights-displacement.

CHRONOLOGY 1977–1993

1. Dana C. Chandler Jr., *If the shoe fits, hear it!: Paintings and Drawings, 1967–1976* (Boston, MA: Northeastern University Art Gallery, 1976). Northeastern University Archives and Special Collections, African American Master Artists-in-Residence Program records, Box 1, Folder 4.
2. Theresa-India Young, "A Statement About My Work," in *African American Artists Works in Traditional Crafts Media: National Conference of Artists: 24th Annual Exhibition*, April 3–May 1, 1982, (Roxbury, MA: The Museum of the National Center of Afro-American Artists, 1982).
3. *The Greater Boston Women Artists Exhibition II* was presented at AAMARP in 1983.
4. Holmes was later included in *Young Black Artists Under 36* (1980), while Thompson and Tinker participated in *Five Women* (1982), alongside Lotus Do, Valerie Jayne, and Weeta Lopes.
5. Edmond Moussally, while assistant to the camp director at the Stay-At-Home Day Camp in Charlestown, MA, in 1963, was later implicated in the cover-up of child sexual abuse at the camp.
6. Kay Bourne, *The Callboard*, *The Bay State Banner*, January 10, 1980, 14–15.
7. Dana C. Chandler Jr., Press Release "rough draft." Northeastern University Archives and Special Collections, African American Master Artists-in-Residence Archives.
8. Vusumuzi Maduna, quoted in "Background," *Vusumuzi Maduna*, https://www.vuzi.org/background.
9. Edmund Barry Gaither, "Heritage Reclaimed: An Historical Perspective and Chronology," in *Black Art—Ancestral Legacy: The African Impulse in African-American Art* (New York: Harry N. Abrams, 1989), 34.
10. Bryan Marquand, Obituaries: James Spruill, 73; actor and founder of influential black theater company, *Boston Globe*, February 11, 2011.
11. "History and Chronology of New African Company," n.d. Northeastern University Archives and Special Collections, African American Master Artists-in-Residence Program records, Box 2, Folder 6.
12. Rebecca Meejoo Choi, "The Black Workshop: Yale University's Margin at the Center," in *Black Architectures: Race, Pedagogy, and Practice, 1957–68*, (PhD diss., University of California, Los Angeles, 2020): 70–129.
13. Reginald L. Jackson, in conversation with Jeffrey De Blois, March 22, 2024.
14. Ellen Banks, "Regarding City Shapes," n.d., Northeastern University Archives and Special Collections, African American Master Artists-in-Residence Program records, Box 2, Folder 12.
15. Lowery Stokes Sims, "Discrete Encounters: A Personal Recollection of the Black Art Scene of the 1970s," in *Energy/Experimentation: Black Artists and Abstraction 1964-1980* (New York: Studio Museum in Harem, 2006): 53.
16. Banks, "Regarding City Shapes."
17. Wanda Coleman, "Bobbi Sykes: An Interview," *Callaloo*, no. 24 (spring/summer 1985): 294–303, https://doi.org/10.2307/2930979, and https://www.jstor.org/stable/2930979.
18. Angélique Stastny, "Anti-colonialism and Black Power: Indigenous Periodicals in the Pacific," *The Funambulist*, no. 22 (February 2019): 42–50, https://thefunambulist.net/magazine/22-publishing-struggle/anti-colonialism-black-power-indigenous-periodicals-pacific-angelique-stastny.
19. Dana C. Chandler Jr., "To: AAMARP Artists; Re: May & June Exhibit (AAMARP Artists), April 4, 1985. Northeastern University Archives and Special Collections, African American Master Artists-in-Residence Program records, Box 2, Folder 6.
20. Marcia Lloyd is featured prominently in *Say Brother* episode 1419, 1984. WGBH-TV Media Library and Archives.
21. Edward Strickland, "Hakim Raquib: On Photography," unpublished. Northeastern University Archives and Special Collections, National Center of Afro-American Artists records, Box 5, Hakim Raquib Folder.
22. Lowery Stokes Sims in conversation with Kofi Kayiga, unpublished interview. Northeastern University Archives and Special Collections, National Center of Afro-American Artists records, Box 5, Kofi Kayiga Folder.
23. Edmund Barry Gaither, brochure copy, "Interior Landscapes: Works on Paper and Canvas," Gallery Light Center, Brookline, MA, 1987.

(SEE ATTACHED): DANA C. CHANDLER JR.'S *URBAN NEWSLETTER ART PIECE* AND THE FIGHT FOR AAMARP

1. Baer's interview appears in the May 12, 1993 issue of *Northeastern News*; reprinted in Chandler's *Urban Art Newsletter Piece.*
2. Sampada Aranke, *Death's Futurity: The Visual Life of Black Power* (Durham, NC: Duke University Press, 2023): 16.
3. Ruth Wilson Gilmore, *Abolition Geography: Essays Towards Liberation* (New York: Verso, 2022): 20, 357.
4. Jeffrey De Blois, email correspondence with author, June 2025.
5. Faye R. Gleisser, *Risk Work: Making Art and Guerrilla Tactics in Punitive America, 1967–1987* (Chicago, IL: University of Chicago Press, 2023): 169.
6. Dana C. Chandler Jr., quoted in email correspondence between the author and Jeffrey De Blois, May 2025.
7. Ida B. Wells, *Southern Horrors: Lynch Law in All Its Phases* (New York: New York Age Print, 1892); and, Fred Carroll, *Race News: Black Journalists and the Fight for Racial Justice in the Twentieth Century* (Champaign: University of Illinois Press, 2017).
8. Jordana Cox, *Staged News: The Federal Theatre Project's Living Newspapers in New York* (Amherst: University of Massachusetts Press, 2023): 10.

CHRONOLOGY 1993–TODAY

1. Khalid Kodi, in conversation with the author, May 7, 2025.
2. Sharon Dunn, "Artist's Statement," n.d., Kay Bourne Papers, Art Box 10, AAMARP Folder, Emerson College Archives and Special Collections.
3. Don West with Brian O'Connor, "Introduction: A Photographer of Purpose," in *Portraits of Purpose: A Tribute to Leadership*, ed. Don West, (Jamaica Plain, MA: Three Bean Press, 2014), 12.
4. Stephen Hamilton, "The Conscious Artist: Identity and Social Responsibility in Boston's Black/Brown Mural Arts," *Now + There*, March 21, 2018, https://www.nowandthere.org/blog /tag/Stephen+Hamilton.
5. Alyssa Vaughn, "The Roxbury Love Mural Has Been Destroyed to Make Way for an Apartment Complex," *Boston Magazine*, July 24, 2020, https://www.bostonmagazine.com /news/2020/07/24/mandela-roxbury-love-mural-destroyed/

SUSTAINING COMMUNITIES

1. Thelma Golden, email to author, August 20, 2025.
2. "The Concept of the Harlem Museum," 1966, Studio Museum in Harlem Archives.
3. "A Proposal for The Studio Museum in Harlem," n.d., Studio Museum in Harlem Archives.

Works in the Exhibition

Unless otherwise noted, all works courtesy the artists

Benny Andrews
Born 1930, Plainview, GA; died 2006, Brooklyn, NY

***Nene*, 1978**
Oil and collage on canvas
50 × 36 inches (127 × 91.4 cm)
Andrews-Humphrey Family Foundation; Courtesy
    Michael Rosenfeld Gallery, New York

Ellen Banks
Born 1938, Boston; died 2017, Brooklyn, NY

***Scott Joplin*, 1982**
Acrylic on canvas
72½ × 48½ inches (184.2 × 123.2 cm)
Addison Gallery of American Art, Andover, MA

Gloretta Baynes
Born 1954, Cambridge, MA

***Ghana*, c. 1992**
Quilted fabric, airbrush paint, photo transfers, raffia,
    and fan
72 × 32 inches (182.9 × 81.3 cm)
Collection of Jemadari Kamara, Boston

Calvin Burnett
Born 1921, Cambridge, MA; died 2007, Medway, MA

***Angela Davis*, c. late 1970s**
Oil on canvas
Approximately 40 × 30 inches (101.6 × 76.2 cm)
Museum of the National Center of Afro-American
    Artists, Roxbury, MA

Ambreen Butt
Born 1969, Lahore, Pakistan

***Feudal prince and his disciple puppets*, 1993**
From the Cognition series
Watercolor and white gouache on handmade Wasli
    paper
8 × 11 inches (20.3 × 27.9 cm)

Dana C. Chandler Jr.
Born 1941, Lynn, MA; died 2025, Gallup, NM

***Pan-African Man*, c. 1970**
Acrylic on canvas
Approximately 36 × 36 inches (91.4 × 91.4 cm)
Museum of the National Center of Afro-American
    Artists, Roxbury, MA

***Roots*, c. 1974**
Acrylic on canvas
Approximately 48 × 36 inches (121.9 × 91.4 cm)

***For the Children We Strive*, 1991**
Photocopy collage printed on board
51 × 36 inches (129.5 × 91.4 cm)

***Urban Newsletter Art Piece*, 1993**
Newsprint
23¾ × 17 inches (60.3 × 43.2 cm)
Northeastern University Library Archives and Special
    Collections

Jeff Chandler
Born 1955, Boston

***Shaman's Trilogy*, c. 2000**
Wood, raffia, feathers, synthetic leather, metal,
    and acrylic paint
71 × 48 inches (180.3 × 121.9 cm)

Allan Rohan Crite
Born 1910, North Plainfield, NJ; died 2007, Boston

***Black Arts movement in Boston*, c. mid-1980s**
Graphite on paper
Approximately 24 × 32 inches (61 × 81.3 cm)
Museum of the National Center of Afro-American
    Artists, Roxbury, MA

Allan Rohan Crite and Susan Thompson
Born 1910, North Plainfield, NJ; died 2007, Boston
Born 1945, Cincinnati, OH

***Freedom, Justice, Equality*, 1989–2012**
Applique and painted quilt
45 × 40 inches (114.3 × 101.6 cm)

Milton Derr
Born 1932, Milwaukee, WI; died 2021, Boston

***Confined*, 1980–87**
Oil on cotton duck
72 × 54 inches (182.9 × 137.2 cm)
Museum of the National Center of Afro-American
 Artists, Roxbury, MA

Sharon Dunn
Born 1946, New York

***Floor Piece*, 1994/2026**
Wood and charcoal with beeswax and turmeric balls
6 × 36 × 36 inches (15.2 × 91.4 × 91.4 cm)

Marlon Forrester
Born 1976, Georgetown, Guyana

***Warrior Dance*, 2014**
Oil and mixed media on canvas
64 × 64 inches (162.6 × 162.6 cm)

L'Merchie Frazier
Born 1951, Jacksonville, FL

***Ogun: God of War to Love*, 1995/2015**
Mixed media assemblage
18 × 12 × 6 inches (45.7 × 30.5 × 15.2 cm)

***Ericka Huggins: Liberation Groceries*, 2019**
Thinsulate fabrics, nylon, and synthetic tape
50 × 40 inches (127 × 101.6 cm)

Tyrone Geter
Born 1945, Anniston, AL

***Girl Reading (Janice Posey)*, c. late 1970s**
Pastel on colored paper
Approximately 56 × 42 inches (142.2 × 106.7 cm)
Museum of the National Center of Afro-American
 Artists, Roxbury, MA

Ricardo "Deme5" Gomez
Born 1975, Santiago, Dominican Republic

Wall mural documentation, 2025
Photographs and projected images
Dimensions variable

Paul Goodnight
Born 1946, Chicago

***A room full of sisters*, 1997–98**
Mixed media
Approximately 42 × 36 inches (106.7 × 91.4 cm)
Museum of the National Center of Afro-American
 Artists, Roxbury, MA

Arnold Hurley
Born 1944, Boston

***Untitled*, 1973**
Acrylic on canvas
48 × 37½ inches (121.9 × 95.3 cm)

Reginald L. Jackson
Born 1945, Springfield, MA

***Things Go Better?*, c. 1970**
Gelatin silver print
27 × 18 inches (68.6 × 45.7 cm)

***FESTAC—The Benin Ceremonial The African
 Meetinghouse 1806*, 1976–77**
From the Urban Ceremonial Mask Series
Chromogenic color print
20 × 20 inches (50.8 × 50.8 cm)

Michael Jones
Born 1959, Brooklyn, NY

***Meditation–Inner Force–Lotus*, 1982–84**
Acrylic on shaped canvas and artist's frame
76 × 66 inches (193 × 167.6 cm)

Shea Justice
Born 1971, Roxbury, MA

***Scrolls of Justice* (excerpt), 2001–present**
Graphite and collage on paper
24 inches × 30 feet (61 cm × 9.1 m)

Kofi Kayiga
Born 1943, Kingston, Jamaica

***Moonlight*, 1987**
Pastel on paper
8¼ × 10½ inches (21 × 26.7 cm)

Khalid Kodi
Born 1961, Sudan

***Excessive Narrative: Echoes of Eden*, 2025**
Oil on canvas
68 × 170 inches (172.7 × 431.8 cm)
Courtesy the artist and Skoto Gallery, New York

Marcia Lloyd
Birth year not known, Philadelphia

***South Dakota Highway series*, n.d.**
Pastel on paper
15¾ × 20 inches (40 × 50.8 cm)
Museum of the National Center of Afro-American
    Artists, Roxbury, MA

Vusumuzi Maduna
Born 1940, Cambridge, MA; died 2007, Cambridge, MA

***La Diablesse as Sentinel*, 1987–88**
Wood and mixed media
82¼ × 10¼ × 10½ inches (208.9 × 26 × 26.7 cm)

Bryan McFarlane
Born 1956, Moore Town, Portland, Jamaica

***I Dream of African Souls*, 1984**
Oil on linen
93 × 137 inches (236.2 × 348 cm) (overall)
Courtesy the artist, AAMARP, Gallery NAGA,
    and Winsome Gallery

Stanley Pinckney
Born 1940, Boston

***Untitled tapestry*, c. 1978**
Resist-dyed fabric
36 × 60 inches (91.4 × 152.4 cm)
Collection of Reginald L. Jackson

Hakim Raquib
Born 1946, Colón, Panama

***The Tent*, 1992**
From the series Canvas Cathedral
Gelatin silver print
28 × 18 inches (71.1 × 45.7 cm)

James Reuben Reed
Born 1920, Kansas City, MO; died 2002, Boston

***The Mask Maker (Portrait of Susan Thompson)*,
    1983**
Acrylic on canvas
Approximately 42 × 28 inches (107 × 71 cm)
Museum of the National Center for Afro-American
    Artists, Roxbury, MA

Rudolph Robinson
Born 1938, Philadelphia; died 1988, Boston

***Street Boy*, 1983**
Gelatin silver print
21 × 16 inches (53.3 × 40.6 cm)
Addison Gallery of American Art, Andover, MA

***TRY BLACK*, 1983**
Gelatin silver print
15 × 16½ inches (38.1 × 41.9 cm)
Addison Gallery of American Art, Andover, MA

Renée Stout
Born 1958, Junction City, KS

***Renée & Sam*, 1985**
Acrylic on canvas
48 × 48 inches (121.9 × 121.9 cm)
Collection of Lauren Thomasson

Edward Strickland
Born 1930, New York City; died 1998, Boston

***Beacon Street Arches*, 1981–82**
Acrylic on board
16 × 12 inches (40.6 × 30.5 cm)
Museum of the National Center of Afro-American
    Artists, Roxbury, MA

Susan Thompson
Born 1945, Cincinnati, OH

***Call of the Ancestors 1*, 2017**
Pieced quilt with applique
54 × 35 inches (137.2 × 88.9 cm)

***Call of the Ancestors 2*, 2017**
Pieced quilt with applique
56 × 31 inches (142.2 × 78.7 cm)

Arnold Trachtman
Born 1930, Lynn, MA; died 2019, Cambridge, MA

Spirit of '76 (Louise Day Hicks and Ted Landsmark),
1979
Acrylic on canvas
77 × 64 inches (195.6 × 162.6 cm)
Estate of Arnold Trachtman; Courtesy Childs Gallery,
Boston

Wen-ti Tsen
Born 1936, Shanghai, China

Peaceable Kingdom, **1971**
Oil on canvas
60 × 120 inches (152.4 × 304.8 cm) (open)

Barbara Ward
Born 1940, Cambridge, MA; died 2013, Boston

New Race II, **1987–88**
Mixed media
Four parts, each approximately 67 × 22 inches
(170.2 × 55.9 cm)
Cambridge Public Library Archives and
Special Collections

Keith Morris Washington
Born 1956, Gary, IN

George Armwood: Front Lawn of Judge Duer's
Home; Princess Ann, Maryland, **1999**
Oil and acrylic on linen
72 × 119 inches (182.9 × 302.3 cm)
Fitchburg Art Museum, Fitchburg, MA

Don West
Born 1937, Boston

Elma Lewis, **c. 1985**
Gelatin silver print
Printed dimensions variable

Edmund Barry Gaither, **c. 1985**
Gelatin silver print
Printed dimensions variable

Rene Westbrook
Born 1958, New York

Strange Fruit, **1986**
Oil pastel, graphite, and turpentine wash on paper
20 × 30 inches (50.8 × 76.2 cm)
Museum of the National Center of Afro-American
Artists, Roxbury, MA

John Wilson
Born 1922, Roxbury, MA; died 2015, Brookline, MA

Study for Martin Luther King, Jr. (Buffalo), **1981**
Charcoal on paper
28½ × 28 inches (72.4 × 71.1 cm)
Estate of John Wilson; Courtesy Martha Richardson
Fine Art, Boston

Richard Yarde
Born 1939, Roxbury, MA; died 2011, Northampton, MA

The Parlor, **1980**
Watercolor on paper
58⅞ × 78⅝ inches (149.5 × 199.7 cm)
Mount Holyoke College Art Museum, South Hadley, MA

Theresa-India Young
Born 1950, New York; died 2008, Boston

Blue Bird, **1981**
Cotton, silk, wool, and synthetic yarns with cowrie
shells
Approximately 36 × 60 × 48 inches (91.4 × 152.4 ×
121.9 cm)
Estate of Theresa-India Young; Courtesy
Jacqueline McRath

Native Dancer, **2000**
Sisal rope, shells, copper, and beads
54 × 12 inches (137.2 × 30.5 cm)
Estate of Theresa-India Young; Courtesy
Jacqueline McRath

Works in the exhibition as of September 17, 2025

Contributors

NORA BURNETT ABRAMS, PhD is Ellen Matilda Poss Director at the Institute of Contemporary Art/Boston.

GLORETTA BAYNES is an artist and current AAMARP resident.

JEFF CHANDLER is an artist and current AAMARP resident.

CONNIE H. CHOI is curator at the Studio Museum in Harlem.

MEGHAN CLARE CONSIDINE is curatorial assistant at the Institute of Contemporary Art/Boston.

JEFFREY DE BLOIS is Mannion Family Curator at the Institute of Contemporary Art/Boston.

SHARON DUNN is an artist and former AAMARP resident.

MARLON FORRESTER is an artist and current AAMARP resident.

L'MERCHIE FRAZIER is an artist and current AAMARP resident.

EDMUND BARRY GAITHER is director and curator of the Museum of the National Center of Afro-American Artists and was special consultant at the Museum of Fine Arts, Boston.

FAYE R. GLEISSER is associate professor of art history at Indiana University at Bloomington.

RICARDO "DEME5" GOMEZ is an artist and current AAMARP resident.

REGINALD L. JACKSON, PhD is an artist and current AAMARP director.

NAPOLEON JONES-HENDERSON is an artist and founding member of the African Commune of Bad Relevant Artists (AfriCOBRA).

SHEA JUSTICE is an artist and current AAMARP member.

KOFI KAYIGA is an artist and current AAMARP member.

KHALID KODI is an artist and current AAMARP member.

BRYAN MCFARLANE is an artist and current AAMARP member.

HAKIM RAQUIB is an artist and current AAMARP member.

RENÉE STOUT is an artist and former AAMARP resident.

SUSAN THOMPSON is an artist and current AAMARP member.

WEN-TI TSEN is an artist and former exhibiting artist at AAMARP.

KEITH MORRIS WASHINGTON is an artist and former AAMARP resident.

DON WEST is a photojournalist and current AAMARP member.

RENE WESTBROOK is an artist and former AAMARP resident.

Reproduction Credits

Unless otherwise noted, all works courtesy the artists, all archival material courtesy Northeastern University Archives and Special Collections, Boston. Materials correspond to the following folders: A103: Northeastern University Photograph Collection; A080: African American Master Artists-in-Residence Program; A060: Jet Commercial Photography Negatives; M042: National Center of Afro-American Artists Records.

Pp. 10–11: Courtesy Dana C. Chandler Jr.; p. 12: Photo by Frank Lerner; p. 13: Photograph © 2026 Museum of Fine Arts, Boston; p. 14: Courtesy Lincoln Cushing and the Timothy Drescher Community Mural Slide Archive. Photo by Eva Cockcroft; p. 15: A103 Box 1, African American Master Artists Folder; p. 16: A060 Box 37, L8907-54; Courtesy Hakim Raquib; p. 17: A060 Box 37, L8907-54; p. 18: Kay Bourne Papers, Emerson College Archives and Special Collections, Art Box 10, AAMARP Folder; p. 19: Courtesy Dana C. Chandler Jr.; p. 20: Photo by Don West; p. 24: Courtesy Martha Richardson Fine Art; p. 25: A103 Box 1, African American Master Artists Folder; p. 26: A080 Box 1, Folder 3; A060 Box 34A, L6987-8; p. 27 Photo by Hakim Raquib. © Estate of Theresa-India Young; p. 28: Courtesy the University Archives and Special Collections Department, Joseph P. Healey Library, University of Massachusetts Boston: Theresa-India Young Papers Box 46, Folder 7; p. 29: A060 Box 34A, L6913-17; p. 30: Photo by Rogier Gregoire, reproduced in "Barbara Ward: A Portfolio," *Callaloo* no. 41 (Autumn 1989): 627; p. 31: Courtesy Hakim Raquib; A080 Box 2, Folder 16. © Tyrone Geter; p. 32: A080 Box 2, Folder 16; p. 33: A080 Box 1, Folder 3; A080 Box 2, Folder 16; Courtesy Gloretta Baynes Slide Archive; p. 34: A060 Box 37, L8907-54; p. 35: © Benny Andrews Estate / Licensed by VAGA at Artists Rights Society (ARS), NY, Courtesy of Michael Rosenfeld Gallery LLC, New York; p. 36: © 2025 Estate of Calvin Burnett / Licensed by VAGA at Artists Rights Society (ARS), NY; p. 37: © Estate of Milton Derr; p. 38: A080 Box 2, Folder 16; p. 39: Courtesy Dana C. Chandler Jr.; p. 40: Courtesy the Estate of Arnold Trachtman and Childs Gallery, Boston. Photo by George Bouret. © Estate of Arnold Trachtman; p. 41: © Stanley Forman; A080 Box 2, Folder 16; p. 42: Courtesy Dallas Museum of Art Archive. Photo by Tom Jenkins; Courtesy Hakim Raquib; p. 43: Courtesy Gloretta Baynes Slide Archive; p. 44: © Wen-ti Tsen; p. 45: Courtesy Hakim Raquib. © Reginald L. Jackson; p. 46: © Reginald L. Jackson; p. 48: Image courtesy Addison Gallery of American Art, Phillips Academy, Andover, MA / Art Resource, NY. Photo by Frank E. Graham. © Ellen Banks (1938–2017); p. 49: A103 Box 1, African American Master Artists Folder; Courtesy Hakim Raquib; p. 50: © The Estate of James Reuben Reed; Courtesy Hakim Raquib; M042 Box 26, Folder 10; p. 51: A103 Box 1, African American Master Artists Folder; p. 52: Photo by Hakim Raquib. © Bryan McFarlane; p. 53: Photograph © 2026 Museum of Fine Arts, Boston; p. 54: Photo by Hakim Raquib. © Michael Jones;

p. 55: Courtesy Gloretta Baynes Slide Archive. © Michael Jones; p. 56: Photograph © 2026 Museum of Fine Arts, Boston; p. 57: Image courtesy Smithsonian American Art Museum, Washington, DC / Art Resource, NY. © Paul Goodnight; p. 58: Photo by Laura Shea. © Estate of Richard Yarde; p. 59: Image courtesy Addison Gallery of American Art, Phillips Academy, Andover MA / Art Resource, NY. Photo by Frank E. Graham. © Rudolph R. Robinson (1938–1988); Photo by Eben Lacasse, M042 Box 20, Folder 2; Photograph © 2026 Museum of Fine Arts, Boston; p. 60: © Renée Stout; p. 61: © Hakim Raquib; p. 62: © Rene Westbrook; Courtesy Martha Richardson Fine Art. © Estate of John Wilson; p. 65: A103 Box 1, African American Master Artists Folder; Courtesy Dallas Museum of Art Archive. Photo by Tom Jenkins. © Kofi Kayiga; pp. 67, 68, 73: A080 Box 1, Folder 4; p. 70: Photo by Hakim Raquib; p. 72: Getty Research Institute, Guerilla Girls 2008.M.14, P.E.S.T.S., 1986-89, Box 7, Folder 1. ©PESTS; p. 74 © Khalid Kodi; p. 75 © Ambreen Butt; p. 76 Photo by Hakim Raquib. © Estate of Theresa-India Young; p. 77 Photo by Hakim Raquib. © Susan Thompson; p. 78: Photo by Hakim Raquib. © Susan Thompson; p. 79: Courtesy Gloretta Baynes Slide Archive. © Gloretta Baynes; p. 80 Photo by Hakim Raquib. © L'Merchie Frazier; p. 81: Photo by Craig Bailey/ Perspective Photo. © L'Merchie Frazier; p. 82: Kay Bourne Papers, Emerson College Archives and Special Collections, Art Box 10, AAMARP Folder; M042 Box 26, Folder 21; p. 84: Photo by Susan Byrne. © Keith Morris Washington; pp. 85, 86: © Don West; p. 87: Photo by Hakim Raquib. © Jeff Chandler; p. 89: Courtesy Fountain Street Gallery, Boston, MA. Photo by Sara Fine-Wilson. © Shea Justice; p. 90: © Ricardo Gomez; p. 92: Photo by Hakim Raquib. © Marlon Forrester; p. 93: Photo by Mel Taing. © Marlon Forrester; p. 98: M042 Box 20, Folder 4.

Front cover: Dana C. Chandler Jr., *Black Man Break Free of the Sucking, Mutherfucking White Egg* (detail), 1974. Offset print. 23 × 17½ inches (58.4 × 44.5 cm). Photo by Hakim Raquib. © Dana C. Chandler Jr.

Back cover: Susan Thompson, *Call of the Ancestors 2*, 2017. Pieced quilt with applique. 56 × 31 inches (142.2 × 78.7 cm). Photo by Hakim Raquib. © Susan Thompson

Endpapers, front, clockwise beginning top left: Michael Jones, *Just-Us!*, c. 1980. Courtesy Gloretta Baynes Slide Archive. © Michael Jones; Left to right: Theodore Landsmark and Dana Chandler, with Chandler's portrait of Landsmark, 1976. A103 Box 1, African American Institute Folder; Benny Andrews exhibition flyer c. 1980. Courtesy Gloretta Baynes. © Benny Andrews Estate; Calvin Burnett in his studio, 1980. A060 Box 37, L9109-27; Dana Chandler with tissue collage, c. 1980. A103 Box 1, African American Master Artists folder. Photo by Bill Fusco

Table of Contents: L'Merchie Frazier, *Ogun: God of War to Love*
(detail), 1995/2015. Mixed media assemblage. 18 × 12 × 6 inches
(45.7 × 30.5 × 15.2 cm). Photo by Hakim Raquib. © L'Merchie Frazier

Foreword: Shea Justice. *Egleston Square Memorial* (detail), 2022.
Watercolor. 30 × 32 inches (76.2 × 81.3 cm). Courtesy Fountain
Street Gallery, Boston, MA. Photo by Sara Fine-Wilson.
© Shea Justice

Preface: Edmund Barry Gaither, Harriet Forte Kennedy, Allan Rohan
Crite, and Dana Chandler, n.d. M042 Box 20, Folder 6

Pp. 23–23, clockwise beginning top left: Arnold Hurley's AAMARP
studio, n.d. A103 Box 1, African American Master Artists Folder;
Arnold Hurley in the studio, 1980. A060 Box 37, L8907-54; AAMARP
flyer c. 1978 featuring Dana C. Chandler Jr. drawing. Courtesy
Gloretta Baynes; Original AAMARP location at 11 Leon Street,
c. 1977. A103 Box 1, African American Master Artists Folder. Photo by
J.D. Levine; Dana C. Chandler Jr., *Land of the Free*, n.d. Courtesy
Gloretta Baynes Slide Archive; AAMARP Newsletter, June 1980.
A080 Box 1, Folder 4

Pp. 96–97, clockwise beginning top left: AAMARP stationary c. 1977.
Courtesy Gloretta Baynes; Nelson Stevens exhibition flyer, 1979.
A080 Box 2, Folder 16; Arnold Hurley in his studio, 1980. A060
Box 37, L8907-54; Dana C. Chandler Jr.'s AAMARP founding state-
ment, c. 1977. Courtesy Gloretta Baynes; Band performing at
AAMARP, 1979. A060 Box 36, L8284-177; Rene Westbrook exhibition
flyer, 1989. A080 Box 2, Folder 16; Milton Derr in his studio, n.d.
M042 Box 26, Folder 13. Photo by Adger Cowans

Endpapers, back, clockwise beginning top left: Left to right stand-
ing: Barbara Ward, James Reuben Reed, John Wilson, Reginald L.
Jackson, Arnold Hurley, Ellen Banks, Theresa-India Young, and
Stanley Pinckney on stage in Dodge Library, 1978. A103 Box 1,
African American Master Artists Folder; *All My Relations* flyer, 1983.
A080 Box 2, Folder 16; Barbara Ward with children, 1980. A060
Box 37, L9109-27; Clem McLarty in his studio, 1980. A103 Box 1,
African American Master Artists Folder; Arnold Trachtman flyer
featuring *Peaceful Demonstration* (1980). A080 Box 2, Folder 16.
© Estate of Arnold Trachtman; AAMARP Artists flyer, c. 1978. A080
Box 1, Folder 3

This catalogue is published on the occasion of the exhibition *Say It Loud: AAMARP, 1977 to Now*.

Organized by Jeffrey De Blois, Mannion Family Curator, with Meghan Clare Considine, Curatorial Assistant.

The Institute of Contemporary Art/Boston
February 12, 2026–August 2, 2026

Support for *Say It Loud: AAMARP, 1977 to Now* is provided by The Kristen and Kent Lucken Fund for Photography.

This publication was generously supported by Wagner Foundation.

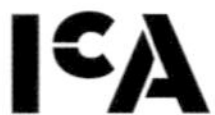

Wagner Foundation

Published in 2026 by the Institute of Contemporary Art/Boston and DelMonico Books · D.A.P.

I꜀A

Institute of Contemporary Art/Boston
25 Harbor Shore Drive
Boston, MA 02210
icaboston.org

DelMonico Books
available through ARTBOOK | D.A.P.
75 Broad Street, Suite 630
New York, NY 10004
artbook.com
delmonicobooks.com

Editor: Jeffrey De Blois
Text Editor: Matthew Christensen
Design, Typesetting, and Production: Rebecca Sylvers and
  Tina Henderson, Miko McGinty Inc.
Publication Manager: Tessa Bachi Haas
Publication Coordinator: Meghan Clare Considine

Printed in Italy by Conti Tipocolor
Color separations by Prographics

ISBN: 978-1-63681-199-4

Library of Congress Control Number: 2025947632

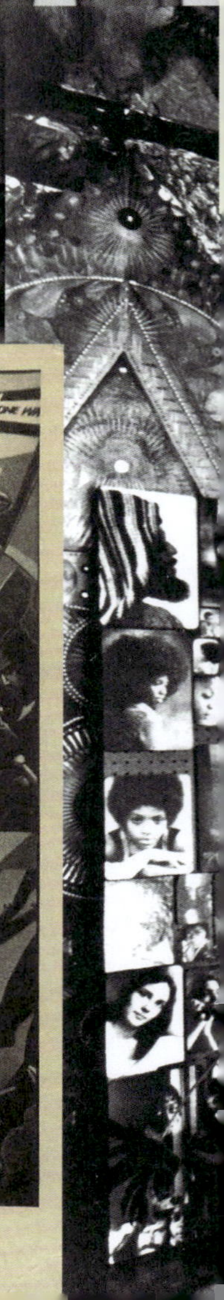

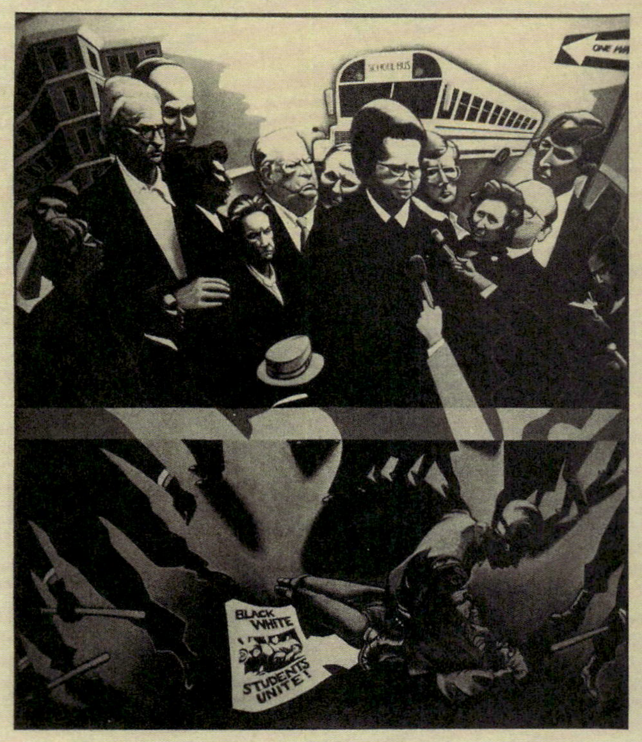

"Peaceful Demonstration" 1980